TOBIAS SMOLLETT

Tobias Smollett

NOVELIST

Jerry C. Beasley

THE UNIVERSITY OF GEORGIA PRESS

ATHENS & LONDON

© 1998 by the University of Georgia Press
Athens, Georgia 30602
All rights reserved
Designed by Erin Kirk New
Set in 10.5 on 14 Monotype Garamond by G & S Typesetters
Printed and bound by McNaughton & Gunn, Inc.

The paper in this book meets the guidelines for permanence and
durability of the Committee on Production Guidelines for Book
Longevity of the Council on Library Resources.

Printed in the United States of America

02   01   00   99   98   C   5   4   3   2   1

Library of Congress Cataloging in Publication Data
Beasley, Jerry C.
Tobias Smollett, novelist / Jerry C. Beasley.
p.   cm.
Includes bibliographical references and index.
ISBN 0-8203-1971-6 (alk. paper)
1. Smollett, Tobias George, 1721–1771—Criticism and
interpretation.   I. Title.
PR3697.B42   1998
823'.6—dc21   97-37492
British Library Cataloging in Publication Data available

William Hogarth, *A Midnight Modern Conversation*
(Engraving, 1732). (Copyright British Museum.)

FOR FLEDA

CONTENTS

The Thomas Rowlandson illustrations dated 1790 are from an edition of Smollett's *Miscellaneous Works* published during that year in Edinburgh. The titles for these illustrations are the author's. The Rowlandson illustrations for *Humphry Clinker* dated 1793 are from the London edition of that year. The Anthony Walker illustration for *Sir Launcelot Greaves* originally appeared in the *British Magazine,* February 1760, and is the first known magazine illustration for a work of fiction.

ACKNOWLEDGMENTS

I want to thank, first, the many dedicated colleagues I have come to know so well and to appreciate so much during my years as General Editor of the University of Georgia Press's series *The Works of Tobias Smollett*. Together they have all taught me more about the subject of this book than I ever thought it possible for me to know. I could not have written it without them. For particular help, advice, and—especially—friendship and support, I am most deeply grateful to O M Brack, Jr., and the late Robert Adams Day. The University of Delaware awarded me a Fellowship in the Center for Advanced Studies for the 1995–96 academic year, allowing me to finish the book much sooner than I could have done otherwise; I shall always remember this generosity with gratitude.

ABBREVIATIONS

Ferdinand Count Fathom	*The Adventures of Ferdinand Count Fathom,* ed. Jerry C. Beasley (Athens: University of Georgia Press, 1988).
Humphry Clinker	*The Expedition of Humphry Clinker,* ed. Thomas R. Preston (Athens: University of Georgia Press, 1990).
Knapp	Lewis M. Knapp, *Tobias Smollett: Doctor of Men and Manners* (Princeton: Princeton University Press, 1949).
Letters	*The Letters of Tobias Smollett,* ed. Lewis M. Knapp (Oxford: Clarendon Press, 1970).
Peregrine Pickle	*The Adventures of Peregrine Pickle,* ed. James L. Clifford, rev. Paul-Gabriel Boucé (Oxford: Oxford University Press, 1983).
Roderick Random	*The Adventures of Roderick Random,* ed. Paul-Gabriel Boucé (Oxford: Oxford University Press, 1979).
Sir Launcelot Greaves	*The Life and Adventures of Sir Launcelot Greaves,* ed. Peter Wagner (Harmondsworth: Penguin Books, 1988).
Travels	Tobias Smollett, *Travels through France and Italy,* ed. Frank Felsenstein (Oxford: Oxford University Press, 1979).

TOBIAS SMOLLETT

Introduction

Tobias Smollett was, in the fullest eighteenth-century sense of the phrase, a professional man of letters. Like another great practitioner of the same vocation in the same century, Samuel Johnson, he managed to achieve at least some measure of success in virtually every literary form. Smollett was, variously, a poet, a playwright, a prose satirist, a pamphleteering controversialist, a translator, an editor and compiler, a historian, a travel writer, a journalist, and, of course, a novelist. Above all, he was a novelist. It is justly for his five works of fiction that he is best remembered.

This is not to say that in his other work he was a failure, or a drudge who merely hacked his way toward a living in a capricious market—and the eighteenth-century publishing market was nothing if not extremely capricious. He was an indifferent poet, it is true, and his two plays—*The Regicide* and *The Reprisal*—are distinguished mainly for being very forgettable.[1] But his translations of Lesage (*Gil Blas,* 1748, and *The Devil upon Crutches,* 1750) and especially Cervantes (*Don Quixote,* 1755) are still considered even by many specialists in those two great Continental writers to be the best ever completed.[2] As a historian he published two major works, a four-volume *Complete History of England* (1757–58) and its five-volume *Continuation* (1760–65), in them rivaling the achievement of his famous contemporary and fellow Scotsman, David Hume.[3] His journalistic endeavors included the founding of the *Critical Review,* which he edited from 1756 to 1763, by his own many contributions and his managerial skills nurturing it into the most formidable and influential or-

gan of its kind and, with the rival *Monthly,* creating the modern institution of
the review periodical. His *Travels through France and Italy* (1766) is by any account one of the most original and impressive works of its kind to appear at
any time during his century. Smollett was, altogether, remarkably versatile, remarkably accomplished—and remarkably prolific. Few writers of any age
have produced so much in so short a lifetime. When he died in 1771, at just
fifty years old, he left behind him a truly vast and varied body of work; among
his contemporaries and near-contemporaries, only Defoe wrote more.

Smollett took up literature when he was very young. He did not set out to
be a great novelist, but rather a great playwright. He left Scotland for England
in 1739, at the age of eighteen, with high hopes that his clumsy tragedy *The
Regicide* would make him both famous and rich. Nothing of the sort happened,
for he could not get his play accepted for production. Wounded and bitterly
disappointed, he turned next to poetry, publishing his moving ballad *The Tears
of Scotland* (1746) in reaction against English persecutions of his homelanders
following the bloody Battle of Culloden in April 1746, and then, with *Advice*
(1746) and *Reproof* (1747), trying his hand at verse satire in the manner of
Alexander Pope. His subsequent efforts in still other forms, it seems, were (at
least initially) less the result of particular enthusiasm or ambition than of occasional opportunity and, in many instances, financial need. The translations
of *Gil Blas* and *Don Quixote,* for example, were booksellers' jobs begun at
about the time when, having achieved no success as a poet, he was writing his
first novel, *Roderick Random* (1748), and readying it for the press. In the case of
Gil Blas, the translation appears to have been completed almost simultaneously with the novel.[4] *Roderick Random* earned him his first success, but it did
not make his fortune; and for the remainder of his career Smollett was always
glad enough to take work for hire or to risk himself with such an undertaking
as the *Critical Review,* gladdest of all during the long interludes in the 1750s
and 1760s when he abandoned the novel because *Peregrine Pickle* (1751) and
Ferdinand Count Fathom (1753), and then *Sir Launcelot Greaves* (1760–61), met
with a discouraging reception. Ironically, it was his translations, and especially
his historical writings and his work on the *Critical Review,* that brought him the
greatest recognition he had ever enjoyed and, for the first time in his life, real
financial security.

I say this development was ironic because, while Smollett certainly threw himself into Grub Street work with a furious energy and an astonishing discipline that (joined with a considerable talent) helped him to complete so much of it with genuine distinction, it is absolutely clear—especially to anyone who knows his biography and has also read widely in the total body of his writings—that his real vocation was that of novelist. It was his fiction that he approached with the greatest imaginative intensity and devotion, investing his stories of wayward or dislocated protagonists with the same sense of alienation that he himself felt as a displaced Scot, and with a virtuosity of style and incident generated by powerful feelings and by a great spirit of fun and (often) a fierce indignation. Apart from the personal disaster of his inability ever to persuade anyone that *The Regicide* was worthy to be staged—a catastrophe of his adolescence from which he never fully recovered—he was more pained by the relative indifference of the response to his second, third, and fourth novels than by anything else in his life except, perhaps, the death of his only daughter in 1763 and the progressive tuberculosis that sickened, depressed, and eventually killed him. If Smollett is best remembered now for his novels, it is no doubt also true that this is exactly what he would have wanted. Nothing, we can be sure, would have pleased him more than to know that one day, more than two hundred years after his death, he would be counted among the "early masters" of English fiction.[5]

It is the novels that I have chosen to write about in the following chapters. One of the strangest facts of modern criticism in the field of eighteenth-century fiction is that Smollett, despite his stature, has until recently received comparatively little attention in the form of extended studies of his work. The other four "early masters"—Defoe, Richardson, Fielding, Sterne—have benefited from a modern British and American scholarly industry that has produced scores of books about each; but, even counting biographies, bibliographies, editions of his letters, and miscellaneous collections of critical essays, only about two dozen books on Smollett have been published in this century.[6] Of these, just half are devoted largely or entirely to his novels, ten of them published since 1950 but a mere seven within the past two decades. Among this last group of books the most recent are Robert D. Spector's study of Smollett's fictional women, Aileen Douglas's work on his consuming interest in the physical body, and John Skinner's theoretical consideration of his novels in relation to issues of genre and gender. The other two most im-

portant books date from the 1970s: Damian Grant's definitive analysis of
Smollett's style, and Paul-Gabriel Boucé's comprehensive treatment of all of
the novels.[7]

It is astonishing to think that Boucé's book is the only one of its kind to appear in more than half a century, and it is now twenty years old. This work is
and will remain an essential contribution for its exhaustive exploration of
Smollett's inspirations and sources and for its studious assessment of his literary devices and thematic structures. I began thinking some years ago, however, that a new study of the novels as a whole body of work was long over-
due—one written from a perspective fresher than Boucé's and conceived so
as to take into account relevant recent developments in the broad field of literary criticism while attending also to revised understandings of Smollett that
have emerged largely in connection with preparation of the definitive edition
of his writings now in progress at the University of Georgia Press.[8] The books
by Spector, Douglas, and Skinner, all published within the last couple of years,
certainly help to provide the kind of innovative critical reconsideration I have
wished for, and together they are a gratifying sign of a new burst of enthusiasm for Smollett among students of early British fiction. But all three approach the novels by pursuing a somewhat narrowly conceived thesis. Spector
sets out to account for and defend their treatment of women; Douglas, drawing heavily upon Foucault, focuses almost exclusively on the cultural significance of their representations of the body; and Skinner, who develops the
broadest critical range, nevertheless proves mainly interested in theorizing
Smollett rather than engaging with him as the author of works of the imagination possessing a particular kind of power and a particular appeal. The need
for a new and comprehensive study of the novels remains.

The book I have written is intended to meet that need. It is by no means
the only one that might be written with such a purpose in mind, but it does
one thing that, to my knowledge, has never been done before: it focuses directly on Smollett *as novelist,* and on his narratives as *texts* that define a certain
way of apprehending and dramatizing human experience. By using literary
theory, biography, and contextual backgrounds only as they serve the purposes of interpretation and assessment, and by emphasizing Smollett's other
writings only as they illuminate the fiction, I have tried to avoid the imbalance

that has limited the effects of much previous criticism. I have my own thesis to pursue, as will become readily apparent in succeeding pages of this introduction; but my discussions of the novels in the chapters that follow are actually a series of close readings, and collectively they are offered as demonstration of a *way* of reading Smollett that honors him for exactly the kind of novelist he was and that makes the complexities of his stories more accessible than they typically have been in the past.

It would be useless and diversionary to speculate here as to why Smollett's novels have been given so much less attention over the years than they have deserved, except to say that they have—rightly—never been seen to match up well with the received critical orthodoxies that have found Defoe so congenial for his masquerading behind ironic narrators, Richardson for his psychological studies of the inner life, Fielding for the beauties of his organic structures, Sterne for his prototypical modernism. The writer who vigorously defied the orthodoxies of his own day, as Smollett so often did, was not likely to find great favor among adherents of the orthodoxies prevailing in a later age—whatever his merit or importance. No critical *-ism* can contain or explain Smollett adequately, whether fashioned for the eighteenth century or in the twentieth. The most recently familiar *-isms* (New Historicism, feminism, Marxism, cultural materialism, and the rest), however, by their introduction of revisionist orthodoxies, are beginning to have a salutary effect upon discussion of his work. Despite the ideological grounding of most of them, or perhaps because of it, the conflict among the competing views they represent has generated productive debate and occasionally real complementarity, opening the field of criticism in a way not heretofore seen. Noncanonical writers are now paid a respectful attention unimaginable only a few years ago; new approaches to reading and to assessment, often very eclectic, have emerged. All of this greatly benefits Smollett, as it meaningfully challenges—even discredits—prepossessions that in the past have so narrowly defined standards of judgment (a good novel was what certain critics, from Henry James to Ian Watt and Wayne Booth, said it was) as to exclude his novels from the kind of consideration they require if they are to be read fairly, on their own terms, so that they might be properly estimated—and, yes, admired. I have sent my book into the opening just described with the hope that it will promote the needed new appreciation of Smollett's achievement, thus helping to restore him to his rightful place alongside his four great contemporaries.

In the remainder of this introduction I should like to outline some of the issues to be taken up later in my readings of Smollett's novels, explain the overall approach and the method followed, and—perhaps most important—raise (and attempt to clarify) two fundamental questions that I hope my reader will consider answered to his or her satisfaction upon reaching the last page of the book. The questions are: First, just what kind of novelist was Smollett?—that is, how does he seem to have conceived his stories, and with what sense of how best to structure their incidents so as to accomplish the literary and other purposes he had in mind? And second (this question has already been hinted at), given the maverick nature of his narrative unorthodoxies, just what was his appeal in his own time?—and how may he best be read now, in a very different time, so that the continued appeal of his work may be recognized and fully felt? As I began writing, I framed these questions for myself as a way of focusing my overriding concerns in the discussions of the novels. And now, as I frame them for the reader, I do so not as a program for special pleading, but rather to provide a similar focus. I have not contrived each detail of every discussion to address the questions directly—that would have been obsessive, and tedious; nor have I made any attempt to conclude each chapter with the flourish of an answer to them—that would have been clever, perhaps, but forced, and so schematic as to be useless as well as inauthentic. The questions, though I believe they are compelling ones, are no more than a guiding principle, a formulated center around which the arguments about individual novels revolve.

The issues that should concern any modern reader of Smollett's fiction are themselves inextricably related to the questions I have posed. It is crucial to remember, for example, that Smollett was a Scot, willingly but always uncomfortably displaced from his homeland, an alien in English culture (including, of course, its literary culture) who ceaselessly sought accommodation while remaining (emotionally, at least) near the periphery, looking on from the vantage point of an observer—an observer who was both detached and engaged. There can be no doubt that this positioning affected his writer's consciousness, as it likewise affected the consciousness of other displaced literary

Scots—James Thomson, Allan Ramsay, David Hume, James Boswell, Henry Mackenzie, to mention only the most prominent. But it seems to have affected Smollett in the extreme, and to have driven him almost inevitably toward the characteristic boisterousness and the irregular shapes of the stories he wrote—stories of "the body at risk," in Aileen Douglas's phrase;[9] stories of outsiders, some of them angry or aberrant or both, and all of them buffeted by a world that is hostile, often vicious, nearly always crazy; stories fractured and episodic, full of intensive language and striking visual effects focused by an acute authorial sensibility that translated feeling immediately into sound and sight.

It was from Glasgow, a city not far from the idyllic Dumbartonshire where he grew up, that Smollett traveled into England, and it was to London he went. Like those countrymen who took a similar journey for a similar purpose (and like the native Englishman Samuel Johnson, who left his Lichfield home almost simultaneously with Smollett's departure from Glasgow), he found Britain's largest city a baffling, unsettling place. The evidence of his novels, and occasionally of his other works, is clear on this point. The sheer number of people was unimaginable, and their bustle overwhelming; the streets were a maze, the air was foul, filth abounded, crime and poverty were rampant, the incessant noise was deafening.[10] Smollett, not yet out of his adolescence, must have felt this new urban environment as something so different from all he had ever known that it almost staggered him. At any rate the shock was certainly a great one, deeply formative, for his novels are obsessively preoccupied with the city as *locus,* as the preeminent place in which are concentrated the most important and vexing conditions of modern life. He no doubt learned early on that one could get lost in a city like London, be hurt by its unexpected cruelties and abandoned to loneliness in the midst of its crowds, as the young Scot Roderick Random is upon his arrival there; one could be maddened by the frenzy, the roughness, the perceived meanness of a city, as Matt Bramble is in Bath and then, like Roderick, in London. It seems beyond doubting that Smollett felt the dislocation of his early days in the English capital for the rest of his life, and that it forever altered his responses to experience, both personal and professional. The feeling was surely intensified by memories of the place of his departure, a much smaller and very different kind of city about which he wrote with fond nostalgia just a few short years before he died:

"Glasgow is the most beautiful town of Great Britain, adorned with a great number of public edifices . . . whose lofty turrets and spires yield a magnificent prospect at a distance."[11]

Smollett's representations of the dislocation of modern life in his novels is by no means restricted to the *locus* of the city—the shipboard scenes of *Roderick Random* serve a similar purpose, with especially horrific intensity of effect. But the city is a constant, and when his protagonists enter the urban environment they are always (with the exception of Ferdinand Count Fathom, who is totally identified with the city and everything it stands for) faced with the sights and sounds of a chaos and, frequently, a viciousness that opposes and threatens the center of moral conviction by which their status as agents in the world is first defined. The result is almost invariably fragmentation of the self—the felt divisions between the world as it is and as it ought to be generate an internal division as well; only Sir Launcelot Greaves, Smollett's one unwavering idealist, altogether escapes this effect. If the city is a natural place for the dramatization of such conflict, and it is that for Smollett, the conflict itself is fundamental to human experience. That Smollett felt this, and that he was beset by a consciousness of its truth for him personally, is made plain in the mock dedication (to himself) prefixed to *Ferdinand Count Fathom,* where he acknowledges his pride of character, his obstinacy, jealousy, and intemperance, but goes on to say that his integrity and sanguinity yet qualify him as generally worthy of esteem. Smollett's personal sense of internal divisiveness is unmistakable here, as is his acute alienation from a world that refuses to honor his best qualities and provokes him into acting out his worst.

One hears echoes of Roderick Random's indignation and self-doubt in this dedication to *Ferdinand Count Fathom,* and portents of Matt Bramble's benevolent misanthropy. This Smollett, the voice of the dedication seems to ask, just who is he anyway? Is he most defined by anger and irascibility, or by decency and generosity? Such questions continually perplexed Smollett, and they surely arose for him in the larger context of the very powerful personal *and* cultural issue of his national identity. If we return for a moment to the crucial matter of his literal alienation, we may imagine this issue for him as an abiding concern: Was he a Scot or an Englishman? Was his character most determined by the traditional values and quiet beauties that were, in his mind, the chief attractions of the homeland he fondly remembered but rarely visited?[12] Or was he now an emotional and moral citizen of England, the adopted country in which he lived and which he loved, but which he scorned for its corrupt politics, its degenerating manners, its social cruelties, its progressive mixing of classes, its insensitivity to the problems of crime and poverty? How could he reconcile the two points between which the question of his national loyalties stretched?[13] The personal problem was no doubt made harder for him by the intensification of the age-old conflict between the two cultures of Scotland and England following the Act of Union in 1707—the effect of the two Jacobite rebellions of 1715 and 1745 was powerful and lasting, and real unity still seemed impossible even as late as the years of Smollett's maturity. With which culture should he identify? Further confounding him was the fact of his desire to succeed as a writer, and in order to do so he had to meet the requirement of the marketplace (not to mention the literary establishment) that he write polite English convincingly; and so he confronted as a lingering crisis what other writers who were rooted in a literary culture not English also confronted, and had to come to terms with: the dislocation from that dimension of personal definition that was determined by his native linguistic heritage.[14]

My point here is the enduring strength of Smollett's feelings of alienation, his chronic concern with divisions in the world as they must be felt with a potentially destructive force by any person with normal thickness of skin. He spent all of his life wrestling with these feelings, facing down the reality that provoked them, and failing to achieve a confident personal spirit of reconciliation.[15] The obstacles to such reconciliation—in other words, to order and harmony in human experience—became the great subject of his writing career, and, except in his historical works (where he distanced himself from his own raw sensibilities and restrained the passions unleashed elsewhere by his imagination[16]), he was unable to project even the possibility of their dissolution—until late in his life when, as he completed *Humphry Clinker,* he at last had mellowed enough to spin out a fantasy that actually brings together not only individuals and a family but whole classes, and even nations. The differences of perception, feeling, and voice that have separated the members of the Bramble traveling party all but disappear as this novel draws to a close: Welshman Matt's servant marries his natural son Humphry, his sister marries the half-pay Scottish officer Lismahago, his niece marries the young Englishman George Dennison, and all of these nuptial festivities occur in the aftermath of Matt's trip to a Scotland he finds Arcadian and of his visit to the English estate of his old college friend Dennison (father of Lydia's groom), which he finds equally paradisal. In this his last work of any kind, Smollett did not change his subject—the alienation of the self; and he did not change his mind about the world as intractably vexing, strange, and hostile—the ending of *Humphry Clinker* is pure fable, by no means a complete repudiation of the moral stance Smollett had taken all his life. But he did finally bring his imagination to rest in a comic vision of hopefulness grounded in a traditionally Christian understanding of the meaning of redemption.[17]

It is impossible to separate Smollett's Scottishness from the other facts of his life that seem to have contributed most to development of the sensibilities and the moral vision characterizing him as a writer. Those facts are many, and while there is no need here to review them all in detail, some are crucial enough to call for brief discussion.[18] I have already mentioned his disappointment with *The Regicide,* evidence enough to him as a young man that the world was utterly unresponsive to his merits. The lingering bitterness he felt over his play's failure to be accepted for production at any of the London theaters led him to pillory both theatrical managers and patrons (among them David Garrick and Fielding's friend George Lyttelton) in the pages of his first two novels.[19] But Smollett was beset by other disappointments in his early years. Though he wanted more than anything to succeed as a writer, he was prudent enough to know that he needed a secure livelihood. For some three years prior to his departure from Glasgow, he had trained as apprentice to two of that city's prominent surgeons, William Stirling and John Gordon, and he must have expected easy entry into the London medical establishment. This he could not gain. We know too little about this period of his life to be clear about exactly what happened; but it is certain that, while many of England's more distinguished physicians and surgeons were of Scottish origin, the medical profession was nonetheless almost a closed circle, and Smollett could not break into it. Possibly in some desperation he turned to the military, and after extended and apparently exasperating dealings with the Navy Office, he shipped as a surgeon's mate aboard the *Chichester,* a British man-of-war that sailed in April 1740 as part of the failed expedition to Cartagena.[20] Following his return to England sometime in the spring of 1744, he did manage to establish a medical practice, though he was never very successful with it;[21] in

1750 he purchased his medical degree from Aberdeen University for £28 Scots, presumably to enhance his standing as a professional man, but within months he had given up his physician's practice altogether.

Smollett's first experience in both of his chosen vocations—as writer and as physician—was, then, one of failure and disillusionment. It is no wonder that many of the facts I have just been reciting are aired in *Roderick Random,* written when—at the age of twenty-six—he was still very young and impressionable. The late chapters (61–63) in which Roderick's prison-mate Melopoyn tells the woeful story of his mistreatment in the world of letters essentially repeat the history of Smollett's failure with *The Regicide;* earlier, Roderick's account of his frustrations with the military bureaucracy (chapters 16–18), and then his hair-raising recollections of life aboard the *Thunder* (chapters 24–37), echo Smollett's own experience in his application for a place as a ship's surgeon and during his service on the *Chichester.* The shipboard chapters have long been recognized as among the most authentic records we have of eighteenth-century Navy life—or, more precisely, of how that life *felt* to the sailors who lived it. It was a brutal, punishing, and dangerous life, and Roderick captures it with a vivid intensity that could only have derived from his author's firsthand encounter with it.

But my purpose here is not to go on seeking out parallels between Smollett's personal history and his fiction. In any case that has already been done for many of the episodes of his first novel, which is, besides, only incidentally an autobiographical narrative.[22] Like almost any writer one can think of, Smollett made free use of his own experience in his earliest work, recreating it imaginatively. There is little to be learned from a mere cataloguing of corresponding biographical and fictional details. It is on the whole sufficient simply to note that Smollett continued throughout his career to draw upon remembered experience and his knowledge of real people and events in filling out the textures of his stories, though the stories themselves bear steadily fewer resemblances to the curve of his own life—until, in *Humphry Clinker,* we read of the autobiographical valetudinarian Matt Bramble, off on a quest to recover his health. A few other salient facts do deserve emphasis, however. One, as hinted in the reference to *Humphry Clinker,* is Smollett's illness. When he left Glasgow in 1739 he was already suffering from a persistent cough that would later develop into fatal tuberculosis; his decision to pursue medicine as a livelihood very likely resulted in part from worry about his own health, which was surely also a reason why, as a novelist, he was obsessed both with the corporeal body and with medical charlatans who exploited human misery for personal gain. It goes without saying, though it has been said many times, that his irascible temperament was as much the consequence of his illness as it was the product of his youthful indignation and his alien status within English culture. Perhaps it is most accurate to remark that all of these causes coalesced to promote a single effect. In any event, Smollett's irascibility got him into literary, legal, medical, and political controversies that deepened it, even as they gave him ventilation.[23]

Like all of his major fictional characters, Smollett was a great traveler, though for the most part only in his imagination. Late in life he traveled for his health, and it was a final visit to his homeland in 1766 that encouraged the emotional relocation revealed in the Scottish episodes of *Humphry Clinker,* a novel he completed five years later, after removing from London to the warm climate of Italy.[24] But the most momentous event of his youth was also a journey—that first ever for him, from Glasgow to London, so formative and, as I have already argued, so dislocating. For Smollett, full living seems to have meant ceaseless motion; the vital body was the body never at rest. During the years following his return from naval service in 1744 he was too busy trying to make ends meet as a physician and writer to undertake many trips,[25] but he was an enthusiastic reader of travel literature, and in 1756 he published a seven-volume *Compendium* of voyage narratives that proved quite popular.[26] His fascination with travel writing was certainly not unique in his time; literally hundreds of works in this vein were printed throughout the eighteenth century, among them Smollett's own *Travels through France and Italy.*[27] As Percy G. Adams has shown in a definitive book, the abundant presence of such works in the literary marketplace reflected a public obsession that novelists besides Smollett—here we need think no further than Defoe and Fielding—also reflected in their own work.[28] The typically episodic structure of so many eighteenth-century novels may have resulted partly from the residual influence of the French heroic romances so popular in the preceding century, and, more importantly, from the example of *Don Quixote,* in Smollett's day the most widely read and admired work of Continental fiction;

but it was preeminently a consequence of rapid, radical, and deeply unsettling cultural change—change that fostered the travel literature, both fictional and historical or biographical, written as a sign of and also as a response to it.[29]

Percy Adams and others have made it unnecessary for me to go on at any length about the nature of the change itself, and its effects on eighteenth-century narrative sensibilities, especially as reflected in travel writing.[30] Several important matters do call for summary attention, however, not because I have anything to add to what is already known by any informed student of the period's history, but because it will be helpful here to bring them into focus. It is worth emphasizing, for example, that the eighteenth century marked the beginning of the accelerated colonial and commercial expansionism which would make England the world's greatest imperial and economic power in the next century. With expansionism came both increased exploration and broadening curiosity about remote and, in some instances, hitherto unknown regions of the globe.[31] The remarkable popularity of works like *Robinson Crusoe* and *Gulliver's Travels* may to some extent be attributed to their success in appealing to—or, in the case of Swift's book, spoofing—this curiosity. For wealthy young men the Grand Tour of Europe became a matter of convention, making still nearer regions of the world objects of intensified interest, and the effects of such fashionable travel—French cuisine and costume, for example, and Italian opera—became strikingly visible in English culture, previously so insular. At the same time the landscape of Great Britain itself was the site of newly vigorous motion and activity. Roads were still atrocious by modern standards, but sufficiently improved to make domestic travel easier than it had been at any time in the past, and numerous popular works such as Defoe's *Tour* appeared to encourage it. Spas at Tunbridge, Clifton, and Bath attracted ever larger numbers of visitors, becoming what we would now call resorts, and indeed Bath was rebuilt by the two John Woods (Elder and Younger) to make it more alluring to people of fashion. Meanwhile agricultural reforms, growing industrialization, and the concentration of mercantile wealth in London and in such newly important ports as Bristol drew thousands off the land, unwillingly or willingly: displaced farm workers relocated to the cities in quest of work; more carters and wagoneers than ever were seen hauling goods to distant markets; affluent merchant families increasingly followed the aristocratic practice of maintaining two places of residence, one in the city and another in the country (or at least the suburbs), journeying back and forth between them as business or pleasure required.

All of this motion coincided with, and indeed was in part a consequence of, the destabilization of English class structure that proceeded relentlessly throughout the eighteenth century. As mercantile wealth gradually increased, and as the middle class grew into unprecedented prominence, the aristocracy simultaneously began to lose its hold on the nation's economy and its centers of political power. Trade, and the newly surging enterprises of banking and stock-jobbing, altered the basis of finance, shifting it from land to money and therefore, inevitably, from country to city. Meanwhile the effects of the 1688 Revolution Settlement created a parallel flux of their own, eroding the position and authority of the Crown and concentrating both power and the means (and will) to exercise it in the halls of Parliament. Parliament men like the ruthless manipulator Sir Robert Walpole may have abused their authority as much as any Tudor or Stuart monarch had ever done, but it was now theirs to abuse.[32] The democratization of English politics, which progressed slowly but inexorably toward two major reform bills (in 1832 and 1867) that created a republican government and reduced the monarch to a ceremonial head of state, was set going in the early years of the eighteenth century. If ever England had truly enjoyed a stable social and political order (a matter for some debate), it simply could not do so any longer, despite occasional appearances to the contrary—and despite the kinds of affirmations (more a matter of nostalgic longing than of anything else) we see so regularly in the endings of popular novels like *Moll Flanders, Pamela, Tom Jones,* even Smollett's *Roderick Random* and *Humphry Clinker.* The old notion that the Enlightenment, with its celebration of science and reason, brought with it greater certitude in English (and Continental) culture has now been thoroughly and justly discredited. In what is surely one of the great ironies of our modern cultural history, the process of discrediting it actually began with that generation of writers who were the first inheritors of the legacy of Enlightenment principles—that is, with those revolutionary spirits of the 1780s and 1790s, William Godwin, Mary Wollstonecraft, and their group of philosophical radicals.[33]

The rhythms of the travel book perfectly captured all this flux, and the energy and tension it generated, while the form also appealed through its subject matter to the reading audience's desire for novelty: for knowledge of new places, new peoples, new ways of being and of coming to terms with experience. Novelty itself can be disruptive—this is one of the lessons of *Gulliver's Travels;* and in the case of travel writing in particular the very structuring of the typical narrative—episodic, with movement by fits and starts—enforces a sense of dislocation: from home and the familiar, and from a norm (or, perhaps more accurately, an ideal) of order. That this was so for the eighteenth century is attested by the unarguable fact that the journey became the primary metaphor for the rendering of experience in novels, which consistently represented life as flux; that it was all very disturbing seems clear from the ways in which most novels (one can bring to mind only a small number of exceptions—*Tristram Shandy,* certainly, along with Godwin's *Caleb Williams* and a very few others) impose order on the disorder of their characters' lives, in the end resolving confusion into clarity, motion into stasis.

Doubtless the most influential fictional example of the journey as metaphor for life was *The Pilgrim's Progress,* next to the Bible the most popular of all books in England from the time of its initial publication (in two parts, 1678 and 1684) through the end of the following century. Bunyan's stunning allegorical tale of a protagonist's total alienation from a world gone crazy with greed, pride, and faithlessness is the best remembered, and certainly the best, among a great number of spiritual narratives (real and imagined, in form both biographical and autobiographical) that began to appear from the pens of Puritans and other Dissenting men and women in the late 1600s.[34] Together, and against a background of new scientific and philosophical empiricism (this was the age of Newton and Descartes as well as of Bunyan), these works provide evidence of an emphatic new individualism that promoted—for the first time on so broad a scale—deeply personal inquiry into the place of the private self within a public world, and indeed within the whole scheme of the Creation. Not all of these narratives are literal journeys, but, like *The Pilgrim's Progress,* they all record spiritual passages from a state of sin and confusion toward redemption and clarity; and though they structure themselves linearly, they linger over specific moments—often traumatic, epiphanic, or both—in the subject's moral and spiritual life. They are episodic, in other words, like travel

books, and they similarly reflect an obsessive curiosity (though about an interior instead of an exterior landscape) and a profound sense of uncertainty or
disquietude.

The impact of such narratives on the first great generation of English novelists is unmistakable. All of Defoe's major works are journeys, either literal or
spiritual or both, and he has been accurately described as the master of the
brilliant episode.[35] *Pamela* and *Clarissa* are stories of confinement, but in both
there is significant movement from place to place as the heroines are tested in
differing environments. Both heroines locate their experience within a context of Scripture, and their stories are accounts of a spiritual passage; Clarissa,
as she nears the end of her trials at the hands of Lovelace, even writes of her
plan to travel to her "Father's House."[36] *Joseph Andrews* and *Tom Jones,* like
Smollett's *Roderick Random* and *Peregrine Pickle,* are novels of the road, and they
thus bear more of the attributes of the adventurous travel narrative than of
the spiritual journey; still, they are biographical in form, and while their protagonists can hardly be described as contemplative or reflective, they all suffer
the buffetings of an unpredictable, hostile world as their mercurial lives proceed, and they all yearn for—and finally attain—both redemption and quietude in a condition of stability.

The restless movement and the fracturing of narrative order we find in so
many eighteenth-century novels, including all of Smollett's, express the age's
general feeling of alienation from earlier, traditional notions of a universal system of being. Even the Church was affected, and it was in fact a contributing
force, as earth-centered latitudinarianism and a still more aggressively ratio-
nalist theology seriously eroded old structures of faith; the fundamentalist be-
lievers of Bunyan's generation, and after them Wesley's Methodists, reacted
directly to such demystification of the Christian religion.[37] The manifold
changes I have been outlining reached into all corners of contemporary life;
they were profoundly revolutionary, and they occurred with such a rush as to
make them almost dizzying. Indeed, the great project of English culture in
this period, in both the public and the private realms, was the development of
meaningful responses to all the newness of things, so that a modern conception, of a different universal system, could emerge: one that acknowledges uncertainty as the source of a pervasive anxiety (or *angst,* to use the term made
fashionable by late nineteenth-century philosophy), promoting an extremely

complex—and not especially comfortable—understanding of the age-old conflict between desire and limitation, between will and possibility, as an essential fact of human existence that, paradoxically, provides the impetus and generates the energy for virtually all creativity.

The eighteenth century's most meaningfully creative *literary* response to the unsettlingly disruptive birth of the modern world was its invention of the novel as we now know it. I mean the English novel specifically,[38] and its astonishingly adaptive capacity to register flux, make it felt, and render it intelligible—even if in the end it is resisted, as it is in, say, *Clarissa,* or *Tom Jones,* or *Humphry Clinker.* The novel turned its attention directly to the individual life, to the realm of private experience, giving it visibility and significance within the larger context of a public reality. This protean new form was able to accommodate, though in varying ways and with differing degrees of subtlety and comprehensiveness, the dimensions of both realms, dramatizing class realignment, the reconfiguration of the hierarchy of political authority, even the process by which the entire nation redefined its role as an increasingly dominant presence in world (not just European) affairs; and it was able to portray convincingly authentic men and women as they struggled, often through great puzzlement, toward clear self-definition in the midst of shifting notions about the proper location of the individual in space, in time, and in a universe of moral ambiguity. Where is home?—is it in the country, on the road, in the city? What is important?—the present moment, lived in a bewildering rush of circumstance, or the timelessness of sacred truth, so regularly objectified in the mythic *locus* of the edenic rural estate? How can moral integrity be preserved in a world so confusing, and so hostile, that its appearances can hardly be penetrated and its power hardly resisted? These are the questions that eighteenth-century novels pose repeatedly, with such insistence that even the reader who comes to them with no knowledge of the period that produced them feels their urgency. It was this shared urgency that made for common ground among the many hundreds of fictional narratives written in the period, and it did more than anything else to unite them—in all their amorphous disparateness—toward the creation of a genre.

Smollett was arguably the best of all eighteenth-century English novelists at making these urgent questions drive his narratives (or, perhaps more accurately, allowing them to do so); they generate the tremendous energy so characteristic of his style and of his intensive way with the details of virtually every incident, and they determine the often erratic structures of his plots. They are, after all, questions about Smollett's own greatest personal obsession, born of the displacement and dislocation he himself had experienced: they are about the alienation of the self, and the compensating desire—in his novels, formally expressed as a quest—for safety, community, and certitude. All of his characters are wanderers, placed directly into the circumstances from which the questions actually arose. Because those circumstances were unpredictable—Chance always rules in a Smollett novel, until the end of the story—and because they were fraught with danger, they could not be organized into an elegant narrative shape, but instead created their own shape, a shape always threatening formlessness. Apparent formlessness was for Smollett a matter of deliberate artistic choice; his novels make it plain that he actively rejected the organic model of narrative construction represented in the works of his rival Fielding, and along with it the authorial posturing of Richardson, who, despite his pretended invisibility as the "editor" of collections of letters, always projected himself into the space between his story and his reader, conspicuously manipulating—so as to control—the potentially unruly details of the former as well as the responses of the latter.[39] Whether Smollett actually considered Fielding and Richardson false models, purposefully repudiating them, it is impossible to know. It is clear, however, that he wished to create a new model of his own. Like all of his great contemporaries he was conscious of himself as an innovator in what Richardson called a "new species of writing."[40] The genuine originality of his conception of the novel as a literary form has never been sufficiently recognized, striking though it is and influential though it has been—Smollett was among the favorites of Dickens, who fashioned his own works partly after his predecessor's example, and his novels lie importantly in the background of much modern fiction.[41]

Just what Smollett's original conception of the novel was is difficult to pin down, as he never fully articulated it. The best we can do is simply to pause reflectively over the most distinctive qualities of the works themselves, allowing *what* Smollett wrote to tell us *how* he wrote, and why. The first thing to note is that, while he was by no means a realist in the familiar literary sense of the term, he was certainly intent upon capturing life as it actually felt to those who lived it. And to him life felt disordered and erratic. He responded to it viscer-

ally, catching at fragments of experience with a ferociously acute power of observation that led him to see each fragment as somehow essential, worthy of
lingering attention and not necessarily connected in any coherent way with all
of the other fragments, equally interesting. His habits of exaggeration—often
to the level of farce, or the absurd—are usually for the sake of laughter
(Smollett is one of the great literary pranksters, and he seems never to have
been able to resist a good practical joke), but they also typically intensify the
immediacy of the individual incident, or fragment of experience, by forcing
from the reader an extended visceral response of his or her own. His method
of achieving this kind of response is consistently that of the verbal picture,
and in fact the visual quality of his writing is so fundamentally important to its
overall effects that I want to return to it presently for fuller discussion in
preparation for more detailed analysis, in subsequent chapters, of its centrality
in each of the novels.

But first it will be best to point to another quality of his work, of lesser but
still real importance, and closely related to the visual: his regular practice of introducing both explicit and implicit references to real people and real historical events for the purpose of authenticating his characters' experience by placing it within a context of the known and the familiar. There was nothing
unusual about the practice itself; most novelists, in an age deeply skeptical
about the value and respectability of prose fictional narrative, did the same
thing with equal regularity. But Smollett's manner of carrying it out *was* unusual, for he frequently mixed real and fictional time, indulging in glaring
anachronisms that would seem merely the results of carelessness if we did not
know that he was a disciplined and accomplished historian who cared about
the meaningful placement of events in their chronological and causal sequence, and if the anachronisms themselves were not so purposeful. There
are instances of this mannerism in all of his novels, but they are especially
conspicuous in *Ferdinand Count Fathom,* his most experimental work and the
one which occasioned his only concerted attempt to outline a theory of narrative composition. "A Novel is a large diffused picture, comprehending the
characters of life," he wrote in the mock dedication (p. 4) to this account of a
predatory villain who indeed encounters all sorts of "characters" in his ram-
blings through Europe and England. The key words here are *diffused,* which
certifies Smollett's defiant conception of an alternative to sanctioned ways of

telling a story, and, of course, *picture,* which proclaims his way of proceeding with such a conception.

In *Ferdinand Count Fathom,* and to a lesser but still significant extent in his other novels as well, Smollett's anachronisms are part of the alternative conception, for they serve to promote the diffuseness he adopts as a compositional strategy. Further discussion of this odd and intriguing habit of merging history and fiction must await later chapters; what needs to be emphasized here, in a general way, is that it gives evidence of Smollett's lack of interest in, his inability to believe in, a principle of linear coherence when, writing as a novelist, he sought to register felt life. His stories are progressive—each has an identifiable beginning, middle, and end; but his imagination apprehended all of experience as fractured, not whole, its bits and pieces an apparent jumble, each powerful enough to arrest attention and movement, and the totality of them all needing to be sorted out so that their meaning might at last be clarified. Not surprisingly for him, the facts of history, when appropriated for fiction, frequently lost their actual reference points in time and became part of the jumble. Nothing gives a clearer sign of Smollett's very modern sensibility than this peculiar approach to the intersection between the real and the imagined. His novels seem constantly to be engaged with the question of just what constitutes the real. Is it what we construct it to be as we record the past, imposing order through the exercise of judgment? Or is it what we know it to be through feeling, which, if intense enough, makes judgment suspect if not irrelevant (because it is artificially imposed) to apprehension of the truth? The answer to these questions lies in the works themselves. The novel was to Smollett—obviously—a truer form of writing than the history book, for it had the capacity to displace the necessary logic and regularity of the factual chronicle so as to expose, by an exercise of the imagination, the illogic and irregularity of actual experience.

I observed earlier that for Smollett, the life lived at its fullest was a life in motion. This is the sensibility that his novels reflect; even the individual incidents over which he pauses so lovingly, or sometimes so impishly, vibrate with energy. They are moments caught in time but not deprived of their human vitality. Smollett's consciousness of all the flux and change of his age was itself a consciousness of movement. He was perhaps sensitized into such consciousness partly by the books he loved to read, among them the episodic *Don*

Quixote, Lesage's picaresque *Gil Blas,* and of course travel narratives. In any case he was clearly fascinated by everything he saw going on around him. It was spectacle of a sort, and like all spectacle compelling even if the busy-ness and force of its activity caused meaning to become elusive as details blurred. But he was repelled, too, and troubled and wounded; his repulsion drove him, as it did Swift, to satire, and to the occasionally vicious pranks he imagined for so many of his characters, most especially for Roderick Random, Peregrine Pickle, and Ferdinand Count Fathom, protagonists of the three novels of his youth. Roderick seems to speak for his author when he says, in chapter 15 of his story, that he was "confounded at the artifice and wickedness of mankind" (p. 73); the astonishment and bewilderment conveyed by these words hint at an interior source for the creation of Roderick and of the central characters of the other two earliest novels as well. Even the idealist Sir Launcelot Greaves seems to have sprung from the same source, and likewise Matt Bramble. Matt's violent railings against the folly and corruption of Bath and London, his furious response to the swelling movements of the "mob" as it crushes his toes on its way to breaking down traditional class distinctions—such fulminations (and there are many others in *Humphry Clinker*) echo similar outbursts from Smollett himself, recorded elsewhere in his writings, and sometimes in his own voice.

Smollett obviously delighted in the representation of what, as a man of extremely conservative social vision and powerful moral impulses, he most feared and most despised: the cacophony and the mercurial instability of contemporary life, with its perceived threats to individual happiness and to the survival of the moral self. The mixture of fascination and indignation surely helped to determine the subject matter and the structures of his narratives, and no doubt it also spurred him to the kind of relentlessly pictorial vividness that would scarcely be seen again in the English novel until Dickens began publishing the monthly parts of *Pickwick Papers* in 1836. I have suggested that the pictorial method is of fundamental importance to the broad effects Smollett achieved as a novelist. That is hardly a strong enough statement, as the visual is in fact the most essential (in the fullest sense of the word) of all the qualities that may be identified in his work. This point requires explanation, lest it seem reductive—and because it is central to a way of reading Smollett that embraces as virtues what many have seen as faults.

If critics have not always recognized the centrality of his pictorialism, other readers have. Dickens certainly recognized it. And it is no mere accident that George Cruikshank, one of the great book illustrators of the nineteenth century, drew illustrations for novels by both Dickens and Smollett. Dickens's own favorite illustrator, Hablot K. Browne ("Phiz"), likewise recreated scenes from Smollett's novels.[42] The finest of Smollett's illustrators was Thomas Rowlandson, whose drawings for *Roderick Random, Peregrine Pickle, Sir Launcelot Greaves,* and *Humphry Clinker* first appeared in editions of those novels in the 1790s and have remained popular ever since.[43] Anyone who has ever read Smollett will immediately understand his appeal to such artists, all of them— like their forebear William Hogarth—gifted at caricature yet able to allow the real humanity of their subjects to show through distortions of feature and quirkiness of bearing.

The pictorial artist with whom Smollett shared the greatest kinship was Hogarth himself. The eccentric painter Pallet introduced in chapter 46 of *Peregrine Pickle* may have been intended as an amused glance at Hogarth, but Smollett cannot have meant to mock him, as he elsewhere refers to him with unfeigned respect and admiration.[44] Hogarth would have been the perfect illustrator of Smollett's novels, as the two subscribed to essentially the same narrative principles, while they also possessed a common visual sense of the world and of people. Smollett used terms from painting and from the drama when, in the dedication to *Ferdinand Count Fathom,* he described the effects he aimed at in his fiction; Hogarth imagined himself a dramatic painter, a creator of visual narrative, and so he would have had an intuitive understanding of what Smollett attempted in words. Hogarth never undertook the task of illustrating Smollett, and there is no evidence that such a scheme was ever proposed to him. He probably would have rejected any proposal of this kind had it been made, as he was a fiercely independent creative spirit who did not depend on the works of others for his subject matter; certainly he did not think of himself as an illustrator, though he completed drawings or series of drawings for a number of literary works, including *Tristram Shandy, Gulliver's Travels, Hudibras,* and *The Beggar's Opera.*[45] In any case the kind of book illustration we associate with the later Rowlandson and Cruikshank was still at a formative stage in the mid-eighteenth century, and among Smollett's novels only *Sir Launcelot Greaves* included illustrations at the time of its initial publication.[46]

Hogarth did not illustrate Smollett, but he must have been a major presence in the minds of the novelist's first readers. He did more than anyone else to make the recently imported Italian form of *caricatura* familiar in English art, and Smollett in his turn adapted the same form as a guiding principle in developing the distinctive style and manner of his character portraits.[47] Whole scenes from Hogarth must have occurred to many members of Smollett's audience as they progressed through his narratives. Robert Etheridge Moore claims as much, arguing for a kind of literal transference as he identifies several scenes Smollett seemingly borrowed straight from Hogarth, though without acknowledgment.[48] Like Fielding, who always acknowledged his similar indebtedness (Fielding's interest in creating explicit fabrics of intertextuality was generally much greater than Smollett's), Smollett apparently was so steeped in Hogarth that he turned naturally to him for specific visual models.[49] There are yet more echoes of Hogarth in Smollett's works than Moore has noted, and in later chapters I shall turn to consideration of the more interesting and revealing of all such parallels. What I want to emphasize here is the way Smollett's various borrowings from Hogarth help to highlight the prevailing visual orientation of his work. Experience taught Smollett how it felt to live in a world characterized by accelerating and baffling flux; the broad cultural and epistemological currents discussed earlier certainly led him to the set of assumptions by which he understood the ways and movements of such a world; and Hogarth, it is clear, showed him a particular method and technique for bringing that world into imaginative focus, for giving it real texture and a direct presence that was the more powerful because it was not strictly representational.

But Smollett's indebtedness to Hogarth goes far beyond the mere appropriation of some of his scenes. For Hogarth's most innovative works, his several dramatic series, added a specific kind of narrative model to those literary models—*Gil Blas* and the picaresque, travel books, *Don Quixote*—from which Smollett learned so much. If it is true (as the eighteenth century believed and as modern narratologists have categorically proclaimed) that narrative shapes our understanding of experience and profoundly affects the way we recreate it as we tell about it, then all of these models combined to determine Smollett's characteristic episodic manner, which was (so he seems to have believed) the only authentic manner for the novelist who would capture life with absolute fidelity to the immediacy of its moral, emotional, and physical dimensions. Hogarth may thus, in an important sense, have been the most influential model of all. In any case a Smollett novel develops in very much the same manner as a Hogarth series: individual scenes define themselves with a graphic intensity and a throbbing vitality of intricate detail so arresting as to make them seem to stand alone, static, unrelated to what has gone before or to what is to come after. There is narrative progress (Hogarth deliberately used the actual word *progress* in the titles of two of his most famous series), but its invisible line is intersected vertically by the scenes, which seem to stop it, suspending both movement and time; the connecting narrative threads must be found within the scenes themselves, for they do not appear between them. Only when all the scenes, or episodes, have been viewed (when they have been visually "read") in the fullness of their detailing does their cumulative effect emerge, revealing in its totality the outline of a story and bringing to clarity the completed pattern of its meaning. The point here is that if we would read Smollett's novels well we must approach them very much as we would *The Rake's Progress* or *Marriage à la Mode.*

By so emphasizing Smollett's affinities with Hogarth I do not mean to suggest that his interest in, and knowledge of, the art of his time was narrow, or that Hogarth was the sole influence upon him. In fact, his knowledge was broad and his interest was very keen. It would be difficult if not impossible to trace direct sources for very many of the visual effects in his novels to particular examples of graphic art. Unlike Fielding, Sterne, and especially Richardson, Smollett almost never alludes to individual paintings or sculptures except in the *Travels,* and, aside from scenes in Hogarth, he seems to have used specific works as models only rarely.[50] But there can be no doubt that his visual imagination was continually stimulated by what he saw in London studios and collections, and during his few journeys to the Continent. Robert Etheridge Moore is simply wrong to say that Smollett "knew literally nothing about any other painter" except Hogarth, and that "his judgments on pictorial art are absurd."[51] It is true, as Moore notes, that in the *Travels* Smollett announced his preference for certain works of Guido Reni over others by Raphael,[52] and numerous readers besides Moore have objected to certain of Smollett's opinions of paintings and statues as expressed in the same work.

The issue is always one of taste; Smollett's tastes did not always coincide with prevailing standards, and he was nothing if not blunt in stating his views. But his eye was attentive and clear, and in his time few lay people other than connoisseurs like Horace Walpole[53] commented so expertly about principles of line and composition or so explicitly about the aesthetic effects of particular works; the very letter in the *Travels* containing the comparison between Guido and Raphael is largely devoted to a detailed (and knowing) review of the art treasures of the Vatican and Saint Peter's Church.

Smollett did not wait until the *Travels,* written late in his career, to begin public discussion of the arts. Indeed, in the very first volume of the *Critical Review* (January to July 1756) he launched into a series of featured notices and articles calling attention to new works of art, to artists, and to new books about both. Little of what appears in the *Critical Review* measures up against modern standards of reviewing in the field, but Smollett's magazine was the first to undertake regular, serious discussion of such subjects, and it thus helped importantly to establish commentary on the arts as a genre of critical writing.[54] During the years of his involvement with the *Critical Review,* first as editor and then as occasional contributor, Smollett wrote more than half of the two dozen or so features concerning the arts, but we may be fairly certain that for much of this time he had a guiding hand in the selection of artists and other topics for consideration even in the pieces he did not write; as editor, he very likely reserved the right to approve final copy before publication, thus ensuring his control of the series.

Overall, the *Critical Review* displayed a particular interest in promoting British (as opposed to Continental) art, too often neglected (Smollett seems to have thought) in other published commentary. Lewis M. Knapp has observed that the *Critical Review* was launched as part of Smollett's grand (and unsuccessful) scheme to establish a British academy of the belles-lettres, by which he hoped to promote the organized study of literature and the other arts.[55] At about this same time—that is, between 1755 and 1757—he possibly struck up an acquaintance with John Nesbitt, cousin to John Wilkes (with whom Smollett was then on the friendliest of terms) and author of the widely read *Essay on the Necessity and Form of a Royal Academy for Painting, Sculpture and Architecture* (1755).[56] Nesbitt's pamphlet was an important contribution to the

long campaign for just the sort of institution it proposed, which was founded
at last in 1768 as the Royal Academy of Arts. No doubt Smollett was sympathetic to this campaign, and the support of the *Critical Review* was surely crucial. Such support was given almost from the very beginning. Among the earliest pieces Smollett wrote for the magazine is a brief, celebratory notice of
new works by the English sculptor Joseph Wilton, which he praises (Smollett
rarely criticizes in any of these features) for their exquisite fidelity to their
Greek models, observing also—and with great emphasis—that they possess
"the strength and accuracy of a *Bona Rota,* with all the taste and delicacy of a
Bernini." He ranks Wilton with Hogarth and Francis Hayman, proclaiming
that these three alone are sufficient to ensure that England's "neighbours on
the continent, will no longer reproach us with want of talent for the arts."[57]
His very next contribution takes up the same theme in a longer and even
more admiring review of Hogarth's triptych altar painting for the church of
Saint Mary Redcliffe in Bristol. Smollett reveals a fine sensitivity to line, color,
and proportion in his detailing of this work's subject matter and composition,
and he finishes with a striking tribute to this quite uncharacteristic, but still
excellent, example of the artist's skill: "if this noble ornament," he says,
"should make its way into our churches [i.e., in copies], it will be the likeliest
means to raise a *British* school of painters." "In the meantime," he concludes,
"we think it would be a just subject of public regret, if Mr. *Hogarth* should
abandon a branch of painting in which he stands alone unrivaled and inimitable, to pursue another in which so many have already excelled."[58]

It is clear that at this time Smollett considered Hogarth the preeminent living British artist, a view no doubt encouraged by his sense of kinship with him
but certainly justified by any meaningful standard of judgment. He did not
discount the accomplishments of others, however. A particularly glowing—
and acute—review of three new prints by Sir Robert Strange[59] lavishly
praises the skill with which the engraver has rendered difficult works by
Nicholas Poussin and Guido Reni, once again using the occasion to celebrate
British art and to argue against its neglect. "Amidst the degeneracy, want of
taste, trifling pursuits, and dissipation of the present age," Smollett begins,
"we find many instances of uncommon genius in all the different branches of
the liberal arts, shooting up as it were without culture, and even unheeded,

like a number of delicate flowers on a common overgrown with weeds, heath and brambles" (p. 375). With impressive perceptiveness and skill, he goes on to argue convincingly that Strange belongs among the finest examples of a peculiarly British genius, a tactic he will use again, in other contributions, as he seeks to raise public consciousness of native artists by trumpeting their merits. One other example will suffice to demonstrate how this is so. In a series of three brief pieces on the works of Thomas Frye, he repeatedly calls upon the taste of his readers, urging them to join him in his festive sense of the "rapid progress we make in the polite arts,"[60] meanwhile revealing his genuine excitement about (and exact knowledge of) the new art of "metzotinto"—or mezzotint, a technique of engraving copper plate by scraping and burnishing certain areas so as to create subtle effects of light and shadow. In these notices (they can hardly be called reviews) Smollett possibly did more than anyone to make Frye's innovative engraving process widely known, understood, and appreciated, and he very likely helped the artist's career into the bargain, as he also helped the cause of British art and artists generally.

Smollett's purpose in publishing such items as I have been describing was in part to mount a kind of public relations campaign, carried out with the help of his fellow contributors. It is impossible to estimate how well he succeeded in this purpose, though the broad popularity of the *Critical Review* makes it likely that he was very successful indeed. But he did not write as a mere polemicist or promotional agent for specific artists and their works. The range of his professional interest was very broad, extending to published commentaries on aesthetics and the history of the visual arts. His review of one such commentary, Daniel Webb's *Inquiry into the Beauties of Painting* (1760),[61] runs to more than eight pages of closely reasoned argument grounded in deep understanding and a genuine engagement with the subject. This review, generally favorable, is distinguished by Smollett's judicious differences with Webb over matters of taste and the proper estimation of works by the great masters, and also by a fundamental disagreement in principle— Webb argues for judgment grounded in precept, whereas Smollett favors a "long habitude of studying pictures and statues, and of comparing one piece with another" (p. 198). Because he had traveled so little on the Continent before the date of this review, Smollett could hardly have encountered firsthand

more than a relative few of the masterworks used by Webb as examples in his
analysis of the constituent elements of successful painting; yet he shows a surprising knowledge of them—gained largely, no doubt, through the many
prints and other reproductions he had seen and admired. His reference to the
need for long study is a little disingenuous, but only a little.

The review of Webb is by itself irrefutable evidence against Moore's claim
that Smollett was wholly ignorant of the arts, and of all artists except Hogarth.
Taken together with the other assorted reviews and notices I have been sampling, it is likewise strong evidence of an abiding preoccupation—it seems to
have been a passion—with visual modes of expression. This preoccupation
coincided with Smollett's particular talent as a writer, and with his personal
way of registering experience by focusing on the most powerful images of
it as generated by feeling and filtered through memory. Here I may return to
the question, raised early in this introduction, of just what kind of novelist
Smollett was. At least one answer to this question should be obvious by now,
and it is this: He was an intensely visual writer whose knowledge of the arts
was broad and deep and whose stories are therefore best read with the closest
possible attention to the explicitly graphic details he so purposefully used to
represent character, environment, and incident.

Smollett's particular habit of rendering experience by picturing it so vividly
makes it clear that he was neither an intellectual like Fielding nor a student of
the interior life like Richardson, but rather a writer who simply recorded tumultuous reality as it *looked,* filling out the representation and giving it vibrancy by adding sound, smells, physical texture, and even taste. Silence is rare
in a Smollett novel, stenches are common, and one nearly always feels it
would be possible to reach out and touch his characters or to walk through
the places where they find themselves; people eat a great deal, often badly,
while foods are always pungent and frequently rotting. Smollett wrote without
much reflection and with even less consideration of the complexities of human motivation. This is not to say that he was not thoughtful, or that he
lacked penetration. On the contrary: Despite occasional carelessness and a
habit of improvisation, he was on the whole a very deliberate novelist who
chose to read the world through its manifest appearances and then to capture

those appearances precisely, in words that make their substance accessible and their meaning inescapable.

Smollett's words consistently project an unmistakable sense of the fragility of all principles of order. Such principles inevitably break down in his novels, making his characters vulnerable to circumstantial uncertainty and threatening to reduce their lives to scattered fragments, until at last order is recreated in mythic endings affirming a system of belief that displaces felt reality. The relation between Smollett's visual technique and his episodic structures is so close as to defeat attempts to say exactly what it is. These two dimensions of his work simply cannot be totally isolated for separate analysis, and so it is only possible to observe that each generates the other in a kind of reciprocal transmission of creative energy. Such reciprocity seems to have come naturally to a writer of Smollett's raw sensibilities. Given his conviction that the world was a dangerous and unstable place, episodic irregularity seems to have been almost a structural necessity in his narratives. Given his personal disposition, and his sense of himself as alien and (frequently) victim, it is no wonder that he felt a compulsion to conjure up pictures of what he wished to condemn or to ridicule; they were the means by which his vivid imagination was able to make moving targets stand still so that he might take sure aim at them. As a moralist Smollett certainly knew the cautionary value of his pictures, and he also knew, intuitively at least, that representation reduces the power of what is represented by defining it through exposure.

This way of approaching the writing of a narrative led naturally to a method involving a system of oppositions. In his novels, Smollett characteristically places the reality of disorder, graphically rendered, in tension with an ideal of moral order that is always in a state of more or less abstraction. The edenic rural estates to which all of his heroes retreat as their stories close are rarely seen, never so clearly as the city or the road. The heroes themselves are fully pictured (Peregrine Pickle, for example, and Sir Launcelot Greaves), but only so long as they are in the world and thus susceptible to it, in danger of seduction by it. When they are finally able to withdraw from it into a mythic space of beauty and tranquility they fade into indistinctness—a condition of strength because it certifies the unity of the moral self with an ideal that is (or so Smollett's practice would lead us to believe) impossible to describe but

more real and thus more powerful than its opposite. In an interesting variation, Smollett offers relatively few details about the appearance of the villainous Ferdinand Count Fathom, instead allowing him to be identified with the
equally villainous world he schemes to exploit, which is anything but vague or
abstract; the effect is a kind of negative representation, and it is balanced by
the idealized portraits of the hero and heroine, Renaldo and Monimia. In the
deployment of his imaginary people Smollett consistently gives his moral idealism both potency and relevance by two means: through comic figures like
Strap (in *Roderick Random*), Hatchway (in *Peregrine Pickle*), and Humphry
Clinker (in the novel bearing his name), who are graphically visualized, but
emphatically for the purpose of provoking the kind of sympathetic laughter
that can take recognition past their ridiculous eccentricity of appearance and
conduct, and toward their more elusive centers of gentle humanity; and
through his heroines, who (particularly those of the early novels—Narcissa,
Emilia, Monimia) embody all virtue but are essentially as self-less and voice-
less as they are conventionally beautiful—they are icons, or statues, constant
and powerful reminders of what is not but ought to be.

Smollett's heroines are all "amiable apparitions," to borrow from Roderick
Random's description of Narcissa upon first encountering her in chapter 39.
Such a reductive conception of the woman is certainly demeaning, as we now
know from hindsight, and recent critics (especially feminists) have sometimes
treated Smollett roughly for it. The real issue here, however, is not deliberate
misogynistic intention, but rhetorical purpose; with respect to his heroines at
least, Smollett was no more the misogynist than other novelists of his generation, including many women. His deployment of characters like Narcissa and
Emilia works strategically because it insistently enforces the reader's sense of
the deep divisions within his imagined worlds: the bright, gentle beauty of his
heroines is always opposed, in a kind of implied dialectic, to the dark, harsh
ugliness (and often the grotesquerie) of the reality that encloses and endangers
them; sometimes that reality is represented in the figure of a misshapen or
otherwise egregiously physical female body, doubly emphasizing the role of
the heroine.

The crucial test for the wayward protagonists of his first three novels, on
the other hand, is somehow to find a way past the threat of permanent and to-

tal alienation from all that is desirable, all that is associated with eternal values—as Roderick is almost forever alienated from Narcissa, Perry from Emilia, and Fathom from everything signified by the ethereal Monimia. In these early novels it is the heroine who draws the hero (in Fathom's case, the hero-villain) toward his redemption, and she does so by simply being what she is—lovely, virtuous, constant: everything the world is not. In *Sir Launcelot Greaves* and *Humphry Clinker,* Smollett plays out a different dramatic relationship between his central male and female characters, but the results are much the same. Aurelia Darnel, rarely ever seen, serves as external definition of what Greaves already is but must struggle to remain in a world that mocks and actively seeks to undo him—she is, for hero and reader alike, an idea rather than a physical presence. Lydia Melford is a more complex figure than any of Smollett's other girls, but through her constant love for the exemplary (as he proves to be) son of her uncle Matt's old friend Dennison, she becomes a primary instrument for bringing about the orderliness and tranquility with which the Bramble family's erratic journey concludes.[62]

In further response to the question of just what kind of novelist Smollett was, then, we may say that he wrote dialectically—relentlessly visual, and as relentlessly episodic, he carefully opposed the calm, clear stasis of moral idealism to the irregularity, confusion, and swirling movement characterizing daily life in the world as he knew it, in the process generating the restless narrative energy for which his novels have always been justly admired. One would suspect Smollett of having pursued a particular system of thought if he were not known to have been so skeptical of all formal systems. He could admire thinkers like his countryman David Hume, but (in his imaginative life at least) he could not approach the interpretation of experience with their cool rationality. His method was the result of something else—the workings of the heart, not the head; he wrote from the realm of feeling, and he cared little for precept or philosophy.

This observation brings me to an additional, final point. If Smollett wrote dialectically, he also proceeded dialogically—in the Bakhtinian sense of the term. His novels always incorporate elements from the multiplicity of competing narrative forms available to the storyteller in his day—the drama and verse satire, of course, and serial painting, but also the many forms of prose narrative. Most of these last I have already mentioned, in a different context: travel writing, the picaresque, various other biographical forms, the romance, the narrative in letters. In his eclectic habits, Smollett was not especially different from other novelists of his period. They all exploited whatever was popular at the time they wrote, not just because they wanted to achieve commercial success by appealing to the heterogenous tastes of the reading audience (though this was no inconsiderable motive), but because they were striving toward definition of the new form in which they practiced. It is worth remembering that when Smollett began writing novels (almost simultaneously with Richardson and Fielding, and not long before Sterne), there was no coherent tradition to guide him. Indeed, the form was hardly a form at all; there was no vast legacy of previous examples such as informed the work of contemporary playwrights and poets, no body of critical theory, no "rhetoric" of fiction. If every serious novelist at the time laid claim to "newness" and innovation, every one also borrowed freely from the narrative types supposedly being displaced.[63]

The convergences of form achieved in works like *Clarissa, Roderick Random, Tom Jones,* and even *Tristram Shandy* gradually provided at least a certain tentative definition of a distinctive genre devoted to the display of ordinary experience in a recognizable world and to the portrayal of familiar characters engaged in a process of self-definition, all developed through a continuous story of substantial length and dense detail. Smollett's own *Humphry Clinker,* the last work of fiction written by the five so-called "early masters," confirmed this definition, though it is actually the most eclectic of all eighteenth-century novels, for it manages to incorporate virtually every narrative type known to its generation of writers and readers—it is at once travel book, biography, adventure story, rogue tale, epistolary chronicle, and comic romance. In this work—his most carefully structured and most coherently plotted—as in his others, Smollett was very little interested in the consolidation of forms. It was their multiplicity that appealed to him, and he took few pains to disguise the seams holding the constituent generic elements of his novels together. The landscape of eighteenth-century fiction writing was as tumultuous and uncertain as the broader cultural landscape Smollett tried to capture in his stories; its disparateness served him well, allowing for tensions among ways of rendering the experience of his characters that expand his readers' means of knowing them, while also promoting the felt resistance to principles of cohesiveness that otherwise distinguishes his stories.

It is as though Smollett (in contrast to, say, Fielding) did not really believe it was possible to achieve a full convergence of forms in a transforming creative act that would produce a single new form. Certainly Sterne did not believe in such a possibility, and these two rivals are much more alike—as experimental writers—than critics and literary historians have generally perceived them to be. The likely truth is that Smollett (in this respect he is very unlike Sterne) did not think about the matter much if at all, and he most assuredly did not theorize about it. He just wrote, purposefully grasping and using whatever formal methods he needed to make his novels do what he wanted them to do—tell stories of mercurial adventures in a manner that would give those adventures full visibility of detail, striking immediacy, and powerful impact. His appeal to his earliest readers resided in the success (it was not always the same level of success) with which he was able to reach their nerve centers of feeling and judgment by giving them a heightened sense of the world they knew both through their other reading and through their own private experience. His appeal today, in a very different time, is about the same. The novels he wrote, with their frequent absurdist effects and their glaring focus upon the dislocation and alienation of the individual, seem unmistakably modern—even postmodern, if we consider especially their deliberate irregularities of form. Read well, Smollett at his best is as interesting and rewarding now as he ever has been, and his works hold up sturdily for an audience steeped in Joyce, Faulkner, Heller, Barth, and Pynchon.

In the chapters that follow, I shall try to read him well, and I hope to demonstrate the truth of what I have been claiming for him in a way that will be helpful both to the general reader and the specialist. The method I have adopted (if it can be called that) is simple to describe. Each chapter takes up a single novel, developing its analysis from the biographical and historical contexts explored in the introduction I am now concluding, but avoiding any formulaic approach and instead allowing the novel under discussion to dictate both organization and critical procedures—Smollett's novels are so very different, in so very many ways, that they defy rigid interpretive schemes and formulas. The chapters are arranged chronologically, as I am interested in (among many other things) the progression of Smollett's career, though I do not see it as an altogether evolutionary progression. Always in view are the two questions raised at the outset of this introduction (what kind of novelist was he? how may he best be read?) and then, over the last several pages, briefly answered in a preparatory way. It is time now to move beyond preparation to discussion of the novels themselves. I begin with *Roderick Random*.

CHAPTER I

Roderick Random

"It does not appear," wrote James Beattie of his countryman Tobias Smollett, "that he knew how to contrive a regular fable, by making his events mutually dependent and all co-operating to one and the same final purpose."[1] Beattie intended this observation as a judgment against all of Smollett's novels, though many readers and critics of subsequent generations would apply similar strictures with especial vehemence against *Roderick Random.*[2] Such dispraise, arising from a fundamental misunderstanding of what Smollett sought to do in his work, hardly diminishes his novels at all, but instead reflects upon those expressing it. Beattie obviously assumed as a standard of evaluation a traditional, pre-novelistic model of narrative born of the neo-Aristotelian critical dogma promoted in the late seventeenth century by Thomas Rymer and other classicists as a way of governing form in the drama.[3] Such a model bore little relevance to the fiction actually written by most of the earliest practitioners of the novelist's craft—Cervantes, Lesage, Defoe, and Sterne among them. Smollett, in particular, deliberately rejected the principle of regularity in the construction of a narrative fable—or at least the kind of regularity Beattie seems to have had in mind. He was an apple to Beattie's orange.

That Smollett did not write as Beattie would have preferred is no proof that he lacked the ability to do so. What he lacked was the will. We can say with assurance that he knew the dramatic model of regularity very well; his youthful *Regicide* follows that model closely, and its failure is not one of form but of language and character—Smollett naively tried to write like the Dryden of *The*

Conquest of Granada (1670), and the result was stiltedly inauthentic. And we know for certain that he was a close reader of Fielding, the chief exponent of organic regularity in contemporary fiction, whom he made no attempt to emulate—though his education in the classics, and his literary awareness, were comparable to Fielding's in every way. Beattie's judgment, it must be said, is absurdly prejudicial; and worse, it begs the real question. What needs to be asked about Smollett—about *Roderick Random,* and about each of his other novels as well—is not whether he "knew how to contrive a regular fable," but a set of different questions altogether: Just what kind of fable *did* he contrive, why did he do it, and what does it mean to the reader who seeks to understand the work as a whole construction?

In the introduction I began the process of answering these questions by elaborating in general terms upon the characteristic form of Smollett's novels—eclectic, episodic, fragmented, pictorial in a way that frequently stops both motion and time; and I suggested some of the personal and cultural reasons why he may have chosen to write as he did. Now, as I turn to *Roderick Random,* it seems important to pause for consideration of some critical principles that will help toward an understanding of the consequences of his choice. Only principles different from Beattie's—different, too, from those of the later readers who have followed his same line of argument—will do, as a fair reading of Smollett requires an approach and a set of premises appropriate to the actual words on the pages of his books. For such principles one must look outside the boundaries of traditional criticism of eighteenth-century fiction and toward the more expansive field of modernist and postmodernist narratological and genre studies, where there is greater tolerance of and respect for the sorts of irregular procedures we find in his erratic stories of adventurers in motion.

Probably the modern theory of narrative most congenial to Smollett is that of Joseph Frank, as set forth in his landmark article on spatial form, published more than half a century ago.[4] Frank has nothing to say about Smollett, but his notion of an essentially anti-Aristotelian narrative structure that legitimately subverts chronology and linearity—or at least diminishes both—in the interest of promoting alternative kinds of effects (specifically through an emphasis on spaces, and on "vertical" rather than "horizontal" representations of experience) is very close to Smollett's own. Frank's essay, offered partly as a response to the pieties of New Criticism, provided a critical framework within which the works of Joyce, Woolf, and other modernists might be read and meaningfully discussed. The essay has been very influential,[5] but so far as I am aware no one has cited it as a guide to reading Smollett. And yet it is just the guide that is needed, for it lends critical authorization to the sort of novel he always wrote—to the "spatial form" he gave to his stories. Smollett is not Joyce or Woolf, but his work shows a similar disruption of narrative principles of causality and temporality; he is in this sense very modern, as I suggested in the introduction to this book, and so it seems strange that to date no modern critic has applied Frank's modernist theory to his work.

The central tenet of Frank's position is simple to state. The chronological model, he explains, is the foundation model of all narrative. Life is experienced sequentially and progressively; and besides, every story told is a series of words, also (and necessarily) experienced sequentially and progressively. In its purest form (that is, in the story told with the strictest fidelity to causality and sequence), the chronological model is nothing more or less than the "regular fable" so prized by those who, like Beattie, see literature as preeminently an empirical exercise in the simplifying definition of emotional, moral, and (most of all) social order. Spatial form of course incorporates chronology and sequence too (both qualities are inescapable in any narrative), and it is likewise devoted to the display of a concern with the human need for order, in both the private and the public realms of experience. But, less grounded in a rigid rationality, it is able to address that need by a structural imaging of the felt stresses working against its fulfillment. In a novel organized by the principles of spatial form, time as a dimension may be reduced in importance relative to space (image, scene, episode), and indeed may apparently (or even really) lose the force of sequentiality, as simultaneity, or disjunction and the disordering of events, takes precedence. Such a novel is disruptive for its reader, whose expectation is that the story in a book will replicate the perceived form of the story of his or her life, lived one day after another in a kind of ceaseless forward motion. But the disruption forces altered perceptions by projecting unanticipated configurations of experience, leading to direct awareness of the reality of disorder, of the rule of Chance in human affairs, of the urgent meaning of intensive moments without respect to their specific placement in time or in a structure of causality (which is often shown to be illusory anyway)—any or all of these.

A novel's commitment to spatial form may be more (Cervantes, Sterne, Joyce, Pynchon, the Heller of *Catch-22*) or less (Defoe, Dickens, Lawrence, the Barth of *The Sot-Weed Factor*) extreme. In certain generic types (the picaresque, for example—a type closely associated with Smollett), says David Mickelsen, one of Frank's most articulate followers, chronology may all but give way to the atemporal juxtaposition of equivalent incidents, and if it is actually "eliminated or at least severely attenuated," "true spatial form appears."[6] The result in such a case is a "shift from the diachronic to the synchronic," and with this shift "the major unifier left is thematic" (p. 70)—indeed, virtually no other unifier remains possible. By "discarding a causal, linear organization," Mickelsen concludes, a novelist may move toward "an organic conception of life, a life in which events are not so much discernible points on a line as they are random (and often simultaneous) occurrences in a seamless web of experience" (p. 77). Mickelsen was not writing about Smollett, or *Roderick Random,* but he might as well have been. Though Smollett is in all of his novels more committed to the representation of experience as progression through time than is the composite generic author of whom Mickelsen speaks, still he favors the synchronic over the diachronic, he cares more about thematics than architectonic regularity, and he emphasizes an organic conception of *life* rather than of form.

What Smollett does as a writer, and what Mickelsen and Frank theorize about as critics, is all very close to another modern configural notion of narrative form, Mikhail Bakhtin's idea of the chronotope, what he describes as "the intrinsic connectedness of temporal and spatial relationships that are artistically expressed in literature."[7] Time and space cannot be separated, says Bakhtin, for each is essential to the other; yet, in some narratives, the former may collapse into the latter, and indeed time can seem like a fourth dimension of space: an intensively visual scene or episode always conveys a sense of motion, which implies passage and thus time, and yet its energy may be so self-contained and its restriction of the reader's eye and mind so nearly complete as to keep it effectually disconnected from other scenes that precede and follow it. The result is the ascendancy of the spatial as the primary mode of the narrative in which such an effect occurs. Bakhtin, who does occasionally at least glance at Smollett, could have been thinking of him directly (though he almost certainly was not) when he wrote that in the "literary artistic chronotope, spatial and temporal indicators are fused into one carefully thought-out, concrete whole. Time, as it were, thickens, takes on flesh, becomes artistically visible; likewise, space becomes charged and responsive to the movements of time, plot and history" (p. 84). Even the most basic understanding of the applicability of Bakhtin's theory—and Frank's—to Smollett's novels can lead to recognition that their particular shaping and texturing are purposeful: time is less important than the spaces his characters inhabit from moment to moment, scene to scene, episode to episode; causality, most often unintelligible in its specific workings, goes by the name of Chance or Fortune. Smollett sometimes wrote hastily, and he often improvised,[8] but there can be no doubt of his intention as to form. As James H. Bunn has observed, "Nice increments of chance repeated over and over again can create vast designs."[9]

Paul-Gabriel Boucé long ago argued, altogether convincingly, that it is thematic urgency and not organic consistency that unifies Smollett's novels; indeed, this argument is the main burden of his fine book.[10] According to Boucé, the earliest of the novels center upon the thematic relations between adventure and morality, and *Roderick Random* is especially successful in its pursuit of these relations, gaining wholeness and coherence from their formal development. Such an assessment anticipates David Mickelsen's more general point about the unifying effect of thematics in narratives constructed from the principles of spatial form, though Boucé nowhere, in any of his discussions of the novels, takes up those principles as a way of further explaining— or justifying—Smollett's irregularities. He thus misses an opportunity to move beyond spirited defense of the novels against hostile or misguided criticism and toward a positive affirmation of their merit as examples of a certain kind of narrative. Still, his argument about their thematic unity remains useful, especially as a model for critical commentary, and I shall have occasion to refer to it again in this and later chapters. Indeed, I hope to demonstrate (among other things) how the spatial form of *Roderick Random* and Smollett's other novels actually promotes recognition of their thematic centers and their articulations of a vision of the individual character as moral agent.

The thematic unity of *Roderick Random* develops by a cumulative process. Time is an issue—Roderick is born, he grows up, he travels, he matures, he gains happiness, and at last he writes his autobiographical story. Smollett, strongly influenced by Lesage and the tradition of the picaresque, did not make his hero a reflective fellow; Roderick shows almost no interest in drawing connections among the many episodes recounted from his memory, except insofar as he describes them in the sequence of their occurrence and presents them as a journey (sometimes literally) through the world, but with an itinerary only superficially foreordained. He initiates little in his life; instead, people and events happen to him, until finally—by his author's contrivance—he comes out all right. Neither time as a measure of his experience, nor sequence as the means of calibrating that measure, is of any real importance to Roderick, or his reader. What does matter is the content of the individual episodes; disconnected and undifferentiated as they are, Roderick recaptures them in vivid rushes of immediacy, all but reliving them as he does so, making it seem almost as though they are happening in the present instead of the past. His loss of distance—his collapsing of the temporal dimensions of past and present—has troubled some readers, who have called it a flaw in Smollett's conception of his character, a failure of artistic discipline that confuses perspective.[11] But this response to Roderick's voice misses one of the novel's primary interpretive points about the potentially overpowering effects of remembered experience, in the process obscuring the meaning of its transmission. It is precisely the undifferentiating immediacy of the telling that gives the major episodes of Roderick's story (and many of the minor ones) their equivalency of impact by placing them in virtual juxtaposition to one another. With no meaningful connections between them, causal or otherwise, their effect is synchronic, to borrow Mickelsen's term; but they must be read individually, until gradually their relations clarify, revealing a coherence of design.

What I have just described, in brief outline, is the spatial form of *Roderick Random*. I might almost have been describing a narrative series of paintings, but that should not be surprising, for it should be clear by now that I see the movement of a Smollett novel as closely resembling that of a Hogarth progress. Novelist and painter alike were intuitive practitioners of spatial form, and the former surely learned a great deal from the latter about how to succeed with it—which he did, in part, by projecting his episodes literally as spaces, filling them with visual details to create pictorial effects. To put this another way, and more emphatically: In a Smollett novel, and with especially relentless vividness in *Roderick Random,* a space is a picture—dense, busy, active, and precise. And, as David Mickelsen says is true of all narratives that work synchronically by the gathering of seemingly disparate effects, the pictures achieve coherence by crystallizing into "two kinds of spatial form: portraits of individuals and tableaux of societies" (p. 70).

Mickelsen uses both terms—*portraits* and *tableaux*—somewhat loosely, or rather nonliterally, to mean simply the vividly captured impression of an individual fictional personage, however detailed the impression might be, and the precisely rendered study of a particular social group within a particular social context—the tableau is, for him, a bit of behavioral reality caught in a kind of stop action, its movement suspended but not halted. The two "kinds" of spatial form—portraits and tableaux—frequently coalesce as Smollett employs them. Typically, a Smollett episode focuses on a central character or characters, while simultaneously projecting a complex representation of a social environment, the whole adding up to a self-contained drama. In *Roderick Random,* for example, the satiric Captain Weazel episode (chapters 11 and 12) features a memorable portrait of a ridiculous *miles gloriosus,* supplemented by lesser sketches of the other characters—a prostitute, a lawyer, and a usurer, along with the captain's wife—aboard the London-bound wagon on which Roderick and Strap have hopped a ride. There is nothing especially original in the conception here; Smollett merely adapts the age-old convention of the journey by coach, which (like countless other storytellers before him, including Fielding in *Joseph Andrews*) he uses as a device for the satiric display of a social microcosm. His purpose, obviously enough, is to expose the pride, pretentiousness, hypocrisy, and downright meanness of the world as reductively defined by the conduct of the eccentric low-lifes he has assembled, all of them measured in part against the innocence of Roderick and Strap, who are astonished by what they see and hear. It is his manner that sets Smollett's use of the familiar convention apart. By beginning the episode in darkness he calls attention to and thus enhances its singular pictorial effect—Roderick hears the captain's formidable blustering and is at first frightened, only to laugh when the voice becomes a body once its owner emerges into the light. He further enhances the same effect by the colorful vigor of the characters' language. The

visual and verbal intensity of the episode serves to stop the forward movement of the journey during which it occurs (paradoxically, of course, as the
wagon keeps rolling on toward the city of Roderick's destination) by causing
both the hero and his reader to forget about it momentarily in their contemplation of the lively spectacle of the captain and company; progression re-
sumes when the wagon arrives in London without ever seeming to have traveled along the road at all, and Roderick's attention turns to new scenes.

The emphasis of this episode is on space as defined by those who occupy it.
There is relatively little detailing of the setting itself; Smollett does not describe the interior of the wagon, or of the inns where it stops. Yet there is a
completeness in the picture as a whole. In its combination of character portraiture with a social tableau, the Weazel episode works in a manner almost
identical to that of the third scene of *The Rake's Progress,* despite the very different content. In Hogarth's drawing we find the same busy-ness of activity,
the same primary focus of the eye upon characters other than the protagonist—only at second or third glance do we see that Tom Rakewell, placed at
the far right of the scene, is being robbed by one of the whores in the dark
room of the Rose Tavern where he has settled himself after an evening of
carousing (and brawling—he has fought with a watchman, whose broken
lantern lies at his feet) in the streets. The room is obviously very noisy; a
dozen characters, all but two of them women (and all vividly caught in their
various motions), are talking, or singing, or laughing as they drink. In the left
foreground a second whore is undressing, and just behind her a porter has entered the room bearing a large shiny platter and a candle, clearly for her use in
some ghastly erotic ritual.[12] The whole is an anatomy of a social microcosm, a
tableau defined by the characters who populate it and capable of being read
without any reference to its place in Tom's inevitable passage toward ruin—
though in a synchronic way it is extremely important as a stage in that passage.
Smollett's Weazel episode is more fully extended, as it shifts from wagon to
inn and back again; but its method is exactly that of Hogarth in his scene of
debauchery at the Rose. Both pictures arrest motion by compelling attention
to their details, and both are carefully framed within the larger narratives of
which they are a part—the abrupt breaks between Smollett's episodes serve
exactly the same purpose as the frames within which Hogarth enclosed each

William Hogarth, *A Rake's Progress,* Scene 3 (1735).
(By courtesy of the Trustees of Sir John Soane's Museum.)

of the paintings in a series and the boxlike borders he always placed around his prints.

I shall return to the Weazel episode presently for a close look at its particular visual qualities—compelling enough in themselves, but deepened and enriched by the language Roderick hears its principal characters speak. Because, as a novelist, he could give his people voices, Smollett enjoyed an advantage over Hogarth, to whom the medium of speech was unavailable; and yet Smollett most often used speech as a way of adding texture to his visual portraits—his characters always say just what one would expect them to, given their appearance, and in just the right tones, accents, and inflections. In Smollett's work, language regularly becomes part of the visual medium. I shall have more to say of this later also; for the moment I wish to focus directly on the matter of his pictorial representations of individuals—all of them elements in the social tableaux he projects in episode (or "space") after episode. Smollett, like Hogarth, was a satirist—he opens the preface to *Roderick Random* by referring to the work as a satire; and though he introduced idealized characters into each of his novels (most of them women), his real enthusiasm was for the portrayal of eccentricity, innocuous or amusing or villainous. For him, again as for Hogarth, characters wore their identities on their skeletons, and as an artist he had the kind of eye that always saw the defining details. Apart from the long tradition of literary satire, he seems to have been strongly influenced—as was Hogarth—by the old Western tradition of the grotesque, by the modern art of *caricatura,* and by contemporary medical theories of the relations between physiology and character, between inner "motions" and outward expressiveness. As a physician he possessed extensive knowledge of such theories, which were altogether consistent with—and actually supported—the assumptions about individuality and satiric representation he adopted from other sources.

The work of, among others, Wolfgang Kayser (on the grotesque), George Kahrl (on Smollett and caricature), and John McAllister (on symptomatology and the representation of character) has made it unnecessary for me to linger over these influences, except to state more fully what they were.[13] The crucial point with respect to the grotesque style or mode, which was associated with the visually gay and fantastic by such early Renaissance practitioners as Raphael, is that it can move so easily beyond playful fancy to images of the ominous and the sinister, as in a work like the famous triptych *The Millenium,* by Raphael's contemporary Hieronymous Bosch, with its proto-surreal joining of human, animal, plant, and mechanical elements in an astonishing tour de force on sin and evil. By a convergence of the nonhuman and the human, the inanimate and the animate, the grotesque makes the familiar unfamiliar, and depending upon the tone or context the effect can be anything from terror to laughter, or sometimes a mix of effects from both ends of the spectrum. With the grotesque, says Kayser, "the laws of statics, symmetry, and proportion are no longer valid" (p. 21); and even in its lighter expressions (sometimes given the name *burlesque*), he continues, the "basic feeling" it provokes is "one of surprise and horror, an agonizing fear in the presence of a world which breaks apart and remains inaccessible."[14] Given his interest in the visual arts, Smollett surely knew at least the rudiments of a theory of the grotesque, especially as it merged with the recently imported art of caricature. Both modes involved distortion—the latter somewhat more mildly, as it rarely mixed inanimate with animate but instead enhanced peculiarities of a subject by exaggerating distinctive features; both, as Kayser has put it, placed the "principle of art as an imitation of beautiful nature" "in jeopardy" (p. 30); and both were congenial to a writer like Smollett, whose sensibilities led him to a certainty of life's irregularity in a world where the brokenness of experience often felt like a nightmare of twisted, misshapen values, discouraging any notion that the generality of nature (human nature, at least) could with any authenticity be represented as beautiful.

George Kahrl has usefully distinguished caricature (which focuses on "tolerable and humorous imperfections") from the grotesque (it is obsessed with "physical abnormalities and the demonic") and from satire (its subject is "irrational and evil deformities"). Satire, Kahrl reminds us, is a nonpictorial mode, and so its objects in Smollett—in *Roderick Random,* characters like Gawky, Potion, Crumple, and Strutwell—are simple stereotypes, abstractions whose names are their only real signifiers; never precisely described, they are not portraits at all.[15] In truth, of course, there is a blurring of satire, caricature, and the grotesque in Smollett's novels, though his real imaginative energies went into the two pictorial modes. His use of these blurs as well, but in general we may say that he reserves the stronger grotesque for characters (like Captain Weazel) who are to be condemned, or otherwise repudiated through severely judgmental laughter, and caricature for those (like Bowling and Strap) whose failings or eccentricities are merely amusing, to be gently laughed at and joyously celebrated as evidence of the rich diversity of life and character, for which Smollett had a deep appreciation. In the earlier novels, the number of grotesque or near-grotesque character portraits is very substantial, in *Roderick Random* actually greater than the number of caricatures, and this is a reason why these works seem so dark, despite their high comic energy. In any case the differences among his portraits are a matter of degree, just as the difference between the grotesque and caricature in visual art is also one of degree, not kind.

What one notices most about all of Smollett's portraits, and in this he is very like Hogarth, is how intensely physical they are. Even characters such as

Bowling and the Welshman Morgan (or Hawser Trunnion in *Peregrine Pickle*), who are known less by the way they look than by their idiosyncratic language of the sea, emit great physical energy by the vividness and rhythms of their speech—the description of Bowling (p. 8) is rather vague and bland by comparison with Roderick's transcription of his nautical lingo, which both traps the old sailor (he can speak no other way) by its extremely limited connection with the world off-board ship, and expresses a profoundly attractive exuberance associated with his innate good-heartedness. Characters more fully visualized typically speak less, or if they are voluble, the greatest emphasis is still on the shapes of their bodies, with their faces usually (but not always) receiving the larger share of attention.[16] As John McAllister has shown, Smollett relied very heavily on contemporary medical assumptions about the appearance and the motions of the body as evidence of the inner life—of the emotional life, that is, whose physical manifestations alone made it fully intelligible.[17] He has often been criticized for inadequate representation of strong feeling[18]— at moments of high emotional stress for his characters their hair always stands on end, their knees knock, their teeth chatter, they tremble uncontrollably, and so on; but, as McAllister makes clear, this practice proceeded not only from literary convention (certainly an important source) but from a medical understanding of the way in which the body always made an emotion a "physiological event" (p. 288), defining the event by actions that were suitable to its cause, and indeed inevitable. By a kind of transference to the realm of moral life, the "goodness" or "badness" of a character could be recognized by both shapes and motions, as the body helplessly gave expressive definition to the spiritual and moral self that inhabited it. With the human character, appearance *was* reality—or if it was not, then the element of disguise itself became a moral issue because the deception of a mask was but a proof that there was some revealing appearance hiding behind it. (Hence the eighteenth century's great agitation over the social institution of the masquerade.) Morality and feeling were thus joined; and for Smollett, whose artistic sensibilities were even stronger than his convictions as a physician, the intensely visual representation of character was almost a matter of inevitability, as was his particular practice—he was a moralist, after all—of exaggeration in creating the caricatures and grotesques whose presence dominates the landscape of his imaginary worlds.

The parallels with Hogarth make it clear that there was nothing unique about Smollett's practice, and other satiric visualists besides the two of them must have felt the same convergence of influences from the graphic arts and from medicine. No other novelist of Smollett's generation, however, relied so heavily upon what was to be learned from those sources about how to project moral and social reality by means neither naturalistic nor anti-naturalistic, to use McAllister's terms (p. 287), but graphically authentic as an interpretation of that reality. In *Roderick Random,* the world the hero encounters, which from the beginning mocks him, swindles him, and generally abuses him in every way it can, is almost entirely defined by grotesques; the only major exceptions are figures like Bowling and Strap, gentle caricatures as they are presented, and Narcissa, the idealized heroine who is very real to Roderick but is never-theless also a projection of his deep desire for beauty, tranquility, and stasis— just as the more darkly presented figures, also real to him, are projections from his fear of cruelty and corruption: moral deviance he apprehends through powerful feeling, and indignation brings about the extreme distortion that creates the physical monstrosities he sees and describes.

The first of the numerous grotesques Roderick meets during the course of his adventures is the charlatan surgeon Launcelot Crab (chapter 7), whose surname is straight from the typifying abstraction of satiric convention, but whose character definition is deepened and vivified by the imaging of his de-formed person.[19] Roderick, only recently rescued from the brutality of his childhood by his uncle Tom Bowling, goes to Crab as apprentice after the apothecary Potion dismisses him because Bowling, owing to an unhappy scrape at sea, can no longer support him. Roderick's description of his new master precedes the account of his experience with him, suggesting the full power of the man's presence to dominate both memory and imagination. The distancing effect of the description (distortion always has a distancing effect) allows Crab's body to be seen whole, and thus to be interpreted as the per-fected example of an avaricious man of no physical grace and possessing a violent, "crabbed" (or sour, churlish) disposition. The Arthurian echo in the first name is an ironic joke that emphasizes the low-life truth about this pre-tended benefactor, whom Roderick immediately recognizes for the fraud that he is.[20] The description is laughing, but it passes beyond caricature to the grotesque by focusing so sharply upon the nonhuman and even inanimate attributes of Crab's appearance, thus emphasizing that what he represents is not harmlessly amusing, but sinister and dangerous. The accumulation of such grotesques in Roderick's world gradually darkens it, causing him to lose distance and, in his growing indignation, to become more and more like the bestial humanity he scourges, leaving himself in need of reformation and redemption—in later chapters (13 and 14) he is variously associated by others with a fox and an orangutan, foreshadowing his decline into dangerous culpability.[21]

The portrait of Crab, who disappears quickly from the novel, is typical of Smollett's practice in *Roderick Random,* and so it will be worthwhile to present it fully here. "This member of the faculty," says Roderick, "was aged fifty, about five foot high, and ten round the belly; his face was capacious as a full moon, and much of the complexion of a mulberry: his nose resembling a powder-horn, was swelled to an enormous size, and studded all over with carbuncles; and his little grey eyes reflected the rays in such an oblique manner, that while he looked a person full in the face, one would have imagined he was admiring the buckle of his shoe" (p. 26). Through the quality of his presence this grotesque defines the space Roderick has entered by signing on with him as apprentice; no other character in the episode is described at all. The episode itself is brief as presented, though it occupies two full years; such compression emphasizes the spatial form Smollett has wrought—real time moves rapidly onward, but autobiographical time, and Roderick's motion through it, are arrested by the force of Crab's memorable image.

What makes his image so powerful, and his presence so dominant as to compel a moment of stasis, is the juxtaposition of surprising details in his appearance as Roderick perceives it. His ludicrous proportions (five feet tall, but ten feet around) are qualified into the sinister by his powder horn of a nose (he is violent, like an implement of war), which is covered by carbuncles (suggesting disease, and the debauchery associated with drink); and his squinty grey eyes, like shiny mirrors that distort perception by angling light downward and away from themselves, betray the deviousness and metallic hardness of his soul. The portrait is unforgettable, and Crab proves to be exactly what his appearance predicts: a heavy drinker who abuses his wife, who may have murdered his earlier apprentice (Roderick's predecessor), who threatens Roderick, and who has extorted sexual favors from his maid servant and perhaps made her pregnant. The character himself was unforgettable for Roderick. What we see is what he saw: a moral grotesque who, as perceived and recreated, becomes a physical grotesque in a convincingly authentic visual representation. Not surprisingly, it was while in Crab's house that Roderick—who had begun his adventures in the great world full of promise and high optimism—sank for the first time into misery and self-loathing, as he suffered from ill treatment and want. "I became such a sloven," he says, "and contracted such an air of austerity, that every body pronounced me crest-fallen"; and he arrived at a flash of insight that is echoed repeatedly through other episodes of his narrative: "my misfortunes," he writes, "had taught me how little the caresses of the world during a man's prosperity, are to be valued by him; and how seriously and expeditiously he ought to set himself about making himself independent of them" (p. 29).

Weazel is just such another portrait as that of Crab, though somewhat less sinister, and there are many more besides in *Roderick Random*.[22] The blustering captain, when Roderick at last sees him, is reduced to an absurdity, the preposterousness of his pretensions to martial ferocity, high military rank, and exalted social class exploded instantaneously. He is another unforgettable figure, and though Roderick's description deflates him, he is still a sign of the kind of crazed, threatening, violent world the hero has now entered. Again we find a crucial juxtaposition of nonhuman with human features, so that the captain is firmly placed in a context of bestiality. He is "a little, thin creature, about the age of forty, with a long, withered visage, very much resembling that of a baboon." "Having laid aside his great coat," Roderick continues,

> I could not help admiring the extraordinary make of this man of war: He was about five foot and three inches high, sixteen inches of which went to his face and long scraggy neck; his thighs were about six inches in length, his legs resembling spindles or drum-sticks, two feet and an half, and his body, which put me in mind of extension without substance, engrossed the remainder;—so that on the whole, he appeared like a spider or grasshopper erect. (p. 50)[23]

Besides gross distortion of normal human proportions, as in the portrait of Crab, Smollett allows Roderick to associate Weazel with (of course) his animal namesake, and with a baboon, a bird (in this instance only implicitly, by reference to his scraggy neck and drumstick legs), a spider, and a grasshopper. No

Thomas Rowlandson, Captain Weazel greets Roderick and Strap (1790).
(From the private collection of the author.)

other character in the episode is so vividly or reductively rendered, and though the overall ensemble effect is important as marking and defining an important moment in the history of Roderick's deeply felt life, it is the captain who dominates the picture his memory has created.

The ensemble effect I have just mentioned produces the second of the two kinds of spatial form identified by David Mickelsen, the social tableau. With few exceptions in *Roderick Random,* Smollett uses his grotesque portraits of individuals to focus his broader drawing of social groups. The much later episode of Miss Snapper (chapters 53–55) interestingly parallels the Weazel episode, as it begins during a coach ride and as Roderick's first notion of the young woman who is the object of his desperate fortune-hunting scheme arrives in darkness through the medium of her speech: she is a smart talker, as her name suggests, impressive in her raillery at a pompous lawyer and skillful in her satiric thrusts at a braggart soldier who, but for differences in his person, might almost be Weazel himself. Roderick will shortly learn to dread her "unruly tongue," though he can admire "the sprightliness of her genius" (p. 331), and he judges that her fortune of twenty thousand pounds will justify his endurance of her saucy ways. But her appearance is against him; in this instance Smollett uses the grotesque body not so much as an expression of the character within it, but as a projected image of Roderick's now perverted moral sense, his corrupt desire to restore himself to the genteel status of his birth by foul means. Miss Snapper may not be so deformed as he had expected her to be from earlier report (one senses that here Roderick rationalizes), but she makes an astonishing figure as he first sees her: "Her head, indeed, bore some resemblance to a hatchet, the edge being represented by her face; . . . and though the protuberance of her breast, when considered alone, seemed to drag her forwards, it was easy to perceive an equivalent on her back which balanced the other, and kept her body in equilibrio" (pp. 326–27). He soon completes the picture: "I perceived that Miss had got more twists from nature, than I had before observed, being bent sideways into the figure of an S, so that her progression very much resembled that of a crab" (p. 331).

Again we find a juxtaposition of the inanimate and nonhuman to the human, and this portrait in particular is a parody of the aesthetic principles of pleasing regularity and gentle beauty that remain Roderick's ideal (it is a moral ideal as well), as he conceived it earlier upon first seeing the perfected female form of Narcissa. Miss Snapper is an even more emphatic and effective definition of the perverse desire into which he has strayed, driven by circumstances of want, than the ancient Miss Withers of an earlier episode (chapter 50)—a "wrinkled hag turned of seventy" (p. 303) whose fortune could not compensate for his revulsion as, with stinking garlicky breath, she flew upon him "like a tygeress" (p. 305). Roderick gives over his fortune-hunting ambitions, interestingly enough, only when he accompanies Miss Snapper to an assembly at Bath and discovers that Narcissa is there. The two images of his competing desires are at this moment simultaneously before him; he must choose, and he does, setting in motion the extended process of his ultimate reconciliation with Narcissa and all that she represents.

Obviously, characters like Miss Snapper and Miss Withers serve by a kind of opposition to set off the beauty and true desirability of Narcissa, just as characters like Weazel, Crab, and the numerous other grotesques—including moral grotesques like the *Thunder*'s surgeon Mackshane (another medical fraud), and its stern Captain Oakhum—serve to illuminate the essential goodness of Roderick, his companion Strap, his shipboard friend Thomson, and his uncle Bowling. Narcissa is actually introduced to Roderick's view (and the reader's) just following his description (chapter 39) of her eccentric aunt, a maiden lady of about forty to whom the benevolent Mrs. Sagely (one of the novel's saints, as her name implies) sends him as a servant after he has been beaten, robbed, and abandoned on the English coast by the agency of the monstrous Crampley, commander of the wrecked ship on which he had last served. A parodic representation of the learned female, Narcissa's aunt is a fully realized grotesque whose appearance betrays the foolishness of her ambitions in poetry—Mrs. Sagely characterizes her as "a perfect female *virtuosi*" (p. 216)[24]—and marks her as slovenly and mad. She provides an illuminating counterpoint to the idealized portrait of the lovely Narcissa (p. 219), who is presented abstractly as an "amiable apparition," all softness and silence and submission, a familiarly drawn heroine of romance. Here is the aunt as Roderick first sees her:

> She sat in her study, with one foot on the ground, and the other upon a high stool at some distance from her seat; her sandy locks hung down in a disorder I cannot call beautiful from her head, which was deprived of its coif, for the

benefit of scratching with one hand, while she held the stump of a pen in the other.—Her fore-head was high and wrinkled, her eyes large, grey and prominent; her nose long, sharp and aquiline; her mouth of vast capacity; her visage meagre and freckled, and her chin peeked like a shoemaker's paring-knife: Her upper-lip contained a large quantity of plain Spanish, which by continual falling, had embroidered her neck that was not naturally very white, and the breast of her gown, that flowed loose about her with a negligence truly poetic, discovering linen that was very fine and to all appearance, never *washed but in Castalian streams.*—Around her lay heaps of books, globes, quadrants, telescopes, and other learned apparatus: Her snuff-box stood at her right hand, at her left lay her handkerchief sufficiently used, and a convenience to spit in appeared on one side of her chair. (pp. 217–18)

This is a tour de force description, justly one of the most famous passages in *Roderick Random.* Like the descriptions of Miss Snapper, Miss Withers, and other unsightly or unladylike women (the prostitute in Weazel's wagon, for example, and also his wife), the portrait of Narcissa's aunt is intended to suggest the corruption of ideal femininity that blights Roderick's world, marking it as perverse and fallen. The details of the portrait are worth careful notice: the unfeminine pose, the crude scratching, the chin mechanized by the comparison to a shoemaker's knife, the dribbling snuff with its disgusting brown trail, the unwashed linen, the dishabille (in which she should not have been seen by a man), the dirty handkerchief, the spittoon. Later we learn that this astonishing woman, who fits and starts unsuccessfully at the composition of poetic lines, is maddened by her own imagination—at times she loses her humanity in the belief that she is a hare besieged by hunters, or she becomes a cat and springs upon her servants, or she painfully retains her urine against the time when the "general conflagration" will be "at hand" (p. 221). The completed portrait, presented after the frenzy of the seagoing chapters, momentarily stops the motion of the narrative because it so fills the space of Roderick's consciousness as to dominate it just at the beginning of a new episode; and because it launches the new episode, in which Roderick meets the ideal woman whose beauteous image will hover in his memory through all of his remaining adventures, it initially dominates that also, overpowering the description of Narcissa by its contractive effect. As a grotesque, Narcissa's aunt is certainly an offense to the idea of the learned lady,[25] but her portrait is effective rhetorically, as are those of the other female grotesques Smollett draws, and so the issue for the reader is not so much whether he was a misogynist, but how he used the pictorial representation of such characters to express the thematic interests he wished to promote in his novel. There can be no denying that the crudeness and bestiality of Narcissa's aunt works, though in a negative way, to enforce the values associated with her niece and opposite, values—of constancy, gentleness, and moral purity—the wayward hero must adopt before he can gain any real happiness.

When Richardson's friend Catherine Talbot wrote to Elizabeth Carter that she thought *Roderick Random* "a very strange and a very low" book, though "not without some characters in it, and I believe some very just, though very wretched descriptions," she no doubt had in mind not only the fictionalized real people (David Garrick, Lord Chesterfield, and others) who figure in the failed writer Melopoyn's grim story (chapters 62–63), about which she goes on at length, but just such grotesques as I have been discussing.[26] She may also have been thinking of such near-grotesques as the effeminate Captain Whiffle (Oakhum's replacement aboard the *Thunder*)—all laces, perfumes, and whines—and the more genial portraits of Bowling, Morgan, and Strap. The last named is by far the more visually represented of these three—as I suggested earlier, we know the eccentric Bowling and Morgan best by their sailor's language; but the descriptions of Strap typically remain generalized, emphasizing facial expressions (of fear, ecstasy, sorrow) and actions (dancing about, stripping to fight), so that we never gain a full view of his body. Despite the high comic energy of his representation, Smollett keeps his function clear by avoiding all risk of showing him too reductively; Strap is always the *idea* of the faithful sidekick, a projection of Roderick's best qualities into the world about him, and—except for the period of his absence from the novel, when he goes to France and acquires the means and the appearance of a gentleman (he yields up both when he meets Roderick once again)—he is altogether denied an identity separate from that of his friend.

Through almost half of the novel's pages, Strap is a significant presence, and his responses to Roderick, and to the world through which they both travel, provide both amusement and a clear measure (frequently through contrast) of the hero's character and behavior. The visual details of his composite portrait are very precisely chosen. At the first meeting of the former schoolfellows in Newcastle (chapter 8), Strap, now a barber, arrives to shave Roderick, and, upon recognizing him, betrays "great emotion," loses control of his hands, and clumsily smears lather all over his old friend's face (p. 32). The lather returns to his own face when they embrace in a "transport" of joy, and for this brief moment the two characters are united directly by the single visible sign of Strap's profession. But it is, most importantly, the exuberant Strap's capacity for unrestrained high feeling and total denial of himself that is established by this meeting, as is shown when he gives up barbering, lovingly devotes his money and his life to Roderick, and gladly follows him along the road to London and a future of adventures. Numerous trials ensue for this good fellow, as Roderick gets him into repeated scrapes and is frequently bad-tempered, impatient, reckless, and disloyal. Strap's appearance and actions are always a reliable register of how Roderick is doing morally, though Smollett's comic manner usually allows his hero and narrator to relieve himself of the full weight of his reader's judgment—thus saving him from complete rejection, when sometimes he deserves it. In chapter 47, for example, when Roderick reports, abruptly and with a mean spirit, that he has lost eighteen guineas at cards with Melinda, the heiress he has been foolishly pursuing, his account of the moment avoids providing a full picture of Strap's response, resorting in-stead to a gesture of displacement with the remark that it "would require the pencil of Hogarth" to display his "astonishment and concern" (p. 283), and turning attention directly to the funny business that follows from the initial shock: "the bason in which he was preparing the lather for my chin, dropped out of his hands, and he remained some time immoveable in that ludicrous at-titude, with his mouth open, and his eyes thrust forward considerably beyond their station" (p. 283). The allusion is to no particular picture by Hogarth, but rather to his manner, and few readers (in Smollett's earliest audience, at least) would have been unable to complete the intended comic portrait by furnish-ing the missing details.[27] That this moment parallels the uncomplicatedly joy-ous occasion of their meeting in Newcastle many chapters earlier clarifies the distance now separating Roderick from the simple goodness represented by Strap, darkening the picture and giving it an arresting intensity of meaning.

One other brief example must suffice to illustrate Smollett's usual practice in the visual representation of Strap. On a later occasion (chapter 52), when Roderick has for once brought home winnings from the tables, he finds his "faithful valet," his "face beslubbered with tears," waiting for him in an agony of consternation, standing silently "like a condemned criminal"—an attitude that changes instantaneously and radically the moment Roderick displays his new stock of cash. With a "wildness in his countenance" caused by initial worry that his friend may have turned thief, he listens to the account of the night's success, and then begins to dance about the room "in an exstacy," growing so frenzied that Roderick believes he has "run mad with joy"—as indeed he has momentarily, for he must be restrained and awakened from his "delirium," the "transports" (as the recovered Strap himself describes them) aroused by the news of such good luck following upon so many late miseries and disappointments (pp. 318–19). Once again the picture of Strap is only partial, but it is vivid nonetheless, a clear physical and visual representation of his oddity, his geniality, his emotional volatility, and his ability to identify totally with the fortunes of the friend to whom he is a loyal companion—it is a caricature, in other words, that catches its subject in the fullness of his energy and, by so doing, defines the essence of his particular humanity.

The other two extensively developed caricatures in the novel, Bowling and Morgan, are no less vivid as presences, though they are given fewer pages than Strap and though Morgan, the good-hearted first mate of the *Thunder,* is presented with even less of a visual flourish than Bowling. When he is introduced (in chapter 25), Roderick gives him a single brief sentence of description, compared with the two sentences (the second quite long) earlier devoted to his uncle. Perhaps because Morgan is so crucial a figure in the gruesome shipboard episodes, Roderick does provide a more precise picture of his body, and especially his countenance. He was "a short thick man," we are told, "with a face garnished with pimples, a snub nose turned up at the end, an excessive wide mouth, and little fiery eyes, surrounded with skin puckered up in innumerable wrinkles" (p. 146). These details do not amount to much, and they are all we get; but they are sufficient to project a good-humored eccentric onto the canvas of the novel. Like Bowling, Morgan is weathered, a veteran of the hardening effects of a life at sea; both men have preserved a decency and an irrepressible exuberance that makes them counterpoints to the foul brutality and darkness of the particular world they inhabit, as is best expressed by their benevolent actions and, most of all, by the comic explosiveness of the language they speak. Twice, Bowling selflessly rescues Roderick from dire distress, first taking him away from the suffering and abuse caused by his cruel grandfather in his native Scotland, and later paying his debts and getting him out of prison; Morgan repeatedly braves the wrath of superior officers to attend to the welfare of the sick seamen under his charge. What we remember most about both men, however, is what Roderick also remembered most, the sounds of their voices. "Come along, Rory," Bowling says to his young nephew after their failed attempt to win a better provision for him from the grandfather's meanness, "I perceive how the land lies, my boy, . . . —let's tack about, i'faith,—while I have a shilling thou shan't want a tester. B'wye, old gentleman," he concludes to the grandfather, "you're bound for the other world, but I believe damnably ill provided for the voyage" (p. 11). "As for a shentleman in distress," Morgan remarks (in strong Welsh accent) to Roderick upon welcoming him to the *Thunder*'s mess, "I lofe him as I lofe my own powels: For Got help me! I have had vexations enough upon my own pack" (p. 147). As George Kahrl has observed, such language is stylized and artificial, but still authentic as a particular kind of colloquial speech—leaving indelible impressions of those from whose lips we hear it, allowing Smollett to transcend the limits of the merely pictorial caricature and engage in "characterization by style."[28]

This tactic—characterization by style—is actually very broadly typical of *Roderick Random,* and indeed of Smollett's novels generally. If we turn now from portraits of individuals to the other kind of spatial form he employs in his work, the social tableau, we will easily see how he uses the tactic when the economies of his narrative call for the accumulation of quick impressions capable of revealing identifying marks of gender, class, disposition, and even profession, toward the completion of a composite picture of an entire social group, or environment, or both. In the Weazel episode, for example, while the captain himself is the pictorial centerpiece who gives focus to the tableau of which he is a part, the other characters are known largely by their speech. The old usurer is precisely described—hollow eyes, shriveled face, toothless gums, and all (pp. 49–50); but, besides the captain, no one else. Miss Jenny, the saucy young prostitute, makes such free use of her tongue that there is no need to picture her in detail; she is a shrew, but a clever one, and her lively voice bespeaks a lively body—and a lively intelligence as well. "Some people give themselves a great many needless airs," she tells the captain and his lady, rebuking them for their obnoxious snobbery in refusing places to Roderick and Strap; "better folks than any here have travelled in waggons before now," and "Some of us have rode in coaches and chariots with three footmen behind them, without making so much fuss about it" (p. 49). The libidinous usurer she disposes of with cutting sexual innuendo, mocking both his greed and his suspected impotence when she asks, "What do you say, Isaac? Is'n't this a good motion, you doting rogue?—Speak, you old *cent. per cent.* fornicator" (p. 49). The captain huffs and blusters, exposing himself as a fraud (he is in actuality a former valet de chambre and procurer to a master who bought him a commission to get rid of him): "Damn you, sir, who are you?" Jenny challenges him; "who made you a captain, you pitiful, trencher-scraping, pimping curler?" (p. 51). Later, Weazel further exposes himself as a coward, following a riotous night of sexual misadventures that finds the confused Strap in bed with Mrs. Weazel, provoking her husband's ineffectual wrath, which cools instantly when the offender proves more than ready to fight him.

The entire episode is an extended vignette in which Roderick, Strap, and the other principals, along with an assorted minor cast of wagonmaster, innkeeper, carousing rakes, and pretended highwayman, are all gathered, like the figures in a comic history painting, in service of Smollett's anatomy of lower-class life. The comparison with scene 3 of *The Rake's Progress,* suggested earlier, once more seems apt, as Smollett's episode actually works to establish definition of a particular space in which Roderick, like Hogarth's Tom Rakewell, is placed at the periphery, nearly invisible, while the characters he observes (in this particular he is different from the oblivious Tom) play out their drama, crowding the scene with their activity and filling it with the noise of their talk. Theirs is a self-revealing drama of hierarchical conflict and social pretension, prideful exertions of authority, sexual jousting, and moral hypocrisy, and as such it is a comic foreshadowing of what Roderick is to encounter, in some manifestation or other, through virtually all of the adventures that lie before him. The episode thus serves a double function. It stands alone as a self-contained unit of Roderick's narrative, bearing no essential connection with the episodes preceding and following it (except, of course, that it occurs along the road to London), and so it can be read, enjoyed, and understood in isolation; yet it also fits crucially into Smollett's overall design because it so vividly displays varieties of human nature and conduct common to all classes, as Roderick's later experience will prove.

The ensemble effect of the parallel episode during which Roderick begins his pursuit of Miss Snapper's fortune works in exactly the same way, though it anatomizes a social group of higher rank. Miss Snapper herself is heiress to a rich merchant, and the other passengers in the coach include her mother, a lawyer, a lieutenant of the army, and a grave, prudish female, supposedly a gentlewoman but later discovered to be only the wife of a nobleman's valet. The soldier, a braggart coward and thus the counterpart to Weazel, takes some direct hits from missiles fired by Miss Snapper's tongue, as sharp as Jenny's and the means of the amused Roderick's first knowledge of her—the coach is dark and, as in the Weazel episode, the travelers initially reveal themselves by their speech. The opening exchange between Miss Snapper and the "son of Mars" is indeed funny. When the latter complains of everyone's pre-dawn silence, observing that he must have "got into a meeting of quakers," the former replies: "I believe so too, . . . for the spirit of folly begins to move." The verbal contest continues: "'Out with it then, madam' (replied the soldier.)—'You seem to have no occasion for a midwife,' (cried the lady.)—'D—n my blood! (exclaimed the other) a man can't talk to a woman, but she immediately thinks of a midwife.'—'True, Sir, (said she) I long to be delivered.'—'What! Of a mouse, madam?' (said he.)—'No, Sir, (said she) of a fool.'—'Are you far gone with fool?' (said he.)—'Little more than two miles,' (said she.)" (pp. 323–24). Miss Snapper alone is enough to justify Damian Grant's description of *Roderick Random*'s language as a "projectile system"[29]—in the violently contentious world of Smollett's novel, says Grant, perhaps "the most dangerous weapon" of all is "the tongue" (p. 137); and Miss Snapper's tongue, though exercised for comic effect, is certainly a threat to anyone who crosses her. She defeats the noisy self-aggrandizements of the soldier and later the lawyer with her volleys, which her hapless mother cannot control, and the contrast between her bold volubility and the gravity of the prude (the only character in the episode given no direct speech) sets her off to great advantage. It is no wonder that Roderick momentarily wonders whether, if he is able to trap her into marriage, he will merely be exchanging the misery of poverty for the greater misery of perpetual (and dangerous) clacking.

Roderick is a minor participant in the drama of this episode (though he does save the passengers from a highwayman), and again he is primarily an observer and recorder. Miss Snapper is the only actor who is fully described, and so, like Weazel, she is a pictorial centerpiece in the social tableau, with the details needed to complete the whole composition accumulating largely through the tactic of characterization by style. The economy of the two chapters through which Smollett develops the composition gives it an arresting power, and the social anatomy that results is precise and striking—Miss Snapper, besides serving as a foil to Narcissa and a walking judgment against the scheming Roderick, is a parody of the coy young heiress on the make in the marriage market, while the soldier, lawyer, and grave lady are types of professional and social fraudulence. Again we have an extended vignette that creates—and *is*—its own narrative space, possesses its own meaning, and is bounded by its own beginning and ending. What does link the Miss Snapper episode with the one that follows it is the coach's arrival at Bath, site of Roderick's rediscovery of Narcissa—and, of course, always in Smollett's work the scene of interesting social display. Because the main order of business at this point is to begin the complicated process of bringing the hero and heroine together at last, Smollett lingers hardly at all over the spectacle of the crowded long room, where Roderick escorts Miss Snapper on their second day in the city; but there is a fine moment when, to everyone's delight and applause, his companion answers Beau Nash's cruel joke about her deformity with a killing verbal thrust (p. 335). By so doing she explodes Nash's pretensions to authority as master of ceremonies and, indirectly, the artificial and entirely silly social rituals over which he presides in this resort of the fashionable.

In the earlier extended episode of Roderick's fortune-hunting attempts upon the heiress Melinda at London and Hampstead (chapters 47–50), Smollett provides a more nearly comprehensive account of high life, including a scene of ogling at the opera (p. 280), an evening card party where the rich coquette proves herself a clever cheat (p. 282), and an assembly where, following a minuet for which he takes Melinda as his partner, Roderick receives a threat from an offended rival—one Bragwell, oafish counterpart to the comical Rourk Oregan, another jealous rival who later sends him a formal challenge (chapter 49). Like the moment with Miss Snapper at Bath, the occasions of Roderick's involvement with Melinda add up to a particular kind of social tableau. Not specifically visual (there is little descriptive detail of either persons or places), it depends upon the reader's awareness of conventional character types (the coquette, the boor, the fop, the comic Irish bungler) to achieve its effect as a broad picture of fashionable custom that is as troubling—because custom is entirely the practice of duplicity—as it is absurd. Through much of the episode Roderick is accompanied by a crowd of London idlers with names like Medlar, Wagtail, and Chatter, whom he joins in pranks and frivolous amusements. In the midst of the social environment he has entered, he is like a lost soul—he is, after all, as Smollett affirms in the preface, a young man of real though "modest" merit (p. xxxv), but his desperate desire for wealth and status has driven him into degeneracy. And as everyone (including the reader) knows, except Roderick himself, he is out of his element and headed for disaster. His friend Banter, speaking of his schemes against Melinda, tells him firmly—and this is a moment of striking clarity: "You are too honest and too ignorant of the town, to practice the necessary cheats of your profession. . . . —Besides, you are downright bashful—what the devil! set up for a fortune-hunter, before you have conquered the sense of shame!" (p. 285). At this point it seems almost as though Roderick is the protagonist of a Hogarthian narrative called "The Fortune-Hunter's Progress," and the impression is renewed in the ensuing adventure with Miss Snapper.

In Bath with Miss Snapper, and throughout his pursuit of Melinda, Roderick is implicated in the social tableaux within which his author has placed him, suggesting the extent to which he has succumbed to the seductions of the corrupt world he should—and, earlier, often does—condemn. When he turns later to gambling, and then at last lands in prison as a swindler, his resourcefulness is totally exhausted and he seems beyond all possibility of redeeming his life. The prison scenes (chapters 61–64) constitute yet another tableau, as do—though in a very different way—the shipboard chapters (24–37), and both are almost unrelievedly grim. These two long episodes actually parallel and illuminate one another. In the first, Roderick is the courageous victim of a crazed structure of power that terrifies and almost kills him, leaving him outraged and scarred; and in the second, he is a committed felon placed in the midst of an equally crazed and isolating environment of abuse where injustice overwhelms justice but where he has no recourse except—convicted at last of moral failure—to sink into despair. The backdrop and context for both episodes is the city of London, Smollett's comprehensive emblem of the modern world, crowded site of rushing activity, deceptions, confusion, and darkness. There the Marshalsea is located, and there Roderick's seagoing adventures actually begin as he is taken by a brutal press gang and forced aboard the *Thunder*. Smollett's representation of life in the city is like a vast, comprehensive tableau because of its concentration of energy, often visual energy, but it is more broadly intended to suggest an almost infinite, altogether perplexing, and nearly overwhelming variety. Roderick only passes through all this variety on his way elsewhere; and it is his passage—painful, frightening, portentous—that is always the focus of the scattered scenes recounted in the dozen chapters (13–23) devoted to his stay there.

The early scenes in London show how inept and vulnerable Roderick is in the world of action he has entered. He is bedaubed with mud by a coach on his very first day there, he gets lost in the maze of the streets, he becomes embroiled in a fight, he is mocked for his awkward Scotsman's appearance, and he is disappointed by the Parliament man (significantly, his name is Cringer) to whom he carries a letter of introduction; and then he is frustrated by the Navy Office, duped by a sharper, and entangled in the sexual conflicts and power politics within the family of the apothecary Lavement, by whom he is briefly employed—and whose house he leaves after an accusation of theft perpetrated by the vicious Captain Odonnell, whom he has thrashed. London is the place of Roderick's immersion in a whole new experiential realm of uncertainty and violence; what Strap says of the city shortly after their arrival is a portent of what is to come for both of them throughout their travels, separately and together: "we have not been in London eight and forty hours, and I believe we have met with eight and forty thousand misfortunes.—We have been jeered, reproached, buffetted, pissed upon, and at last stript of our money; and I suppose by and by we shall be stript of our skins" (p. 72).

What happens to Roderick in London is but a prelude to what awaits him aboard the *Thunder*, scene of so much greater cruelty and so much more sinister darkness. For good reason, his adventures at sea constitute for many readers the most memorable portion of his entire story. In addition to the fact that they are a harrowingly accurate account of what life was like for an eighteenth-century sailor, and quite beyond their effectiveness as a savage commentary upon the ineptitude of the Naval administration and its officers, they develop powerfully as an immediate personal record of rage and of terror provoked by wilfully vicious authority. As a microcosmic representation of the world at large they reveal Smollett at his darkest; in this extended tableau the villains are almost unimaginably evil, while the victims—Roderick, Thomson (an apparent suicide), Morgan, all the *Thunder*'s sick and wounded—are virtually helpless in the face of their perversity. As an elaborated episode the shipboard adventures dominate the second quarter of the novel, stopping its forward action for fourteen chapters and establishing their integrity as a completed narrative in their own right, yet crucial to the overall effect of the novel as a whole, and particularly to its persistent thematic emphasis on the near-hopeless plight of innocence in the grim arena of human experience.

Roderick, always an alien in English culture because he is a Scot, is more than ever the outsider on board the *Thunder,* where he observes cruelties heretofore totally foreign to his moral imagination and endures torments altogether beyond anything he thought possible among civilized people. But those who wield authority on the sea are, with few exceptions, not civilized at all, except in the superficial sense of possessing the rank that confers their authority upon them. Captain Oakhum, the surgeon Mackshane, the midshipman (later a commander) Crampley: these men are monsters, signs that the world they control is morally upside down. It is by the agency of such men, and their equally corrupt superiors in the military bureaucracy, that Roderick is forced into the sailor's life through a conscription policy of impressment Smollett clearly abhorred, necessary though it was thought to be in a time of war. He is thereafter witness to the deplorable conditions of the sick berth, to the cruelty of putting the ill and injured to work so as to reduce their number, and to the debacle of Cartagena, with its needless casualties; and he is himself persecuted for his resistance to what he sees—accused as a spy and mutinist, he is chained to the poop deck during a bombardment and left to fear for his life, while watching as his mates are blown to pieces.

Smollett is never more graphically visual than in the shipboard chapters, while the intensity of the pictures he contrives calls forth the most violent language in the entire novel. At times in these chapters Damian Grant's descriptive phrase—"language as projectile"—is especially apt, but in a particular way; when Roderick is at his most astonished, outraged, or terrified, he is also at his most impotent, and so language is his only medium of expression—

action is denied (he cannot do anything meaningful to relieve the suffering he sees; he cannot save himself by escaping the danger that threatens him), and language alone must suffice. Roderick fires off words like shots, as though they could kill what he condemns and fears. But they cannot. Because of their explosiveness and precision, what they do for the Roderick who narrates (and for his reader) is vivify remembered details instead of displacing them, whether he is an observer taking in a whole scene—as in his initial view of the sick berth—or a solitary individual looking outwardly, and helplessly, at a moment of apocalyptic horror that overcomes him—as in the battle during which he is fastened to the deck.

Here is Roderick's description of the sick berth as he descends to it with Morgan on his first night aboard ship. The progression of the description reveals his pained amazement, as his words move the eye across the whole ghastly scene and focus it, not upon the separate bodies but upon the horrid effects—offenses to other senses besides that of sight—of their plight. "Here I saw about fifty miserable distempered wretches," he says,

> suspended in rows, so huddled one upon another, that not more than fourteen inches of space was allotted for each with his bed and bedding; and deprived of the light of the day, as well as of fresh air; breathing nothing but a noisome atmosphere of the morbid steams exhaling from their own excrements and diseased bodies, devoured with vermin hatched in the filth that surrounded them, and destitute of every convenience necessary for people in that helpless condition. (p. 149)

The cadences here are those of a ship's cannon in battle; the rhythms are relentless in their movement, almost without a stop; the words are increasingly volatile as the passage proceeds—"miserable distempered wretches," "suspended," "huddled," "deprived," "noisome atmosphere," "morbid steams," "excrements," "diseased," "devoured with vermin," "hatched" in "filth," "destitute." In some sense Roderick's description may be a defense, an attempt to distance the scene so as not to be drawn into it; but if so, his own words betray him, for if he does not permit himself to see any of the "distempered wretches" as individuals, he is irresistibly engaged by the reality of their crowding in a dark hellhole of an airless space, by the stenches rising from the putrefaction of their flesh and their loss of control over bodily functions, by the dirt in which they lie and the tormenting creatures it breeds, and—most of all—by their perceived hopelessness. In turn, of course, the whole vivid picture, because it is so gruesomely unforgettable, becomes a mighty judgment against an authority, and a set of worldly values, that could by indifference allow such a scene of hideous suffering to occur, its victims sunk into an anonymity so total that they do not even exist as men.

The shipboard chapters keep Roderick's eye very busy indeed, moving it regularly from the perspective of distanced engagement exemplified in his description of the sick berth to the alternative perspective caused by enveloping and overwhelming circumstance. His experience as a prisoner on the poop deck in the midst of his ship's encounter with a French man-of-war is simply the most glaring and dramatic instance of the latter. "I endeavoured to compose myself as much as possible," he writes of this occasion,

> by reflecting that I was not a whit more exposed than those who were stationed about me; but when I beheld them employed without intermission, in annoying the foe, and encouraged by the society and behaviour of one another, I could easily perceive a wide difference between their condition and mine: However, I concealed my agitation as well as I could, till the head of the officer of Marines, who stood near me, being shot off, bounced from the deck athwart my face, leaving me well-nigh blinded with brains.—I could contain myself no longer, but began to bellow with all the strength of my lungs; when a drummer coming towards me, asked if I was wounded; and before I could answer, received a great shot in his belly which tore out his intrails, and he fell flat on my breast.—This accident entirely bereft me of all discretion: I redoubled my cries, which were drowned in the noise of the battle; and finding myself disregarded, lost all patience and became frantick; vented my rage in oaths and execrations, till my spirits being quite exhausted, I remained quiet and insensible of the load that oppressed me. (pp. 167–68)

I have quoted this passage fully because it speaks for itself. Roderick, wholly isolated and helpless, modulates from a measured language of determined resignation to frenzied expressions of frenzied feeling. Two visual details—the falling of the Marine and the drummer—are enough to vivify the horror; the splattered brains and entrails are almost more than we can bear to see, yet we cannot help focusing upon them—they are the "load" that oppresses Roderick's trapped, stationary body as his voice involuntarily gives expression

to his terrifying loss of control in an increasing crescendo of yelling and cursing, adding to the noise of the battle but overwhelmed by it and at last un-
heard. The description is pictorial and more, as it draws the reader into a complete identification with Roderick through its fitful rhythms, the increasing
urgency of its transitive verbs (from "endeavoured" and "beheld" to "bellow,"
"tore," "vented"), and, still more, by its emphasis upon sound—"cries,"
"oaths," "execrations." If throughout his story Roderick is a character to
whom things happen, and he is, it is not always entirely because he is passive,
or inept, or foolish, but rather sometimes because the world seems to insist on
happening to him—and by doing so proving its hostility to the essential
goodness that he represents, however wayward he might be. There is no better evidence of his role as victim than the passage just quoted and discussed;
and the passage is, like the description of the sick berth (and like any number
of other passages in these chapters[30]), an indictment of the structure of authority within the microcosm of shipboard life, and of the moral bankruptcy
of the world that endorses such authority.

The extended story of Roderick's adventures at sea takes its own definite
shape and form as a self-contained serial narrative developed by the accumulation of extremely precise pictures of intensive moments of experience, all
adding up to one elaborated tableau of a social space. But the story reverber-
ates outward into the remainder of the novel, too. Roderick loses everything
when Crampley and his henchman beat, rob, and abandon him after their
shipwreck, so that when he meets Narcissa it is in the character of a servant.
Now completely dispossessed of his birthright as a gentleman, he feels the
hopelessness of his love for her with a painful force. It is this more than anything that propels him into the waywardness that marks most of the second
half of his narrative as, despairing of the happiness he seeks and believes he
deserves, he turns fortune-hunter and eventually gamester—too often for-
getting the ideal image of Narcissa, so remote from him, and, at the tables,
yielding up all faith in Providence as well, while casting his lot with Fortune,
or Chance. He does all this partly because he is trapped in a paradox. Chance
does indeed govern the world as he knows it, so it seems that little could be
lost by bowing to its apparent preeminence. But Narcissa is an embodiment
of the good, in the grand scheme of things much more than the lovely "apparition" he first takes her to be (it is important that he sees her as "not real"

in just this way), and she holds out the promise of ultimate redemption through the very Providence Roderick denies; heaven will surely contrive some "unforeseen event in our behalf," she writes to him (p. 371) even as he descends headlong into degradation. Ironically, it is after the point of their renewed acquaintance at Bath, when her image begins to haunt him with greater frequency and power than ever, that he most denies her, his hopes sinking continually lower—with good practical reason, of course, given the conduct of her vicious brother and guardian—until at last, desperate and defeated, he commits the crime that gets him thrown into the Marshalsea.

Roderick is sent to prison because he has broken the law, but it seems clear that Smollett wants us to believe the world drove him to it by laying down so many obstacles in the way of his native goodness and his legitimate desire for happiness. He is guilty, but also—and as usual—a victim. How could he have done other than what he did? Was it within his power to resolve the paradox that beset him?—to repudiate Chance, affirm Providence, and then rejoice in a triumph? Obviously it was not. The ambivalence of his situation as he enters prison is almost palpable. In truth, as I have argued elsewhere,[31] Smollett punishes his hero not so much for his crime as for his spiritual submission to the world and its corrupt, cruel ways—by scourging it he becomes a cynic, seduced by his own indignation into giving up commitment to an ideal standard of morality and conduct. But then, having punished Roderick, Smollett goes on to rescue him by the Providential agency of Bowling, at last giving him a father, his beloved Narcissa, and a return to his ancestral estate—as if to say that, for the lonely, battered individual, there can be no redemption except by the miracle of benevolent intervention. The mythic ending, like that of a fable, resolves the practical dilemma of Roderick's life—how to have what he desires and deserves; but it does not remove the paradox that, even more than Chance, has seemed to rule it.

The darkness of the prison chapters may in some degree be attributed to the somber story of Melopoyn, with all its sorrowful details of the poor poet's many disappointments. The effect of this story is to underscore Roderick's continued sense of the world's injustices, an effect achieved in part by his sympathetic identification with his melancholy new friend and his pained response to such verses as an elegy in imitation of Tibullus (pp. 376–77), which seems to forecast both his own death (as the only possible end to his cares) and the eternal loss of Narcissa. After reading the poem, Roderick tells us, he drank himself into a sleep from which he "awaked in the horrors," his imagination "haunted with such dismal apparitions" that he was "ready to despair" (p. 377). And he did despair. After hearing Melopoyn's complete story in all its sad length he fell into such a despondency that even games of cards, billiards, and bowling had no cheering effect; and he "grew negligent of life," he says, "lost all appetite, and degenerated into such a sloven, that during the space of two months, I was neither washed, shifted nor shaved; so that my face rendered meagre with abstinence, was obscured with dirt, and overshadowed with hair, and my whole appearance squalid and even frightful" (p. 397). It was at this moment, his lowest, that Bowling arrived and, his punishment ended, Roderick was blessed with release and the beginning of a new course of experience leading to his final happiness. The very thing he had ceased believing in—Providential benevolence—redeemed him. Only later, after meeting his father, did he come to any meaningful recognition that his adversity had been partly his own fault and that, instead of being merely the victim of the world, he had learned from his experience in it.

The extended prison episode is less complexly developed and less visual than the much longer and more varied account of Roderick's time aboard the *Thunder,* though of course Melopoyn is very detailed in his story and often explicit in his references to those members of the literary and theatrical establishments who had so tormented him by their false promises and failed integrity. Roderick himself is pictured very vividly, as the passages just quoted make clear, and so is Melopoyn—to Roderick's eye he is an "apparition," all "wrapp'd in a dirty rug, tied about his loins with two pieces of list, of different colours, knotted together; having a black bushy beard, and his head covered with a huge mass of brown periwig, which seemed to have been ravished from the crown of some scare crow" (p. 375). When Roderick first meets him Melopoyn is, in other words, just such a figure as Roderick himself becomes by the end of his stay in the Marshalsea; Smollett's descriptions ultimately unite the two young men in a bond of identification, making it clear that Melopoyn is, in part, a projection of Roderick's own hopelessness. The other prisoners are not pictured at all; indeed, only one inmate besides Melopoyn, his old acquaintance Beau Jackson, engages Roderick's direct attention, and his hapless, forced cheerfulness is a sobering indicator of what life is like in this nether world. On the common side of the prison are nothing but "naked miserable wretches" (p. 375)—like the men seen earlier in the *Thunder*'s sick berth—so that the entire place appears another hellhole for the victims of a world that may have been offended by their crimes but has committed a greater crime by reducing them to such degradation and anonymity.

As an anatomy of a social organization or structure Smollett's prison episode remains largely abstract, but as a microcosmic representation of suffering humanity it is like a tableau, riveting attention by compelling the reader's engagement while forestalling thoughts of any future movement for Roderick outside the prison walls. The effect exactly repeats that of scene 7 of *The Rake's Progress,* where Tom, also sunk low, is similarly beset by enervating miseries—his wife abuses him, the turnkey presses him for garnish money, his mistress is in such convulsions that she neglects their child, and he has just learned that John Rich, manager of the Covent Garden Theater, has rejected the comedy lying on the table, an effort he had hoped would redeem his fortunes (here is a direct connection with Smollett's Melopoyn). It is impossible not to suppose that Smollett had Hogarth's famous picture in mind when writing his prison chapters, and it is very likely that his audience also had it in mind when reading them; these chapters gain visual density by means of implicit intertextual reference. Despite differing subject matter in the two scenes from *Roderick Random* and *The Rake's Progress,* the resemblances are unmistakable, for both center emphatically upon the hopelessness of a degraded life confined within a small, dark, enclosed space from which there is no means of escape and where there is no apparent possibility of redemption.

Roderick is redeemed, of course, unlike Tom (who ends his progress in Bedlam), and his story fairly races to its conclusion following his release from prison. Smollett's readers have often complained about the abrupt contrivances of this ending, finding them awkward and unconvincing. There is some justice in such complaints, for signs of haste in the composition do appear, as the erratic, fragmented, chaotic course of Roderick's life is suddenly resolved into orderliness and quietude; and there is a bit too much reliance on easy romance convention to suit this novel, in so many ways unconventional. Yet, to judge the ending of the work a total failure, as some have done, is to deny both its significance and its overall appropriateness to the kind of novel Smollett actually wrote. Again: Everything in Roderick's story—every move-

William Hogarth, *A Rake's Progress,* Scene 7 (1735).
(By courtesy of the Trustees of Sir John Soane's Museum.)

ment, every fit and start and shift—makes it clear that there can be no other
kind of ending except that by which he is removed from the world that has so
baffled him and which would obviously continue to do so until it utterly destroyed him. The argument of the ending is a philosophical one; its strategy is
that of the satirist who projects a fantasy that repudiates what is and affirms
what ought to be. Why may not this strategy be as acceptable—and as successful—in prose narrative as in verse? in a novel as in a formal satire?

But there is another point to be made here, and with it we return to the
larger question of the novel's overall form. What David Mickelsen has said in
his analysis of *The Golden Ass* may be usefully applied to *Roderick Random.*
Apuleius's work, says Mickelsen, is "most meaningfully envisioned" as a series
of "thematically related episodes" developing in a "potentially endless cycle"
that is all at once halted arbitrarily, in a "problematic" abrupt ending.[32] But

there is a literary logic to the abruptness, Mickelsen argues, and it arises both from the narrative's spatial form (that is, its juxtaposition of equivalent episodes) and from the discontinuous, apparently directionless, and relentlessly accumulating details of the adventures it records. Avoiding organically regular structure as unsuitable—inadequate, really—to the story it wishes to tell, a work like *The Golden Ass* is not driven by its form toward an inevitable ending, but instead scatters itself over the perceived formlessness of experience and must finally just be stopped so that protagonist, reader, and author too may all find release. The ending of *Roderick Random* is far more neatly conceived and executed than that of *The Golden Ass,* as its story is on the whole much more deliberately progressive. But the broad structural similarities between the two works are very clear. In both, a distinctive kind of formal design creates a formal necessity of its own, producing an ending that is no mere contrivance but rather is an essential expression of the work's overall meaning.

To his satirist's instincts and his moralist's convictions, then, Smollett added a particular sense of literary purpose in bringing his first novel to its conclusion. The narrative from which this conclusion follows is that of a restless traveler, an outcast, a Scot suffering from severe dislocation in a strange land, a young man whose innocence combines with his aspirations to doom him to a tempestuous career of frustrating and often dangerous adventures. The journey of his life is a fretful one because he cannot control its direction or in any way appear to move it toward the resolution he wants. As a response to the turbulence of contemporary life, *Roderick Random* is itself formally turbulent, its hero's voice and actions (or reactions, as is more often the case) alternately registering rage, pain, astonishment, and despair as he is tossed about by violent circumstance. The energy of his narrative is a product not of its forward motion, but of his vividness in representing the forceful characters who confront him as graphic scene follows upon graphic scene, episode upon episode, each defining a space enclosing a particular experience or set of experiences, the spaces connected only through the most superficial linearity—Roderick travels from Scotland to London, then he goes to sea, then he meets Narcissa, and so on. Twice Roderick's narrative is displaced altogether by the interpolated story of another person: the history of Nancy Williams, a "harlot's progress" almost in the manner of Hogarth, fills virtually all of two long

early chapters (22 and 23), its only seeming relevance a tenuous parallel between its subject's sufferings and Roderick's own; the story of Melopoyn, already discussed, dominates the prison chapters, momentarily focusing the
reader's attention away from Roderick, but establishing its somewhat greater
relevance by its effect of intensifying and increasing his despondency.

Time passes as erratically as Roderick passes through the world, and as his
story passes before the reader's eye. The account of Roderick's childhood and
youth is compressed into the first six chapters; time stops as Nancy Williams
and Melopoyn tell their stories; we do not really know how long Roderick is at
sea, or the duration of his fortune-hunting schemes. The important relation
between real time and fictional time is deliberately blurred, the one collapsing
on to the other as the shipboard adventures and Melopoyn's tale—both conspicuously based on Smollett's actual experience from about 1740 until the
period when he was writing *Roderick Random*—are told as though they had occurred almost simultaneously. The introduction of such anachronisms is of
much greater significance in *Ferdinand Count Fathom,* as I shall try to show in a
later chapter. But it is clear that in his first novel Smollett was already experi-
menting with a technique by which he might, through a rearrangement of his
reader's sense of history, convey an interpretation of experience that would
emphasize the reality of its uncertainty, its baffling randomness, and its
chaotic progression in every life. Like his disruptions of linearity and causality,
Smollett's vagueness about time and its movement in *Roderick Random* contributes to a particular structural and thematic effect. The spatial form and the
meaning of his work are, in other words, inseparable, one and the same. In
this respect he is not all that different from Sterne, whose *Tristram Shandy* is
even more radically disruptive of conventional expectations about narrative
form—as progressive, organic, purposefully coherent—but who has never
suffered the charge of carelessness or ineptitude too often leveled at Smollett
for his performance in *Roderick Random.*

James H. Bunn has suggested, correctly I think, that while Smollett developed a narrative imaging of randomness as an epistemological position in
Roderick Random, thus catching at a major anxiety of his culture (shared by,
among others, David Hume), he did not go so far as to articulate a theory of
randomness itself[33]—he was, after all, not systematic thinker enough even to
have been interested in doing that. Bunn's argument, in one of the shrewdest

discussions of Smollett's novel to have appeared in the last two decades, assumes a kind of structural integrity for it, a coherence grounded in the very directionlessness others have seen as a fault in its design. Here it seems important to acknowledge also the importance of what Paul-Gabriel Boucé has implicitly defined as *thematic* structure, the notion that, more than anything, it is (as Boucé puts it) the "conscious recurrence of particular moral themes" that holds Smollett's seemingly formless novel together.[34] In *Roderick Random,* says Boucé, the overriding theme is that of the "apprenticeship to life" (p. 100); as the story of a determined quest for personal fulfillment, the novel engages its hero in a painful conflict between the desire for adventure and the necessity of moral purpose. This conflict is elaborated by the continual display of subsidiary themes: "psychological violence" and its consequences, to Roderick and others; a "compulsive need for vengeance," as felt by the hero throughout his adventures, and the encounters with brutality into which they take him; and a "perpetual dialectic of reality and appearance," developed as a means of emphasizing the deceptions by which the world confuses Roderick, deflects him from moral purpose, and finally entraps him (pp. 106, 107). Boucé is of course right; these themes run through every episode of *Roderick Random,* helping each to a center of urgency and, because of their continuity, filling the spaces between them. In the absence of a rigid linearity, and given the disconnectedness of the story's movement, such continuity is essential to narrative coherence.

To thematic consistency Smollett adds a consistency of strategy by projecting a range of opposed characters, values, and settings, creating a dualism by which his novel's obsession with the collision between good and evil is illuminated, until at last it dissolves in the ending. The very presence of characters like Bowling, Strap, Thomson, Mrs. Sagely, and (of course) Narcissa sets off the darkness of the novel's villains, arguing the wrongness of a world in which dispossessed goodness (as exemplified by Roderick) finds so little hope of coming into its just inheritance of happiness and tranquility. Narcissa, so central to Roderick's longing for access to the good, is an abstraction in a context of particulars so grotesque (her aunt, Miss Withers, Miss Snapper) that she can only be understood negatively, by contrast to them. The arcadian ancestral estate to which Roderick retreats in the end, after his release from prison and the discovery of both father and fortune, is another abstraction, the geographical counterpart to Narcissa, who grows big with child as the novel closes upon the fulfillment of Roderick's aspirations for (besides status) love, quiet, and certitude. Like Narcissa, the Random estate is not pictured at all except through conventional references to its beauty; instead, it is negatively understood by implicit comparison with the graphically rendered environment of violence, chaotic movement, and sinister darkness that its brightness displaces. For Smollett personally, and for at least some of his first readers, the comparison was no doubt made even more forceful by the location of the Random estate in idyllic Scotland.

Here we are, focused upon the novel's ending once again. I shall close this chapter with one last word about it. Far from denying randomness, as James H. Bunn suggests in stating his only real reservation about the integrity of the novel's structure,[35] the last pages of *Roderick Random* actually affirm the reality of it by rejecting it with the force of myth. The myth is essentially that of Christian deliverance, as defiant of logic and the laws of causality as the orthodox belief in the complete transformation of the moral and spiritual self by the providential agency of divine grace. The massive accumulation of details in assorted character portraits, the varied social tableaux, the erratic adventures, and the scattered scenes and episodes by which Roderick's narrative proceeds certainly do not lead naturally, much less inevitably, to the stillness with which it concludes. Nor were they intended to do so. Smollett's point, as we understand it if we allow his work the legitimacy of its full design, is that there can be no final release from pain, anxiety, and dislocation except through deliberate and complete withdrawal from them. That, of course, is not possible in real life. But a novel is not life; it is instead a product of the imagination, which can make the impossible seem possible through fantasy—more precisely, through metaphor, for a novel is nothing but an elaborated metaphor bearing the most tenuous analogical relation to actuality, which it can re-create as its author wishes. Seen whole, *Roderick Random* is just such an elaborated metaphor, a fable in which desire and merit are at last redeemed from all that would thwart them and brought by the force of a transforming imagination into that rarified region of fantasy where goodness prevails, hope is fulfilled, and suffering is no more.

CHAPTER 2

Peregrine Pickle

Roderick Random is, like all of Smollett's novels, an elaborate exercise in eclec-
ticism. As the preceding chapter should have made clear, it incorporates conventions of the travel book, the rogue (or picaresque) biography, the whore's
tale (Nancy Williams's interpolated story), the memoir, and the romance—
with wayward Roderick as the wandering dispossessed hero who finally re-
gains his birthright along with his true identity as a gentleman, and Narcissa as
the fair heroine who is his inspiration and, in the end, his reward. *Peregrine
Pickle* is all this and more. Smollett's second novel borrows just as freely from
the very same popular kinds of narrative, but it adds to its eclectic mix the
scandal chronicle, or secret history (Lady Vane's long detailing of her amours
in chapter 88), and an account of a contemporary *cause célèbre* (the story of
Daniel MacKercher and James Annesley in chapter 106) that bears attributes
of the exemplary biography and the trial narrative. Indeed, *Peregrine Pickle* is in
every sense more ambitious than *Roderick Random*; it is about twice as long
(four volumes instead of two), it includes a far greater number of incidents, it
develops a broader geographical sweep over much of England and the European continent, and it introduces a vastly larger cast of characters. It is as
though Smollett decided, after the considerable commercial and critical success of his first novel, to pull out all the stops in an effort to top himself.

The results were mixed at best. The work was not very well received,
though Lady Vane's memoirs created a momentary sensation and though
Smollett otherwise stirred considerable controversy by his attacks on Field-

ing, Garrick, Lyttleton, the earl of Chesterfield, and other prominent figures in contemporary literary and political life. Sales were slow, and no second edition was required for seven years.[1] Smollett was mystified, and embittered; he imagined a conspiracy among booksellers, and among those he assaulted (along with their friends), to discourage reviews of his work and bury it in oblivion.[2] It naturally did not occur to him that *Peregrine Pickle* might be a lesser novel than *Roderick Random,* despite its greater bulk, or that it might deserve something other than an enthusiastic reception.

Actually, the novel deserved better than it got from the public and from critics. Surely it has as much to recommend it as, say, Richardson's sprawlingly tedious *History of Sir Charles Grandison* (1753–54), whose seven volumes enjoyed wide celebrity and repeated editions from the time of their initial appearance. *Peregrine Pickle* bears up well in any comparison with *Grandison,* or for that matter with Fielding's somber *Amelia,* with which it competed directly for readers in the year 1751. It is no better than either of these works, but certainly no worse. *Grandison* and *Amelia,* it might be noted, were the last novels by their authors, written when their powers were declining. Unlike his great rivals, however, Smollett was in no decline when he wrote *Peregrine Pickle;* if anything, as a young writer (he was one month shy of thirty when the novel came out) he was still gathering his imaginative forces. Those forces were, alas, still somewhat scattered. As I have observed elsewhere, what we see revealed in *Peregrine Pickle,* in "rawest and truest form," are the "essential qualities" of a novelist still in the apprenticeship stage of his career and furnished with more energy than discretion and tact; the work is less successful than it might have been because it unrestrainedly and ill-advisedly "subordinates art to exuberance."[3]

Its high energy and inexhaustible exuberance are among *Peregrine Pickle*'s greatest attractions, of course. What is missing in the novel is not invention or narrative skill but discipline. In this respect it is the weakest of all Smollett's fictional works, though from the late eighteenth century onward it has been his best known and most admired after *Humphry Clinker* and *Roderick Random.* It develops by the same principles of spatial form as *Roderick Random*—it is filled with portraits of quirky individual characters, many of them (Grizzle Pickle, Hawser Trunnion, Jack Hatchway, Tom Pipes, the painter Pallet, Cadwallader Crabtree) among the most memorable eccentrics Smollett ever created, and it offers tableaux of an abundant variety of social groups, from the university types with whom Perry indulges his youthful appetite for dissipation, to the assorted culturemongers (both English and European) portrayed in the famous episode of the "Entertainment in the Manner of the Ancients," to the "College" of Grub Street writers the hero joins late in his career, as his fortunes wane and he slides toward misery and despair. Some of the portraits and tableaux are as visually powerful as anything to be found in his first novel, suggesting that Smollett had not drifted totally away from his most basic instincts as a writer, instincts sharpened—as we know—by deliberate fidelity to narrative principles modeled by his contemporary Hogarth.

But he is less faithful to those instincts in *Peregrine Pickle;* or, more accurately, like his hero he expends his energies recklessly. The overly long interpolations devoted to Lady Vane and the moral heroics of the "melting Scot" MacKercher (as Smollett dubbed his countryman in his earlier poem, *Reproof*[4]) disrupt the novel's compositional integrity, while many sections of the story display a kind of compulsive pranksterism—jokes and acts of mischief succeed one another with a gratuitous relentlessness, few of them adding meaningfully to development of the main plot line or to the definition of Perry's character, except insofar as they give evidence of his irrepressible spirit and his inability to resist displays of superiority to those (including his kind benefactor, Trunnion) he makes the victims of his unbridled—and sometimes cruel—sense of fun. The jokes and pranks are themselves often ingenious and just as often hilarious, signs of an astonishing fertility of invention. Their cumulative effect, moreover, when taken with the more substantial episodes of the novel, is to enforce a kind of simultaneity of action, very like that of *Roderick Random* in its undermining of an apparently progressive chronicling of the hero's life, beginning with his birth in troubled family circumstances and ending with his final happiness in marriage to an idealized heroine, with—along the way—a full detailing of his disappointments in amorous relationships and of the many frustrations of his quest for validation of his legitimacy as a gentleman. In this respect, too, Smollett is true to his writerly instincts, which leaned toward fragmentation, diffuseness, and spatiality and decidedly away from the niceties of organic form. But *Peregrine Pickle* is so diffuse, so unregulated, that it is unable to achieve the concentration of effect created by the more efficient compression of incident in *Roderick*

Random, and indeed in all of Smollett's other novels, not excepting *Ferdinand Count Fathom* and *Sir Launcelot Greaves,* usually counted lesser performances. Loss of compression results in loss of intensity, and though *Peregrine Pickle* is finally intelligible as a composite serial picture of contemporary life and characters, the picture is not quite in focus; it lacks something in vividness. In his second novel as in his first, we may say, Smollett purposefully wrote from a set of Hogarthian narrative principles, but he was never less successful in adapting the painterly manner of projecting a wholeness and clarity of vision.

Over the years a number of well-meaning critics, most notable among them the unabashed Smollett enthusiasts Rufus Putney and Paul-Gabriel Boucé, have mounted determined arguments claiming for *Peregrine Pickle* a structural integrity that not only redeems the novel's apparent formlessness but actually crystallizes its extravagant disparateness into a clear center of meaning.[5] Putney, in his very important essay, discovers eleven distinct divisions within the narrative, all of them growing from Smollett's aim to develop a broad and varied satire of high society, with the continuing thread of the love story providing emotional and especially moral urgency in a way that personalizes the satire by highlighting Perry's growth into worthiness as he survives adversity—and the folly of his own social ambitions—and is at last able to fulfill his longing for Emilia. Boucé adopts a similar approach and arrives at similar conclusions, identifying "five major articulations" which, for him, make it easier to distinguish the structure of *Peregrine Pickle* than that of *Roderick Random.*[6] Though Boucé's comparative evaluation both surprises and baffles, it is otherwise impossible to take serious issue with either of these two earnestly ingenious assessments, as far as they go; both Putney and Boucé are accurate in their slightly different descriptions of separate structural elements in *Peregrine Pickle,* and they correctly point to the significance of each within the overall narrative sequence of the work. But in their desire to demonstrate coherence they overlook texture, subordinating the evidence of the actual words on Smollett's pages to the pursuit of a thesis which, though certainly not wrong, is inadequate to explain the full aggregate effects of all of those words—effects that reveal, besides the particular purposefulness Putney and Boucé rightly claim for the work, a corresponding uncertainty in the development of many individual incidents and episodes. The valor of committed partisans cannot rescue *Peregrine Pickle* from the just charge that it is a flawed performance whose excesses and failures of artistic judgment are as glaring as its triumphs and many delights, which they sometimes threaten to obscure.

Part of the problem with the novel seems to have been a confused conception of its hero on Smollett's part. Unlike Roderick Random, Perry is born privileged, to an affluent English family, and though he suffers comparable abuses in childhood (his mother rejects him, and his henpecked father neglects him), Trunnion takes him in and gives him both a comfortable home at the garrison and the opportunity for a fine education at school and at the university, in addition providing him with ample finances. From the point at which Perry turns prankster in his very young boyhood, it grows increasingly difficult for him to hold the reader's sympathy or to be credible as the good-natured fellow his author wishes us to believe he is. Perry is not an alien, as Roderick is, but he acts like one; he is driven not by Roderick's just rage and indignation but by some inner need to trick the world in order to satirize it, to expose people to ridicule (and sometimes pain) whether they deserve it or not—and frequently they do not, as in the instance of his deliberately treading upon the Commodore's painfully gouty toe at the age of three (chapter 11). It is significant that Trunnion is his first victim, and a regular target thereafter—along with many fools and knaves, of course, among them the schoolmastering pedants Jennings and Keypstick and his aunt Grizzle, whom he mortifies by drilling holes in her bedpan (chapter 14). Funny as many of Perry's pranks are (their effects are often heightened by the participation of the ingenious Hatchway), their sheer number and the frequent inappropriateness of their objects suggest that Smollett was not in full control of his own love of high-spirited mockery; by indulging his personal compulsion he not only distended the narrative but skewed his novel's vision of its hero. As Damian Grant has remarked, if Perry was intended as a vehicle of meaningful satire, he is a failure because he does not discriminate when taking aim at the world; he lacks fixed moral principles and is a mere scattershot critic for whom life is actually no more than "a practical joke (this is all his 'practical satire' amounts to), endlessly and tediously repeated."[7]

No doubt Smollett meant to project Perry as a fellow of divided sensibilities trying to make his way in a divided world; this was his successful strategy with Roderick Random, and he would use it again, with even greater success, when imagining the character of Matt Bramble in *Humphry Clinker. Sir*

Launcelot Greaves and *Ferdinand Count Fathom* achieve many of the same effects, though they locate all divisiveness externally. The strategy collapses in
Peregrine Pickle because, while the world it so elaborately represents is certainly
split between goodness and villainy, there is little real tension within Perry
himself; instead, there is only inconsistency. His occasional acts of kindness
and generosity do not balance against his frequent cruelties, as the latter—like
his relentless pranks—seem unmotivated; he is compulsively greedy, opportunistic, profligate, promiscuous, predatory. His gambling and his aggressive
social climbing betray unmitigated acquisitiveness and raw ambition, while his
dissipation of the fortune bequeathed by Trunnion ultimately signifies moral
as well as economic bankruptcy; his attempts to seduce Mrs. Hornbeck (beginning in chapter 45) and the "fair Fleming" (beginning in chapter 56) are
only slightly less egregious as breaches of decency and good nature than his
impulsive decision to purchase the "nymph of the road" from her mother
(chapter 95) and recreate her from a vulgar country girl into a lady of fashion.
His worst offense, of course, is his scheme against the virtue of Emilia
Gauntlet, the idealized heroine who loves him faithfully but whom he
would willingly destroy in order to gratify his voracious appetite for succulent
female flesh.

It is simply impossible to believe Smollett's narrator when he tells us—as
he repeatedly does—that Perry is, after all, good in his heart, but misguided.
The representation of his character goes in an entirely opposite direction for
most of the novel. Even at the end, when Perry has been chastened by loss
and imprisonment and does actually manage to reform, the shadow of his earlier ways darkens the reader's judgment of him. The final transformation of
the consummate villain Count Fathom is more credible, because it is more
consistent—radical though it is—with the fundamental conception of his
character in its relation to other characters in his story. We can accept Perry's
reformation because we know it is the stuff of fable, but we cannot really believe that he had it in him to do it all along. If Smollett believed it, and surely
he did, he was unable for most of the novel to show (or did not understand
that he needed to show) his hero in meaningful conflict with the world's manifest corruptions, and he failed to dramatize any internal struggle between basic goodness and powerful, dangerous desire. The narrator's reassurances
about Perry's merit cannot counter the behavior he records, and his occa-

sional caveats against the hero whose exploits he clearly relishes ring hollow—most especially such remarks as the following, made when Perry is about to launch his campaign against Emilia: "Sorry am I," he writes, "that the task I have undertaken, lays me under the necessity of divulging this degeneracy in the sentiments of our imperious youth" (p. 353).

Perry is much more the initiator than Roderick Random; he makes things happen through most of his story. Active rather than passive, he flings himself into a world governed by Chance with the aim of dominating and controlling it. Ultimately he proves unequal to his ambition and is undone—but (unlike Roderick) as much by his own hand as by the force of circumstance, which his behavior only abets. He is not so much dispossessed by his cruel family as he dispossesses himself by squandering the fortune Trunnion gives him. He grows up mistrusting the world, always ready to mock or scourge it and to devalue the people he meets so that he might abuse them without bearing any burden of responsibility or guilt. His mother's monstrous treatment of him may well be a reason why Perry behaves as he does, though Smollett seems to consider character formation and motivation unimportant. There is, of course, the strong possibility that Perry was conceived out of wedlock, which would help to explain his mother's otherwise unaccountable hatred for him— his illegitimacy, if ever discovered, would embarrass her irretrievably and almost certainly cancel the comfortable property relations established by her quick marriage to Gamaliel Pickle.[8] And illegitimacy is, besides, a kind of symbolic dispossession which, though Perry seems to have no hint of it, might (in his author's mind) provide some justification both for his frequently outrageous conduct and for his social drivenness. But Smollett leaves this possibility in such a state of indeterminacy (in effect, he drops it after chapter 4) that it adds nothing in the way of depth to his hero's character. Perry is all shallow compulsion and sparkling intelligence, fertile wit and active libido; he hardly changes at all through the novel. Indeed he seems incapable of change, until in later chapters he is recast in the role of victim, becoming a bit more substantial and thus sympathetic after he has been swindled by crooked financial speculators and betrayed by lying politicians, who leave him defeated and despairing, weakened and ready for the softening influence of Emilia.

Only one thing seems really unmistakable about Smollett's conception of Perry: that he meant him as yet another proof of the world's power to over-

come individual will and desire, however forceful and determined their expression. The confident, savvy young Englishman of his second novel is
finally no better able to establish his own security and happiness than the be-
leaguered young Scot of his first; both must be rescued by their author in the
enactment of a mythic ending. Beyond this, little is clear. In gravitating away
from the moralized version of the picaresque romance he developed in *Roderick Random*—episodic, roguish, with every incident directed toward a definite
satiric purpose and with a decided emphasis upon his hero's genuine capacity
for redemption[9]—Smollett seems to have been unsure just what he wanted
to do instead. *Peregrine Pickle,* with its delight in roguery for its own sake, is in
many ways closer to the picaresque than anything else he wrote, but it stops
short of being a latter-day *Lazarillo* or *Gil Blas*. It is almost an inverted romance, with a twist on the familiar theme of dispossession and restoration
turned upon a hero who is anything but idealized; yet, it manages only to be
something less than that—the record of a reprobate and degenerate brought
to a romance ending. Perry is close to criminality on many occasions, but
Smollett did not make his story into an elaborated criminal biography, a study
of the aberrant figure, the rebel or the deviant whose crimes are a judgment
against the society that created him and against the darkness of human nature
itself. There can be little doubt that *Peregrine Pickle* was intended as an experiment in fashioning an original narrative from familiar materials; it is a bold experiment, but it fails to define itself adequately in relation to the established
generic types whose conventions and devices it exploits, so that it does not
quite manage to become something new in its own right. The failure is largely
owing to the murkiness of Smollett's understanding of the character and function of his hero. He would solve this problem of understanding in his next
novel, *Ferdinand Count Fathom,* an even bolder experiment achieving much
greater clarity of purpose and vision in a tightly developed narrative that is
one of the eighteenth century's most skillful and powerful evocations of the
criminal in action.

There is another problem of uncertainty in *Peregrine Pickle*. Smollett was not
yet comfortable with third-person narration—in fact, he was never fully
comfortable with it, though he used it twice again, somewhat more happily, in
Ferdinand Count Fathom and *Sir Launcelot Greaves*. It was not his natural mode.
Roderick Random and *Humphry Clinker* succeed so remarkably because, in each

work, Smollett wrote from his truest instinct, creating characters whose self-expression is unimpeded by a narrator's intelligence, voice, and mediating presence and thereby catching directly their unguarded responses to the world exactly as they felt it. What the autobiographical narrative of his first novel and the letters of his last lack in distance they gain in immediacy and authenticity; *Peregrine Pickle* is short on both of these attributes, though it certainly attempts them, while it also suffers from a confusion of perspective. In a Fielding novel, narrative omniscience works triumphantly, since meaningful apprehension of experience in *Tom Jones* or *Joseph Andrews* always depends upon calculated distance; in a Smollett novel, the same manner layers in an obstruction between character and reader. *Peregrine Pickle* makes one wonder what it might have been like if the story had been told in the hero's own voice. As it is, the novel gives us all of Perry's action but little of the feeling that generates it; in fact, Perry seems not to have very much genuine feeling, despite his frequent outbursts of anger and frustration and his periodic effusions on the subject of his love for Emilia. For the most part, all we have to trust for the transmission of such feeling as he does possess is the narrator's voice. The voice is not an ineffectual one; on the contrary, it is distinct and powerful. But it is often less than convincing when recording anything more than action. What we notice most are the narrator's responses to the imagined reality of the novel, while those of Smollett's characters are often blurred and only partially defined because their own voices are muted, drowned out.

Peregrine Pickle deliberately sets out to be a different kind of novel from *Roderick Random;* I do not mean to fault it for failing to be something other than the work that was intended. Smollett clearly wished to try his hand with the narrative technique Fielding had used with such success in *Tom Jones,* and that he admired so much in *Don Quixote;* in doing so, he no doubt planned to forestall repetition of the criticism that the voice in *Roderick Random* was too autobiographical to be credited as a product of art. But by deciding not to adopt Fielding's cool magisterial manner in his new novel, Smollett made a Fieldingesque concentration of aesthetic and rhetorical focus impossible, and he simply did not compensate by imagining a different stance that would ensure a comparable effect; unlike his rival, Smollett was most interested in the passionate impulses acted out by his characters, and he allowed the frequently obsessive volubility of his version of the omniscient narrator to get in the way of his representation of those impulses. In each of his other novels, the obsessions of his characters drive the narrative. In *Peregrine Pickle* the hero is obsessed (as prankster, as social climber, as sexual predator), but one feels that it is the compulsions and urges of his author, impersonated by the narrator, that make the story go.

I have already mentioned one of those compulsions, Smollett's own unrestrained pranksterism, which so distends his novel, with instances of it frequently leading nowhere. There were others, personal agendas that had little to do with the story he wished to tell. All of Smollett's novels include elements of the personal (here we may remember the Melopoyn story in *Roderick Random*), but in *Peregrine Pickle* they are out of control. His prolonged and bitter attacks on contemporaries—Fielding, Garrick, and the rest—certainly gave his work a contemporary relevance and a measure of historical authenticity, but they were for the most part manifestly self-indulgent and transparent, not in the least disguised by being delivered in the voices of assorted members of the College of Authors whose meetings the hero attends beginning in chapter 101—voices utterly undifferentiated from that of the narrator.[10] Smollett later realized that these attacks were gratuitous as well as mean-spirited, which is why he deleted most of them from the second edition of the novel. Surely he felt their intrusiveness upon the integrity of his work. In any case it is clear that his enmities had cooled (Fielding was dead, while Garrick had helped to arrange for production of his comedy, *The Reprisal,* in 1757), and he actually seems to have felt apologetic—in a letter to Garrick dated 27 January 1762, he noted a kind reference to the actor in his *Continuation* of the *Complete History of England,* remarking that "in giving a short sketch of the liberal arts, I could not, with any propriety, forbear mentioning a gentleman so eminently distinguished by a genius that has no rival. Besides, I thought it was a duty incumbent on me in particular to make a public attonement in a work of truth for wrongs done him in a work of fiction."[11]

The other major intrusions in the work, Lady Vane's memoirs and the MacKercher story, are more difficult to account for except as a kind of commercial opportunism. Smollett wanted to sell books, and he actually engineered a minor public relations campaign that pitted his version of Lady Vane's history (probably he wrote it from materials she gave him) against Dr. John Hill's competing *History of a Woman of Quality: or, The Adventures of Lady*

Frail, published a little more than two weeks before *Peregrine Pickle.*[12] Moral judgments against the Lady Vane memoirs are beside the point (though there have been plenty of them, from the very beginning), not merely because the transgressions against sexual standards and codes of proper marital conduct they record look tame in the late twentieth century. But it is possible to convict Smollett of a failure of artistic vision for including both these memoirs and the history of MacKercher. Like the attacks on his literary enemies, they are rendered in voices (Lady Vane's; a prisoner's, addressed to Perry in the Fleet) hardly differentiated at all from that of the narrator, and so they add to the confusion of perspective discussed above. They are impossible to justify as in any way relevant—or even appropriate—to the narrative as a whole. From time to time Smollett partisans, among them Putney and Boucé, have attempted to defend both interpolations as contributions to the story of Perry's passage through the world's arena of instructive experience, but with very little success.[13] The real test of their status as irrelevancies is that, as their topical value has long since faded away, the modern reader can take them in only with the help of an elaborate scholarly apparatus. Many readers would add that they are tiresome.[14]

Smollett's problems with *Peregrine Pickle*—the confused conception of the hero, the difficulties with narrative voice, the unrestrained authorial urges and compulsions—are real and limiting but, finally, not fatally crippling. He almost gets away with them because in other respects the novel offers (as I remarked earlier) so many triumphs and delights. Even the two interpolations of which I have been so critical may be called interesting attempts at studies of private character in a context of history. Lady Vane, who tells her own story (or such is the illusion), imparts to her personal life a public significance, projecting a constructed version of her real self into a work of fiction in a way that blurs distinctions between the actual and the imagined, the objective and the subjective, validating each in a relation of mutuality and reciprocity. The story of MacKercher works in reverse toward the identical effect; told by another, it thus begins from a public perception of MacKercher's actions with respect to the unfortunate Annesley, moving toward a subjective construction of his character as a selfless, benevolent, courageous man. By the logic of this procedure the construction in each story becomes the truth as the objective merges with the subjective, history with fiction, all very seamlessly. If "history" can merge with fiction, Smollett implicitly asks by the inclusion of historical interpolations in a work of the imagination, may not the opposite also be true? This, of course, is the question novelists of his generation were always posing as they sought to justify their work in the midst of skepticism about its value and legitimacy; hence their avoidance of such labels as *novel* and *romance* in their titles, and the prominence of terms like *history, life, memoirs, travels, adventures,* and *letters.*

In *Peregrine Pickle* Smollett intricately complicates relations between history and fiction by choosing the particular stories of Lady Vane and MacKercher as his most conspicuously elaborated explorations of them. The main time frame of his novel places the grown-up Perry's adventures at about (or just before) the date of its publication—that is, the late 1740s to about 1750. The Annesley case, which began in the early 1740s, was still current and controversial at this time, and MacKercher was a well-known London figure; but Lady Vane's amorous exploits, recounted as though they were still in progress, actually occurred in the 1730s, and there is evidence that by 1750 her beauty was too faded to have caused Perry—or any other potential lover—to be smitten by her. There were personal connections between the two historical figures; both knew Smollett, and it was probably MacKercher, one of the many men in Lady Vane's former life, who introduced her to the novelist.[15] The point here is not simply that Smollett confounds relations among biography, history, and fiction, but that he does it so complexly. The author of *Peregrine Pickle* was actually acquainted with two historical figures introduced into his work and given so much space as almost to constitute them major characters—not in the main plot, certainly, but in the work as a whole, which thus contains competing narratives of fictional and real people. One of these narratives—Lady Vane's—conflates fictional and historical time in an unusually glaring instance of the way in which Smollett's novels often seize upon facts only to remove them from historical sequence and reconfigure them in a different narrative context.

To Smollett the novelist, it is history as a revelation of conduct or character that is important, not the placement of a particular historical moment—or personage—in time. To the factual chronicler, linearity and temporality are essential; to the novelist, they do not have to matter. What does matter to Smollett, in *Peregrine Pickle* as in his other works of fiction, is the movement of his principal characters through space. Perry moves through time, too, of course—like Roderick, he progresses from birth, to childhood and adolescence, to a long and mercurial course of adventures, to final quietude in happy marriage; but it is the places where he pauses, their circumstances and their people, that are always his primary focus, and his author's. Like the track of the Bramble family's journey in *Humphry Clinker* (and rather like the hero's progress in *Roderick Random*), Perry's path as a young man on the go describes roughly the shape of a circle—from home and the garrison to school (at Winchester) and university (at Oxford), to a circuit of France and the Low Countries, to Bath and then London, and finally home again. His journeying is several times interrupted for side trips back to the garrison (Smollett's way, perhaps, of suggesting where he is truly anchored), but it remains a forward motion. Though time is real (this novel, unlike *Roderick Random,* more or less regularly tells us just how long the hero has been in this or that place[16]), it is of only relative importance, subordinated to the juxtaposed incidents and episodes whose placement within the circular movement emphasizes their equivalency of value while underscoring the simultaneity and synchronicity of their overall effect. Indeed, the image of the circle itself strongly suggests the synchronic rather than the diachronic. All this is certainly the result of a considered design, which Smollett managed to follow despite the problems with artistic discipline described above. The design derives largely from the broad outlines of travel narrative, always a model for Smollett but more important to the conception of *Peregrine Pickle* than of any of his other novels besides *Humphry Clinker.* In some ways, it might be said, *Peregrine Pickle*—which includes extended accounts of the customs, art, and people of many of the places its hero visits—is Smollett's most systematic adaptation from popular travel writing, and it adds the variation of a parody on the Grand Tour.

The travel book effects are sometimes very conspicuous because so deliberate. A case in point is the episode in chapter 46 during which Perry visits the Palais Royal in Paris, where he meets Pallet and the unnamed physician. His encounter with these new acquaintances will lead to further adventures, but for the moment the focus is upon their reactions to the pictures hanging in the galleries. These are represented as an index of Parisian high culture, which Smollett by no means disapproves. His manner is unusual, however, a variation upon the familiar practice of travel writers, as there is almost no specific

detailing of the exhibited works, but instead an elaborated exposure of the
poor judgment and worse pretentiousness of Perry's companions, both En-
glishmen. Here, then, while part of the object is to call attention to a major
Paris attraction (major, that is, for anyone—like Perry and his author—who
enjoys the painterly arts), the aim is actually to ridicule the boorish ignorance
of English travelers and thereby to make the attraction itself more appealing
to those of real taste and discernment. Perry concludes that Pallet and the
physician are "false enthusiasts" (p. 228), utterly unable to appreciate what
they see—and, as it turns out later, they are equally unable to profit from their
other experience of the unfamiliar lands into which their journey takes them.
In his adaptation from travel narrative, Smollett actually provides not a tour
guide, but a guide to touring—a conduct book, so to speak, for travelers. Severely critical of other cultures, especially the French, he rarely misses an opportunity to display his British sense of superiority throughout Perry's excur-
sions into France, Flanders, and Holland; but he is most concerned about the
character of the traveler and his need to be informed and sensible so as to observe clearly, wisely, and therefore profitably. Hence the ironic importance of
Jolter, Perry's silly tutor, as a foil to his charge. No matter what the evidence
to the contrary, Jolter always praises the French immoderately; he is a Fran-
cophile whom no mistreatment can convert—France is the "land of politeness and hospitality," he announces as he and Perry are about to land at
Calais, where they are promptly subjected to the extortionist tactics of water-
men and porters. Thereafter he continues to believe that politeness permeates
"all ranks and degrees" of French society, "from the peer to the peasant," and
that a foreigner, "far from being insulted and imposed upon by the lower class
of people, as in England," might expect to be "treated with the utmost reverence, candour and respect" in this idyllic land where, moreover, the fields are
"fertile," the "climate pure and healthy," the "farmers rich and industrious,"
and "the subjects in general the happiest of men" (p. 189).

   The folly of Jolter's enraptured assessment of the French is not lost on
Perry, his author, or his reader. Elsewhere Smollett exposes arbitrary abuses
of power by French aristocrats, who are able to command the ruin or imprisonment of anyone who offends them (chapter 44), and the abject submission
of the common people, who are "so much inured to the scourge and insolence of power, that every shabby subaltern, every beggarly cadet of the no-

blesse, every low retainer to the court, insults and injures them with impunity" (p. 211). There are scenes at a masquerade, others along the French roads and at inns, and a visit to a theater in Lisle followed by a conversation upon the relative merits of French and British drama (chapter 55). As Perry's tour takes him into Flanders, Smollett continues the travel book format, showing the sights of Antwerp (chapter 67), where Pallet falls into ignorant raptures over the paintings of Rubens; of Rotterdam (chapter 69), where there is a gentleman who possesses "a very curious cabinet of curiosities" (p. 346)—what would now be called a tourist trap; of the Hague and Amsterdam (chapter 70), where Perry witnesses the wonders of a windmill operated by a miller who powers it (in the absence of wind) by passing his own gas, and is then regaled by an evening of theater featuring a tragedy so badly acted that it is transformed into a farce. The effects of some of these episodes put one in mind of Swift, suggesting that Smollett is not only exploiting travel literature as a way of exposing his hero to the world, but making fun of its conventions.

In any case the focus is most often upon Perry himself as he responds to what he observes, which is a panoramic scene of human pride, folly, and corruption. Only in his *Travels through France and Italy* does Smollett give us a more comprehensive range of sights, sounds, people, customs—and impressions, for in that work, as in *Peregrine Pickle,* the emphasis is decidedly upon the responses of the traveler, a thinly disguised impersonation of Smollett. That the perceptions in *Peregrine Pickle* are more Smollett's than his hero's is suggested by the fact that they are almost always given in the voice of the narrator. They do not change Perry much; he continues his pranks and his exercises in sexual promiscuity—it is during his travels on the Continent that he undertakes his campaigns to seduce Mrs. Hornbeck and the fair Fleming. He may be more cultivated than his companions Pallet and the doctor, or most of the other people he meets along the way, but he does not gain in moral depth or grow in wisdom. His failure to do so is thus not only a sign of Smollett's indulgence of his own xenophobic desire to mock whatever is not British, or to expose the boorishness of certain British travelers, but it is also an index of the pointlessness of the Grand Tour as undertaken by Perry in conformity with the common practice of young men of wealth and social pretension. His tutor, or governor, is unable to guide him; and Perry himself is given mostly to consorting with low characters and prowling in low places. It is typical of him that in Amsterdam, having "visited every thing worth seeing" (p. 349)—not one of the sights visited is named—and laughed at the farcical tragedy, he is most interested in "the Spuyl or musick-houses, which, by the connivance of the magistrates, are maintained for the recreation of those who might attempt the chastity of creditable women, if they were not provided with such conveniences" (p. 350). To one of these houses he goes for a night of debauchery—like Hogarth's Tom Rakewell at the Rose Tavern[17]—that ends in a brawl. Amsterdam, Paris, and the other Continental cities Perry visits are sites of corruption that draw him in, and though they are not represented in any great detail they function as settings in the same way cities always do in Smollett's work, as emblems of the seductively wicked and dangerous modern world. It is not until later chapters of the novel, when the scene changes to London, that Smollett assigns to the city the fullness of this emblematic significance, but Perry's experience in the Continental cities where he pauses is crucial to our understanding of his adventures as a traveler.

Perry, all restless energy, is always in some kind of motion, of course—from place to place, scene to scene, escapade to escapade. The uncontrolled spatial form of his story becomes a major reason why it is so distended, but Smollett's very practice of the form also occasions the memorable visual effects with characters and social groups that are among the real satisfactions provided by the novel. Smollett may not always be at his most focussed or vivid in *Peregrine Pickle,* but he nowhere surpasses the best of its portraits and tableaux. The first of his great successes with portraiture come in the opening two chapters when he introduces Grizzle Pickle (maiden aunt to Perry, who is not yet born) and Hawser Trunnion. At thirty, as her Christian name suggests, Grizzle is already aging and graying; the very sound of her name further suggests a face lined, dry, and drawn, and since the word *grizzle* was a common descriptive term for a roan horse, we also learn from it something of this imposing lady's shape and gait. It is worth noting here the economy of Smollett's procedure. By her name alone he makes Grizzle into a grotesque figure—oddly formed, wizening into spinsterhood, and bearing nonhuman attributes. When he turns to actual description he has only to add a few details to complete the picture of a comical female whose appearance and presence also hint at the sinister—and indeed Grizzle is the first to abuse the child Perry by swaddling him too tightly during his mother's confinement (chapter 6) and then, later, by "thrusting pins into his flesh" (p. 29). Only recently arrived in the country with her brother, Perry's father, she possesses a fortune of five thousand pounds and, while exuding piety, is clearly—like her counterpart Tabitha Bramble in *Humphry Clinker*—libidinous and on the make for a husband (she will, of course, soon catch Trunnion). She "never expressed any aversion for wedlock," we are told ironically, "but, it seems, she was too delicate in her choice, to find a mate to her inclination in the city: for I cannot suppose that she remained so long unsollicited; tho' the charms of her person were not altogether enchanting, nor her manner over and above agreeable" (p. 2).

From this point forward—in Smollett's typical descriptive manner for his grotesques and caricatures—the hand gets heavier. "Exclusive of a very wan (not to call it sallow) complexion, which perhaps was the effect of her virginity and mortification, she had a cast in her eyes that was not at all engaging, and such an extent of mouth, as no art or affectation could contract into any proportionable dimension: then her piety was rather peevish than resigned, and did not in the least diminish a certain stateliness in her demeanour and conversation, that delighted in communicating the importance and honour of her family" (pp. 2–3). Interestingly, Smollett softens the character (if not the image) of Grizzle later in the novel, possibly intending to hint at something about the gradual influence of the basically sweet-tempered Trunnion—he is a crude and gruff man, but he spreads benevolence all around him, and even his eccentrically stiff, proud, self-absorbed wife appears not to be immune to it. First, however, Smollett stamps Grizzle's portrait indelibly with explicit evidence of her essential sterility of soul (and body) by detailing the grimly comic episode of her false pregnancy (chapter 10), after which, we are told (chapter 11), "she could not bear the sight of a child" (p. 51). Perry, at three years old already rejected by his mother, is rejected by Grizzle as well when Trunnion, to whom she is now married, takes him in. Deprived twice over of the nurturing love of a mother, the boy is forced to grow up without any gentling restraints upon either his childhood rambunctiousness or, later, his adolescent libido. Smollett never makes an issue of this deprivation in developing the character of his hero, but it does seem to have figured into his conception at least to some small extent; Perry's utter disregard for the selfhood of the women (including Emilia, until the very end) whose bodies he desires surely results in part from his lack of any model of the woman as feeling person. In any case, Grizzle is a very important presence in the early pages of the novel because of her negative effect upon the emotional and moral environment into which the hero is brought as a little boy. The intensity of Smollett's portrait of her underscores that importance.

Hawser Trunnion is an equally important presence. He first appears in chapter 2, introduced by the landlord of the inn where Gamaliel Pickle, anxious to escape the carping of his sister, quickly begins to spend his evenings after settling in the country. It is the landlord who first characterizes Trunnion as a former seaman who, in his obsession with maintaining this identity, "keeps garrison in his house, as if he were in the midst of his enemies, and makes his servants turn out in the night, watch and watch (as he calls it) all the year round" (p. 5). When Trunnion enters the room, his appearance confirms the eccentric character of him already given. "He was in stature at least six feet high," we are told, "tho' he had contracted an habit of stooping, by living so long on board; his complexion was tawny, and his aspect rendered hideous by a large scar across his nose, and a patch that covered the place of one eye" (p. 7). Blustering, loud, fussy, he is established at once as a figure of powerful as well as comical energy.

Soon after this dramatic introduction, however, Smollett begins to undercut the initially imposing character of the Commodore, projecting him as a failure both as a husband and as a father (he had also failed as a naval officer). He fails in domestic life not because he is unable to get his wife pregnant— her infertility is clearly the reason for that—but because he is unable to control her and, additionally, because as a prankster himself he provides a negative model for his godson Perry after giving him a home in the garrison. All this is true, notwithstanding his benevolence and essential good nature. The garrison is Trunnion's bastion against a mocking world that he finds mystifying, a bad and dangerously threatening joke; he has battened down there, hoping to protect himself against it and firing off his pranks as a defensive assault.[18] But he allows the new Mrs. Trunnion to erect "a Tyranny" (p. 51) over him and his household, undermining the security he has achieved, and so he turns to Perry, whose "certain oddity of disposition" (pp. 51–52)—his mischievousness, that is—matches his own; though the boy torments him with his thoughtless antic cruelties, Trunnion clearly sees in him an extension of his own character and an extremely promising instrument of his unarticulated desire to retort the world's joke upon itself. Out of his element as a seaman upon land, and misguided as a moral tactician, Trunnion is not the surrogate father Perry needs; he is on the whole no more effectual than the hapless Gamaliel, his real father, whose weakness cannot withstand his wife's desire to disenfranchise their son and drive him away.

But Trunnion at least possesses a generous spirit. His kindness to Perry as a child provides a lasting framework for an ideal of human relations; it is this ideal that will be affirmed in the end, when Perry at last reforms his ways and is able to achieve real happiness. And it is also true, at a more fundamental level, that if Trunnion is generally a failure as husband and father, he is certainly a lovable one. Smollett lavishes such affection upon him as to make any other assessment impossible. There is no fonder scene in all of Smollett's fiction than the one in chapter 8 detailing the picture of Trunnion tacking to his wedding—and never getting there. This scene has been so often praised, and so often discussed in minute detail, as to make any extended commentary upon it here redundant. So I shall be brief about it.

The single most important thing to say is that the slow zigzagging of the Commodore's motion is sublimely funny. It is, besides, both a sign of his almost indescribable eccentricity and a reflection of his seaman's hesitant way of going at a landlubber's world—and here, at a landlubber's circumstance: marriage—he does not understand. Trunnion's bizarre progression equally amuses the spectators who witness it, the author who imagined it, and the reader who follows it. It is an unusually striking example of characterization by style, to use George Kahrl's phrase once again,[19] though with a variation, as the style represented is that of action rather than speech. But, as in many other places elsewhere in the novel, we also get Trunnion's speech, a salty spewing of sailor's lingo here occasioned by the approach of a messenger sent by the bride to discover the reason for the groom's delay. Admonished to hurry, the Commodore replies: "Hark ye, brother, don't you see we make all possible speed? go back and tell those who sent you, that the wind has shifted since we weighed anchor, and that we are obliged to make very short trips in tacking, by reason of the narrowness of the channel; and that as we lie within six points of the wind, they must make some allowance for variation and leeway." To the messenger's uncomprehending suggestion that he and his crew simply proceed straight ahead to the church, Trunnion answers: "What! right in the wind's eye? . . . ahey! brother, where did you learn your navigation? Hawser Trunnion is not to be taught at this time of day how to lie his course, or keep his own reckoning. And as for you, brother, you best know the trim of your own frigate" (pp. 36–37).

This scene is almost enough in itself to fix the comic dimension of Trunnion's presence permanently, without further description of his body. But Smollett provides that too. As his horse runs madly away with him, lured by the noises of a hunt, he is seen in vivid close-up—as an "apparition," and then as the subject of a "picture." "The commodore's person was at all times an object of admiration," says the narrator, but "much more so on this occasion, when every singularity was aggravated by the circumstances of his dress and disaster.

> He had put on in honour of his nuptials his best coat of blue broad cloth, cut by a taylor of Ramsgate, and trimmed with five dozen of brass buttons, large and small; his breeches were of the same piece, fastened at the knee with large bunches of tape; his waistcoat was of red plush lapelled with green velvet, and garnished with vellum holes; his boots bore an intimate resemblance both in colour and shape to a pair of leathern buckets; his shoulder was graced with a broad buff belt, from whence depended a huge hanger with a hilt like that of a backsword; and on each side of his pummel appeared a rusty pistol rammed in a case covered with bear-skin. The loss of his tye-periwig and laced hat, which were curiosities of the kind, did not at all contribute to the improvement of the picture, but on the contrary, by exhibiting his bald pate, and the natural extension of his lanthorn jaws, added to the peculiarity and extravagance of the whole. (pp. 38–39)

Thus Smollett, here working as a consummate visual artist, completes the finest of all his many caricatures, sketching a body absurdly dressed in clothes of competing fashions (old and new, of the land and of the sea, of the warrior and the bridegroom) that accentuate the eccentricity already hilariously defined by the zigzag motion earlier described. From this point forward in the novel he adds relatively few visual details to his portrait of Trunnion, but few are needed, as there is little further to be known either about the Commodore's oddity of character or about his vibrancy and energetic geniality.

These qualities are all displayed in their most expressive physical manifestations upon our first encounters with him.

The other memorable eccentrics of the novel—Hatchway, Pipes, Pallet, Crabtree—are presented with a similar verve and economy, though Smollett does not lavish upon them quite the same affection or detail. Hatchway and Pipes, like Trunnion, are first introduced by the landlord in chapter 2, the former as a one-legged lieutenant admired for being "a very brave man, a great joker" who "hath got the length of his commander's foot," the latter as "a man of few words, but an excellent hand at a song concerning the boatswain's whistle, hussle-cap and chuck-farthing—there is not such another pipe in the county" (p. 5). Neither is ever described with much greater precision than this; instead, they are known best by their relations first to the Commodore and then to Perry, to both of whom they are loyal companion and servant, respectively. Hatchway the prankster characteristically situates himself on the world's blind side—as he does with Trunnion upon their initial appearance together in the inn, so that he might play tricks upon him undetected; indeed, we first see Hatchway as he pilfers his master's tobacco, drinks his liquor, and makes faces at him "to the no small entertainment of the spectators" (p. 8). As a practical joker he is a man who talks little but speaks much through his usually antic deeds. Eventually he will turn his talents to the task of abetting Perry in some of his most ambitious pranks, against Trunnion and then against the world at large; in effect he carries the model of the Commodore's own pranksterism into the period of Perry's adventures beyond the garrison. Pipes is still less visible than Hatchway, though he is an equally real presence who will play a bumbling Strap to Perry's Roderick Random, and will be just as badly treated for his faithfulness. His kind and genial spirit is signified by song, and his characteristic posture, established during the scene in the inn, is that of quiet and retiring modesty: "knowing his distance," he takes his station "in the rear" as Trunnion blusters into conversation with Gamaliel Pickle, exerting himself only to play his boatswain's whistle (rather badly, and very shrilly) at Trunnion's command, closing the scene.

With both Hatchway and Pipes, Smollett adroitly practiced the economies of characterization by style to achieve their complete definition as eccentrics—caricatures—whose presence, one-dimensional though it is, makes them memorable. The trick, one that Dickens would later employ with equal success (having learned it from Smollett), was that of absolute consistency within a limited range of action, first signaled by the nautical names, so obvious as to be dead giveaways to their identities—"Hatchway" may be slightly obscure to a modern audience, but Smollett's first readers would have easily understood it to mean that the victims of the lieutenant's pranks are destined to keep falling into the openings for ridicule and humiliation created by his ingenuity in perpetrating them. With Pallet and Crabtree, the other two real triumphs of comic characterization in *Peregrine Pickle,* he was more expansive and more precise, as their functions in the novel demanded much greater complexity of presentation. Pallet is actually far more than Smollett's readers have usually taken him to be. He is, variously, a voice, partly ironic, for the expression of Smollett's own xenophobia; a vehicle, comic but not at all ironic, for the affirmation of modern over ancient values in art and aesthetics; a painter of great energy and an abundance of entrepreneurial spirit, but no talent; an ignorant traveler (as suggested earlier), full of enthusiasms but lacking in knowledge, judgment, and taste; a laughable buffoon whom Perry (and his author, and the reader) cannot help liking and, in his eventual distress, sympathizing with despite his repeated blundering and his many offenses against good sense.

Crabtree, the misanthrope who figures so largely in the latter phases of Perry's adventures, is a somewhat less complicated yet more substantial figure—a presence who darkens our view of the hero's approach to the world by narrowing his pranksterism into a revelatory acting out of its real significance, which is that of the cynic's undifferentiating exposure and repudiation of virtually everything about the entire spectacle of human activity as it passes before his eye. If *Peregrine Pickle* is primarily a satire, as Damian Grant, John Skinner, and others have maintained, then it is most intensely and traditionally so after Crabtree comes upon the scene. It seems possible that Smollett meant his misanthrope as an exposure and renunciation of the extreme satirist's bitter sensibility and posture of superiority—in an echo, perhaps, of Fielding's Man of the Hill in *Tom Jones.* That he chose to make Crabtree the most important instance of the grotesque in the novel certainly hints that this is so.

In any event Crabtree, and likewise Pallet, are given full visual representation in a manner that highlights their complexity—and, in the case of Crabtree, his quite sinister singlemindedness. Pallet is in certain ways the more interesting and important of the two characters. He figures in the novel over a longer span of pages (from chapter 46, when he is introduced, to chapter 96, when he last appears); and, as a painter, he directly raises the issue of Smollett's concern with the visual in art, including narrative art. That he comes upon the scene as Perry is about to view the paintings in the Palais Royal is surely no accident; that his appearance is that of a gauche coxcomb is certainly deliberate, as it underscores his lack of taste and style. Although "seemingly turned of fifty," we are told, he "strutted in a gay summer dress of the Parisian cut, with a bag to his own grey hair, and a red feather in his hat, which he carried under his arm" (p. 224). His admiration for his traveling companion, the pedantic physician—a "man of vast learning," he calls him, "and beyond all doubt, the greatest poet of the age" (p. 224)—further exposes him, as do his volubly ignorant commentary on the paintings he views and his manifest failure to understand the simplest principles of line and composition.[20]

At the moment when we first meet him Pallet is a visual presence, comical and, though a fool, engaging. Very shortly thereafter, the "Entertainment" episode (chapter 48) pictures him as Smollett's unwitting ally (and Perry's) in revealing the folly of the entire idea of such a dinner, together with the physician's excessive—and obsessive—reverence for the ancients. The lunacy of the occasion is highlighted when Pallet drinks of the soup maigre, prepared by adaptation of a Roman recipe (it is dashed with sal armoniac, or ammonium chloride, a particularly foul expectorant); when "this precious composition diffused itself upon his palate," we are told, he "seemed to be deprived of all sense and motion," while he "sat like the leaden statue of some river god, with the liquor flowing out at both sides of his mouth" (p. 237). In drag at the masquerade to which he later accompanies Perry (chapter 49) he is a figure of pure fun who has to be rescued from a ravisher; arrested for his lack of decorum and sent to the Bastille, he appears to Perry extremely distraught, and garbed in "a dishabille" that is "truly extraordinary" (p. 251)—as described by the narrator in gleeful detail, after which Perry teases the poor man with false news of the court's judgment that, to be released, he must submit to castration. Folly and ineptitude make one inevitably the impotent victim of jokes, so Perry appears to believe. But, much farther on in the story, Pallet is also the instrument of a joke against Perry himself, for just at the moment (in chapter 60)

Thomas Rowlandson, Perry and his new acquaintances at the
Palais Royal (1790). (From the private collection of the author.)

when it seems he has at last made a conquest of the fair Fleming with whom he has been traveling through the French countryside, Pallet bursts upon them astride a jackass; the spectacle and the noise terrify everyone (Pallet, too) and infuriate the frustrated lover, who never again comes so close to fulfillment of his desire for this ravishing lady. Thought mad for this escapade, Pallet is almost committed to Bedlam, and upon his reprieve (by Perry's intervention) he is shown all disheveled, "standing with a woeful countenance, shivering in his shirt" (p. 306).

Pallet's condition here is only slightly less dismal, but much more comical, than that in which he is found later, in London (chapter 96), when he is in genuine dire distress and approaches Perry for assistance with a scheme to dispose of one of his paintings by lottery:[21] "Tho' the weather was severe," as Perry observes,

> he was cloathed in the thin summer-dress which he had wore at Paris, and was now not only threadbare, but in some parts actually patched; his stockings, by a repetition of that practice known among œconomists by the term of *coaxing*, hung like pudding-bags about his ankles; his shirt, tho' new-wash'd, was of the saffron hue, and in divers places appeared through the crannies of his breeches; he had exchanged his own hair for a smoke-dry'd tye-periwig, which all the flour in his drudging-box had not been able to whiten; his eyes were sunk, his jaws lengthened beyond their usual extension; and he seemed twenty years older than he looked when he and our hero parted at Rotterdam. (pp. 603–4)

Even Perry is moved by this sight, and he buys six chances, seconding the narrator's compassionate response to the once clownish painter, now reduced to little more than a pathetic beggar.

Smollett is more extensively and consistently visual in his portrayal of Pallet than in his presentation of any other character in the novel. It would be hard not to assume that this manner was calculated, out of a sense of appropriateness. How else should a painter be portrayed but visually, in a novel that purposefully—and on numerous occasions—calls attention to its author's preoccupation with visual art? Pallet is most definitely intended to make the reader think of Hogarth—if there were no other clue, his expressed preference for the "roast beef of old England" (an allusion to Hogarth's popular print, *The Gate of Calais, or The Roast Beef of Old England,* 1748) during the "Entertainment" episode (p. 238) would be enough. Nothing, no one, was sacred to Smollett, and his comic painter certainly is something of a joke at the expense of Hogarth's personal eccentricities. But still Hogarth was for Smollett "the inimitable" one (p. 75), and so Pallet—vulgar sometimes, and silly, but lovable and full of attractive energy—seems even more a tribute to the real-life artist's own fund of inexhaustible comic energy and, by extension, a celebration of his achievement through a tongue-in-cheek reversal upon it. Pallet actually has his own story in *Peregrine Pickle*—it is a "Painter's Progress" of sorts, jokingly ironic, developed in discrete episodes, or pictures, leading its protagonist toward failure and obscurity instead of success and acclaim. It is impossible to imagine even one of Smollett's first readers, especially those who were critical of Hogarth's aesthetic values, entrepreneurialism, and (legitimate) pretensions to superiority among British artists (there were many such [22]), missing the import of this story.

Pallet's "progress," of course, his "story," cannot really be separated from Perry's except for the purposes of a discussion like this one. The point is that its form—episodic, fragmented, spatial—exactly replicates that of the novel as a whole, which is to say that it is an emblem of Smollett's Hogarthian narrative method. Smollett does not give Cadwallader Crabtree a similar "story"; as I have already suggested, Crabtree is a less complexly imagined figure than Pallet. But in his way he is more central—to the plot, at any rate—because he is, during the crucial last stages of the novel, the chief instrument by which Perry acts out his increasing cynicism. A parody of the Mentor figure so familiar in eighteenth-century narrative (he "teaches" Perry how to join with him in exploiting his talents as conjuror and magician for satirical purposes), he helps to darken the hero's perceptions while sharpening them.

Crabtree is, of course, a fraud. He pretends that he cannot hear so that people will speak freely in his presence, revealing bits of gossip or embarrassingly personal information that he can enjoy as he scorns them. Smollett may have taken the idea for his character from Lesage's *Le diable boiteux* (1707) and its central character, a demon named Asmodeus who accompanies a mortal, Don Cleophus, as they wander through Madrid, mischievously lifting the roofs from houses and exposing what is within; Smollett had translated this work (as *The Devil upon Crutches*) in 1750, and so it must have been still on his mind as he wrote *Peregrine Pickle*—perhaps it lay behind his decision to bring the talents of Crabtree and Perry together in a satirical enterprise. But discovery of the source for Crabtree is ultimately not of much importance; it is his role that matters, and the way Smollett presents him.

The old misanthrope first appears in chapter 76, as Perry attends a fashionable gathering at Bath in the midst of idle schemes to seduce women and to amuse himself with scandal in the form of "the secret history of characters" (p. 380). An irreverent, foppish wag delivers the initial (and crucial) description of Crabtree in an impertinent address: "Your servant, you old rascal. . . . I vow to Gad! you look extremely shocking, with these gummy eyes, lanthorn jaws, and toothless chaps. What! you squint at the ladies, you old rotten medlar? . . . I see you want to sit. These wither'd shanks of yours tremble under their burthen" (pp. 380–81). And then, as the company laughs, the wag compares Crabtree to a monkey chained in the room: "you had best survey him," he says, for "he is of your own family" (p. 381). Crabtree, thought by all to be deaf, has of course heard the insults, but by pretending ignorance of them he turns the joke back upon the aggressor, whom (it appears) the monkey much more nearly resembles, and wins the day.

This is a funny and satisfying moment. The superior wit triumphs, which is just as it should be in an arena of comic action; at some level Smollett surely delights in his misanthrope, troubling figure though he is. The comic moment is followed, however, by evidence that the fop's visual portrait of Crabtree as a grotesque was an accurate one after all. Perry discovers that "every sentence he spoke was replete with gall; nor did his satire consist in general reflections, but in a series of remarks, which had been made through the medium of a most whimsical peculiarity of opinion" (p. 381); and he watches as the old man brutally humiliates a young officer and member of Parliament who unwisely talks of military affairs he does not understand. He immediately (in the next chapter) approaches Crabtree, requests and hears an account of his bitterly hard life, and receives from him the ultimate wisdom he has learned from his experience: that "the characters of mankind are every where the same; that common sense and honesty bear an infinitely small proportion to folly and vice; and that life is at best a paultry province" (p. 386). At this point their alliance begins, and they set out to cheat those whom their clever advertising convinces of Crabtree's abilities as a soothsayer and conjuror, taking their money for the privilege of mocking them.

For Perry this is all a matter of good sport, though he pursues the scheme with an enthusiasm that betrays more than a slight measure of angry cynicism; for Crabtree such fraudulence is a way of life, and he draws Perry inexorably into sharing his singleminded misanthropy as the world grows more difficult and treacherous all around him. Crabtree's harsh sentiments concerning human nature, just quoted, sound very much like Smollett's own as occasionally expressed elsewhere,[23] and they resemble those of Matthew Bramble in the early pages of *Humphry Clinker.* In the later prison episode Perry echoes them, and acts radically upon them, as he contemplates all the "shocking examples of the vicissitudes of fortune continually before his eyes" and decides to withdraw himself "from all society" (p. 748)—he becomes, like Crabtree, the complete satirist: isolated, bitter, enclosed by the misery of his own imagined superiority. The ending of the novel repudiates this stance, of course; as Perry adopts it completely he sinks helplessly into a "forlorn condition, with an equal abhorrence of the world and himself" (p. 748), and it is from this condition that his author rescues him by a providential gesture identical to that employed at the close of *Roderick Random.* As further evidence of the repudiation Smollett actually softens Crabtree in the final chapters, making him a loyal (and even kind) friend to the young man whom his counsel and example had encouraged in a morally disastrous course of life.

It would perhaps be an exaggeration to say that Crabtree is projected as a monster, but he is certainly a grotesque—moral as well as physical. The wag's description of him holds; his lantern face, squinty eyes, toothless mouth, and spindly legs add up to a misshapenness typical of all of Smollett's grotesques, and the suggestion of his physical affinity with the monkey imparts the non-human attribute that settles the question of how he is to be understood as a visual conception. The efficiency of Smollett's presentation of Crabtree is the most notable quality about him as a character portrait. Like Launcelot Crab in *Roderick Random,* he is exactly what the description of him shows him to be: an absurdity, a joke, but a sinister presence whose shadow looms as a pall descends upon the hero's life. If any reader is confused by Crabtree, betrayed into applause by the ingenuity of his shifts to mock the world, a return to the initial description of him will have a clarifying effect.

Peregrine Pickle, vast though it is, contains fewer such grotesques as Crabtree than *Roderick Random;* I have already noted that the novel is, on the whole, less intensely visual than Smollett's first. Perry himself, however, is more fully drawn than Roderick—as a visual presence, with an actual body, seen and described. Roderick, quite naturally, rarely manages the kind of distance necessary to see and to portray himself, but the third-person narrator of *Peregrine Pickle* is easily able to gaze upon its hero and draw verbal pictures of him—indeed, this is perhaps the sole advantage gained by Smollett's decision to employ a posture of omniscience in this novel. Most of the descriptions of Perry, it must be said, are perfunctory: at three years old he is a "handsome, healthy and promising child" (p. 51), and at eleven he is "remarkable for the beauty and elegance of his person" (p. 63); as a young man he possesses the same physical attractions, we are often reminded, together with a brightness of eye and sharpness of wit that distinguish him from all others of his sex and station. But on those occasions when Smollett looks most closely at Perry's actual qualities as a person—his capacity for really substantial responses to the world—he becomes strikingly visual in his rendering of him. Such occasions are relatively rare, but they are important because, in the aggregate, they redeem Perry from the shallowness that characterizes both his nature and his author's usual presentation of it.

As John McAllister has observed, these occasions typically arise when Perry is stressed by sexual and emotional frustration caused by failure in an amorous encounter.[24] Other kinds of failure and disappointment can cause vividly expressive reactions in him too, as when, late in the novel, he is denied admission to the house of Sir Steady Steerwell, the minister from whom he has expected the preferment that will restore his fallen fortunes. "This prohibition, which announced his total ruin, filled him with rage, horror and despair," says the narrator; "he cursed the porter," "vented the most virulent imprecations upon his master," and "returned to his lodgings in a most frantic condition, biting his lips so that the blood ran from his mouth, dashing his head and fists against the sides of his chimney, and weeping with the most bitter expressions of woe" (p. 667). When Pipes, in an agony of worry, forces his way into the room where this noisy display is occurring, Perry threatens to shoot him. Such moments provide strong evidence that Perry, by nature given to excess, is always—as McAllister has put it—at risk of falling victim to his own "constitutionally 'warm' passions which explode in paroxysms of violent release when they have been blocked or frustrated" (p. 126). Smollett typically describes those paroxysms with close attention to specific physical details.

His failures with women frustrate Perry most of all, and with the greatest regularity, as his passions are warmest when they involve the female sex. His outbursts in response to such failures are extreme, and sometimes even dangerous to his health. When Pallet rides the jackass into the midst of his near-seduction of the fair Fleming, he is thrown into the "most violent pangs of rage and disappointment," and he fiercely attacks both the painter and his mount, driving them off in a panic of pain and fear (p. 297). When Emilia, the most frequent cause of risible passion for Perry, sets him into a frenzy of jealousy by flirting with a soldier at her brother Godfrey's wedding, his reaction is expressed in precisely noted physiological symptoms: the sweat runs down his face profusely, the color vanishes from his cheeks, his knees totter, and his eyesight fails (p. 589). This is a very real disorder, and it causes him to faint. Earlier, when Emilia reviles him for an attempt to seduce her, he raves "like a Bedlamite," turns delirious, and must be bled before his "paroxysm" can subside. Such behavior, to borrow McAllister's phrase, amounts to "more than conventional lover's swoons" (p. 126); it is instead a sign that Smollett was putting to use his knowledge of current medical theory to display a pathology of violent emotions in response to erotic or other powerfully affecting experience. Smollett the eighteenth-century physician naturally assumed that external appearance gave direct and visual—readable, like a text (or a painting)—expression to internal motions of feeling and qualities of personal character; hence, as we know, the many caricatures and grotesques in his novels. He was most effective with Perry's character when he allowed that assumption to govern the presentation of him. It is certainly true that for the most part Perry is more driven by pure energy than by authentic feeling; but when Smollett now and again gives him occasion to feel, he becomes as passionate and vivid a character as Roderick Random, and he is even more graphically portrayed. At such moments his inner life becomes as public and accessible as Roderick's always is, and it enters the sphere of communal action where his pranks, and the other manifestations of his creative—but frivolously directed—energy, take place. When this happens, Perry seems a character of genuine substance, worthy of his author's talent after all.

Smollett is at his absolute best in *Peregrine Pickle* when he is most Hogarthian, and he is most Hogarthian in the finest of the many tableau scenes that are so crucial to the spatial form of his novel. The first such scene occurs very early, in chapter 2, when Gamaliel Pickle meets first Trunnion, and then Hatchway and Pipes. Together with the landlord, who provides the introductions, these odd characters make a little society of eccentrics whose presence is striking enough to arrest the motion of the story before it even gets started. I have already discussed the visual qualities of this scene, which are typical of Smollett's method in developing others later in the novel. There is no need for further discussion of the same scene here, except to say that its exuberance, its vivid language, and its emphasis on quirks and pranks set a tone and establish a mood for the narrative that is to follow. It is, besides, a brilliant performance, an instance of virtuoso comic writing justly described by George Kahrl as "one of the great episodes in English literature."[25]

Hogarth, obviously, was constantly on Smollett's mind as he wrote. His characterization of the painter as "inimitable," noted earlier, certainly hints that this is so, not to mention (again) his portrait of Pallet and his very pointed allusion to *The Gate of Calais, or The Roast Beef of Old England* during the "Entertainment" scene. In chapter 40, as Robert Etheridge Moore has observed, he actually borrows quite directly from the *Calais Gate* print in his portrait of the cook at the inn in Boulogne where the hero and his party spend a day while their chaise is being repaired.[26] "This phantome," he writes, "was a tall, long-legged, meagre, swarthy fellow, that stooped very much; his cheek-bones were remarkably raised, his nose bent into the shape and size of a powder-horn, and the sockets of his eyes as raw round the edges, as if the skin had been pared off." The description goes on at length in detailing the appearance of this odd fellow, mentioning the faded handkerchief covering his head, the bag ("at least a foot square") containing his hair, his tucked apron and linen waistcoat, and his rolled silk stockings, concluding that altogether he looked "like a criminal in the pillory" (pp. 194–95). Smollett's cook is an exact copy of the figure who occupies the center of Hogarth's composition. In the upper left corner of his picture, incidentally, Hogarth placed a self-portrait in profile, and the resemblance to Smollett's Pallet is unmistakable.

The Gate of Calais is a densely textured narrative of a moment in the actual experience of its artist. Hogarth was arrested on the very spot in August 1748 for sketching the French fortifications; in his drawing we see (on either side of

William Hogarth, *The Gate of Calais, or The Roast Beef of Old England* (1748).
(Copyright Tate Gallery London.)

the cook) two sentinels, apparently ready to make the arrest but (like the fat
friar) distracted by the sight of the great joint of English beef resting in the
arms of the cook, who probably serves in a posh English hotel. There are
signs of poverty and hunger all about, contrasting with the lusciousness of the
beef and suggesting the inferiority and squalor of French life by comparison
with British, which is also (such is the strong implication) open and free while
the French citizens of Calais are enclosed within the city gate, where they can
be narrowly seen (with a broad sky above and beyond them) through its opening. Each face in the picture registers the life of a particular feeling character,
each body is in a particular motion, and the whole is a tableau extremely critical of the microcosmic society Hogarth is representing—as critical, indeed,
as Smollett is in his representations of French culture in *Peregrine Pickle,* and

on this score as on others, the intertextual relations of the two works serve to remind us of the important affinities between the novelist and the painter.

Hogarth created one of his most dramatically exquisite moments in *The Gate of Calais,* with every line of his composition contributing significantly to the high energy of the scene overall. Smollett repeatedly strives for similar effects in the important tableau scenes of *Peregrine Pickle.* When Perry and Godfrey arrive in Bath, that sinkhole of corruption and silly fashion (as Smollett regarded it), they repair immediately to the billiard tables, where Godfrey outsharps a gang of sharpers by proving superior not only with his mast, or cuestick, but as a confidence man. To Smollett, gambling of any kind was anathema, the symptom of a blighted society and, as metaphor (one he frequently used—we have but to recall the latter chapters of *Roderick Random*), an unmistakable sign of capitulation to the rule of Chance. Gambling was rampant in eighteenth-century Bath, and in this episode Smollett has Godfrey (with his ally, Perry) use the professional gambler's deceptions against the whole enterprise of gambling itself, betraying a remarkable knowledge of those deceptions and giving Godfrey complete control of them. The game-playing is detailed over several pages, and the scene culminates in a vivid description of the assembled sharpers as they realize what is happening and calculate their substantial losses. The effect is theatrical, and Smollett catches the whole ensemble of actors in a moment of arrested motion. He begins his description by focusing intensely upon their faces, revealing the turmoil they feel by tracing the physiological changes manifested in their complexions, in the process introducing strong elements of the grotesque. The "visages of these professors" underwent a transformation with each of Godfrey's quick successes, we are told: "from their natural colour" they "shifted into a sallow hue; from thence into pale; from pale into yellow, which degenerated into a mahogony tint"; until finally, "they stood like so many swarthy Moors, jaundiced with terror and vexation." The player whose skill has been so surprisingly overcome goes pale, the carbuncles on his nose taking on a "livid appearance, as if a gangrene had already made some progress in his face," while his hands shake and his whole body shows signs of the most awful "trepidation." When his final shot goes awry and seventeen hundred pounds are lost, his fellow conspirators are sent into a frenzy "of the most violent emotions. One turned up his eyes to heaven, and bit his nether lip; another gnawed his fingers, while he stalked across the room; a third blasphemed with horrible imprecations; and he who played the partie, sneaked off, grinding his teeth together, with a look that baffles all description, and as he crossed the threshold, exclaiming, 'A damn'd bite, by G—d!'" (p. 369).

Here, as in the later scene when Crabtree makes a fool of the young officer, superior wit wins out in a dramatic moment of great satisfaction. In this instance the triumph is also moral, however, as Godfrey, Perry, and the narrator all rejoice in having "so effectually destroyed such a nest of pernicious miscreants" (p. 369). The episode is a narrative tour de force, a self-contained drama that accumulates its details to create a memorable study of social corruption complete with a climactic visual flourish, when the reader's eye narrows to a focus upon the composite image of conspiratorial faces as their colors change to reveal, at last, the darkness that lies behind them. Smollett was exceptionally gifted at capturing scenes like this one, and though they are not so frequent in *Peregrine Pickle* as one could wish, when they occur they display his great power as a social observer who is able to make his readers see, and judge, the spectacle of folly and vice that characterizes the world through which his hero moves.

In several of the most successful tableau scenes in the novel Smollett seems to have been very directly influenced by Hogarth as he developed his visual conception. The two drinking episodes in chapters 24 and 93, when Perry plunges himself into dissipation amongst a group of university idlers and, later, a set of profligate young noblemen in London, bear striking resemblances to Hogarth's *Midnight Modern Conversation* (1732), a startling representation of drunkenness as a kind of social disease.[27] The latter of Smollett's two episodes includes only scanty details, emphasizing instead the narrator's summary judgment against such youthful revels, carried on, he says, at "a certain tavern, which might be properly stiled the temple of excess," and leading almost inevitably from drinking to gaming, in which Perry, now "insensibly accustomed to licentious riot," indulges with impetuous abandon (p. 582). This episode clearly parallels the earlier one, however, and the reader's response to it is thus informed by echoes; once more, Smollett practices a method of economy that he would have been wise to rely upon with much greater regularity in *Peregrine Pickle*.

The drinking scene in chapter 24 is managed with such mastery, and is so detailed and precise, that it easily provides the visual framework for its later counterpart. It commences with a descriptive phrase that seems deliberately chosen as a way of calling to mind the model of *Midnight Modern Conversation*. Such "midnight consistories," says the narrator, always afforded Perry abundant opportunities for the practice of his skills in satire and mockery, owing to the foolishness of the participants, a "club of politicians" he considered "wrong-headed enthusiasts" (p. 114). Perry drinks less in this scene than he does in the later one, but he is drawn into riotous behavior by the irresistible temptation to expose the "grave characters" of the club in "ridiculous attitudes." His success in doing so may be measured by the description of the absurd but morally outrageous debacle that follows his proposals for escalating extravagance.

> They . . . broke their glasses in consequence of his suggestion, drank healths out of their shoes, caps, and the bottoms of the candlesticks that stood before them, sometimes standing with one foot on a chair, and the knee bent on the edge of the table; and when they could no longer stand in that posture, setting their bare posteriors on the cold floor, they huzza'd, hollowed, danced and sung, and in short were elevated to such a pitch of intoxication, that when Peregrine proposed that they should burn their perriwigs, the hint was immediately approved, and they executed the frolick as one man; their shoes and caps underwent the same fate by the same instigation, and in this trim he led them forth into the street. (p. 115)

Smollett clearly borrows the tone of his scene from Hogarth's engraving, along with numerous details, achieving a comparable density and craziness of effect. Hogarth's table is surrounded by equally noisy and dishevelled revelers, one of whom (the figure in the rear) seems to be leading the festivities and urging his companions on; overturned candlesticks, obviously used for drinking, lie scattered about; periwigs, though not burned, are askew on several heads; one reveler (at the far left) appears to be singing; a heap of empty bottles is on the floor. Instead of spilling into the street, Hogarth's drunks— several of them, at any rate—appear to be sickening, and one is stretched on the floor vomiting, his broken glass clutched in his hand. The two scenes— Hogarth's and Smollett's—are intensely dramatic because they so carefully develop a narrative of profligacy, excess, and debauchery. The novelist, limited to words, manages somehow to match the vividness and admonitory emphasis achieved in the painter's graphic rendering of this narrative, making it a self-contained vignette—an ensemble portrait of dangerous folly—that all but stops the larger story of Perry's frivolous evening, indeed—just for a moment—halts the progress of the main plot for a close look at the real meaning of what, in more traditional constructions of the drinking scene (to which both Hogarth and Smollett were responding), was regarded as a celebration of conviviality.

The best, most famous, and most extended of all Smollett's tableau scenes in *Peregrine Pickle* is, of course, the "Entertainment in the Manner of the Ancients." The episode, almost ten pages long (233–41), has numerous agendas, not least of which is the exposure of the doctor's pedantry. Most interesting of all is Smollett's decision to make the painter Pallet a vehicle for representation of his preference for modern aesthetic values as opposed to classical. What he writes here is not at all *about* the visual arts, or even about aesthetics generally, yet it manages to hint at questions of artistic expression in a way that is hard to miss. The farce of the dinner itself, with its hideous gastronomic effects on the participants, emphasizes the folly of obsessive reliance upon old formulas—in this instance, recipes—in a creative act; the doctor, all silliness and pretension (as in his poetry), simply does not recognize the inappropriateness of what he attempts, and in trying to imitate the ancients he misses the point that what they did cannot be done again in the modern world without inevitable failure. In a charming and pointed irony, Smollett spoofs himself by modeling the dinner upon the riotous feast staged by Trimalchio in the *Satyricon,* by Petronius.

It is the prominence of Pallet in the scene, and the implied presence of his model Hogarth, that unmistakably proclaims its serious (if also tongue-in-cheek) concern with aesthetic issues and modernist values. Appropriately enough, Smollett will later make a joke of Pallet's painting of *Cleopatra,* suggesting the artist's bad judgment in undertaking a history painting upon a classical subject—and in doing so he looks ahead to his one reservation about Hogarth's triptych altar painting for Bristol's Church of Saint Mary Redcliffe, expressed in his otherwise admiring review of that work, where he remarks that such a performance wastes the genius of one unrivaled in the art of drawing scenes of contemporary life.[28] In the "Entertainment" episode, Pallet quite viscerally rejects the doctor's ridiculous aesthetic by the reactions of his stomach to the concoctions that are served. And Smollett, because he is so particular in arranging the details of the scene, promotes the values associated with the real-life Hogarth by creating a tableau worthy of Hogarth himself. Those details are too many and too minute to permit a full account of them here; but, from the elaborate description of the disposition of the guests around the table, to the introductory flourish for each dish, to the picturing of individuals as they are convulsed by what they eat, the cumulative effect makes for yet another of Smollett's unforgettable representations of a group of eccentrics, each a type of human folly—or worse. Besides the pretentious doctor and clownish painter (and Perry, of course), he brings into the scene a French marquis, an Italian count, and a German baron, all of whom Perry "knew to be egregious coxcombs" (p. 234). The addition of these characters gives the assembled company an international cast, extending the range of the episode's typologies—silliness is to be seen the world over, Smollett was no doubt thinking. When the Italian and the German are found in a homosexual embrace as the feast ends, Perry (and his author) are outraged, while this conclusion to the occasion only further emphasizes its perverseness—homosexual acts, says the narrator, are "abominable" (p. 242).

It is a comic perverseness, but with its dark side; the values upon which the episode centers were important enough to Smollett so that he clearly took their corruption to heart. There is an air of closeness, airlessness, even gloom about the hotel rooms where the dinner occurs; no reference is made to light of any sort; the odors are overpowering; the whole scene, while farcical, bears comparison with the drinking scene of chapter 24, though here the reveling is aborted by the foulness of the food and drink. When Perry finds the Frenchman "puking" up the soup (p. 238) we have an implicit, but clear, allusion to the grimness of *Midnight Modern Conversation,* which was so important to the conception of the earlier episode. Smollett's dinner even more closely parallels Hogarth's *Election Entertainment,* the first in a series of four pictures (1753–54) satirically treating the nasty conflict between Whigs and Tories prior to the election of 1754. Smollett could not have been influenced by this work in developing his own "Entertainment" episode, which predates it; it seems possible, however, even likely, that Hogarth was influenced by

William Hogarth, *An Election Entertainment* (1753–54).
(By courtesy of the Trustees of Sir John Soane's Museum.)

Smollett. Questions of influence aside, what is important is the way Hogarth's graphic rendering of his scene illuminates Smollett's own verbal painting.[29] There is a comparable crowding of those assembled, the atmosphere of riot and folly is rampant, the moral darkness is almost palpable, and every figure is a highly individualized eccentric, a caricature of a human type—the glutton, who has made himself ill and is being bled (far right); the rake, more interested in women than politics (upper left); the drunk, who is falling over as he passes out (lower right); and so on.

But Smollett's scene is funny too, and its humor is a major reason for its success as a commentary on social folly and aesthetic numbskullery. By the time it begins, both the doctor and Pallet have been fully projected as caricatures who, in the words of George Kahrl, "perfect two incongruous, recurring types of human personalities, not in isolation but in association and conflict."[30] By complementing each other as they do, they effectively create the whole range of comic oppositions within which the tensions of the scene generate their hilarity. The others present—the Frenchman, the Italian, and the German—are less individualized, but are all versions of the fop or dandy, and thus immediately recognizable as physical presences. Smollett focuses his greatest imaginative energy on detailing the dishes and their effects upon those who eat them; except in *Humphry Clinker,* when Matt Bramble launches into his tirade about London food, he is nowhere so graphic about gustatory matters. The characters of the scene, meanwhile, are given life by their actions. As Damian Grant has observed, Smollett achieves a remarkable vividness here by the kind of precision Bergson considered the very essence of comedy.[31] Smells, facial expressions, the doctor's minutiae in describing the courses as he presents them, the crashing of the table as one of the guests lurches away from it, his bowels in convulsions—these particulars and others gather themselves into a teeming picture of absurdity. One of the most laughable moments in the episode comes early, during the long paragraph in which Smollett develops an almost cinematic view of the guests as they try to understand where they are to sit (pp. 235–36); they have never before been asked to "repose" on couches while dining, and their confusion and clumsiness cause a collision that destroys the Frenchman's curls and leaves the German barepated, with the powder from his damaged wig filling the whole room. This paragraph, Grant rightly says, is the best in the whole chapter, as "the fine touch" of Smollett's extremely careful prose exhausts all the comic possibilities of its subject (p. 142).

Later in the novel, still employing Pallet and the doctor as his comic vehicles, Smollett renews his concern with the subject of visual aesthetics when (in chapter 67) Perry's travels take him to Antwerp, the birthplace of Rubens. Pallet, "elevated to an uncommon flow of spirits" (p. 332) at the prospect of breathing the same air once also breathed by his idol, predictably makes a fool of himself, failing to recognize Rubens's masterpieces when he sees them— because Perry, unable to resist a joke, has told him they are by others—and praising inferior paintings he wrongly finds to be in "the stile of Peter Paul" (p. 334)—again as a result of Perry's joking. But Smollett modulates away from irony when, with Pallet and the doctor, Perry visits Antwerp Cathedral to view the *Descent from the Cross;* he allows Pallet to voice his genuine admiration for "the Flemish school" of art (p. 336), with its familiarizing of religious subjects and its close fidelity to the details of actual, felt experience. It is the doctor who seals the solemnity of this praise by scoffing at Rubens for a modern trivializer, and his mean-spirited pedantry—for valuing Rubens above the ancient poets he says that "Pallet's eyes ought to be picked out by owls" (p. 336)—makes the painter's warm enthusiasm seem all the more valid.

Smollett's preoccupation with the painterly arts in *Peregrine Pickle* is important to any meaningful understanding of the work's most important and successful effects. Above all Smollett prized clarity, precision, immediacy, and narrative or dramatic coherence in a picture—just the sort of visual acuity and relevance to familiar life he admired so much in Hogarth and tried himself to achieve through the medium of words. Art, he believed, ought to tell the truth in images that make it accessible and unmistakable. Though he devotes relatively little additional space to overt expression of concern with visual art following the episode at Antwerp, it remains important in the background as other episodes of the story unfold. After Perry's return to England from his travels on the Continent, aesthetic issues give way to larger moral issues, which they actually help to clarify. If the artist's responsibility is to tell the truth, Smollett emphasizes, it is because truthfulness and accuracy of both perception and expression are fundamental moral obligations in human activity of all kinds, private and public, in domestic life and in social and political interchange as well as in works of art.

But the world as Perry knows it, in Europe and then—most especially—in his homeland, is all deception, disguise, masking, and fraudulence. Bath, the resort of the fashionable, is represented as a major outpost in a national system of corruption emanating from its center in London, home to a "great company of adventurers, who employed agents, in all the different branches of imposition, throughout the whole kingdom of England" (p. 365)—fortune-hunters, sharpers, confidence men, and extortionists. We have already seen how Perry and Godfrey beat this system in a game of billiards, using its own tactics against it and routing at least one of its nests of "pernicious miscreants." It is at Bath, however, that Perry meets Cadwallader Crabtree, and his new friendship with this misanthropic fraud draws him deeply into complicity with the very corruption his ingenuity, and Godfrey's, has exposed. Perry has always participated in the world's deceptions, of course; his pranks have depended on strategies of duplicity, and so have his exercises in amorous adventuring. But from the Bath episode onward (that is, from about the middle of the novel) his character darkens. It is during this episode that he begins his scheming against the faithful Emilia's virtue; it is from Bath that he travels to the city of London, that maze of moral confusion and chaotic emblem of modern life, where he carries out his schemes with Cadwallader, falls into disastrous profligacy and extravagance, entangles himself with lying politicians and a crowd of mercenary writers (the College of Authors), exhausts the fortune Trunnion has left him, and lands in prison.

Smollett brings Perry to this point of collapse, it is clear, as a way of resolving tension between his desire for adventure and the moral imperative that, as the providential ending of the novel proclaims by bringing him happiness in the wake of punishment, ought to govern in human affairs. Paul-Gabriel Boucé has gone so far as to say that, in *Peregrine Pickle* as well as *Roderick Random,* this tension provides thematic consistency and, simultaneously and inevitably, generates both the meaning and the erratic structure of the narrative.[32] The adventurer, says Boucé, by "launching out on the roads of life" (p. 100), travels away from a moral center and into an arena where innocence is lost and the self is at risk of corruption and even destruction; rescue and redemption are made possible only by crisis, which leads to the kind of recognition that justifies the reward of safety, quiet, and even bliss that comes with retreat both from adventuring and from the desire for it. Adventuring, in other words, must give way totally to morality.

Boucé may overstate Smollett's view of the incompatibility between the adventurous spirit and moral agency, but it is certainly true that the ending of *Peregrine Pickle,* by duplicating that of *Roderick Random,* affirms an essentially satiric view of human life in a world of action—it is only by withdrawal, say these two novels, that one can escape the need for satire. Both novels combine a version of satiric misanthropy with the sentimentality of the romance ending. The combination works admirably in *Roderick Random;* it is only minimally successful in *Peregrine Pickle* because the hero is less sympathetic, more guilty, and, as I argued earlier in this chapter, altogether unequal to his author's claim that he is a figure of genuine moral substance. Smollett makes a nearly fatal error in imagining Perry capable of wishing to seduce Emilia. The effect of the attempted seduction, which is truly vile, is nearly irretrievable; the reversal that follows later, when Perry repents and is forgiven after suffering

loss and imprisonment, hardly seems justified—it is both facile and unconvincing. To understand why this is so one has only to imagine Richardson's
Clarissa forgiving Lovelace for drugging and raping her, and then making him
happy by marrying him. Still, Perry's schemes against Emilia provide for some
of the most powerful moments in the novel, so one would not wish them
away. Not surprisingly, given Smollett's concern with truth-telling, the culmi-
nation of the seduction effort comes when (in chapter 82) Perry persuades
Emilia to accompany him to a masquerade—a ritualized celebration of masking and disguise. The darkness of his purpose is set off by the light farce of the
parallel episode much earlier, when he goes to another masquerade with Pallet, who is in drag and thus becomes the butt of cruel but very funny jokes
perpetrated by his companion. The masquerade evening with Emilia turns
equally cruel at Perry's hand, but there is nothing funny about it.

In describing the evening's events Smollett gives us another tableau scene,
complete with an account of the dances performed; but all details are blurred
except those immediately concerning Perry and Emilia. He is "dressed in the
habit of Pantaloon, and she in that of Columbine" (p. 405)—an oddly ironic
pairing of costumes (both derived from the Italian *commedia dell'arte*), as Pantaloon is a type of the innocuous and foolish old man, while Columbine, in
traditional associations, is both his daughter and the flirtatious mistress of
Harlequin. In Emilia's case the irony is harmlessly intended, but in Perry's it
signals real danger. He is neither innocuous nor a fool. In what is very probably a deliberate echo of Lovelace's treatment of Clarissa, he brutally deceives
this woman he professes to love, drugging her champagne with "a stimulating
tincture" (p. 405) and then leading her away, not to the safety of her uncle's
house (as she supposes), but to a "strange place" (a bagnio) where he pleads
with her upon his knees to "crown his happiness," addressing her as "Divine
creature" and "My dear angel," and then offers her his pocketbook (containing notes for two thousand pounds) in exchange for her favors (pp. 406, 407).
Her outrage at this insult provokes him all the more, causing him to determine upon "a vigorous assault" in obedience to "the furious dictates of his
unruly and ungenerous desire" (p. 408).

Emilia stops the rape with words. Aside from Lydia Melford in *Humphry
Clinker,* she is Smollett's strongest heroine, and here she discovers for the first
(and last) time that she has a distinctive, powerful voice. She rebukes Perry

firmly, humiliating and unmanning him. "Sir," she cries, "you are unworthy of my concern. . . . As for your present attempt upon my chastity, I despise your power, as I detest your intention. . . . Sir, your behaviour on this occasion, is in all respects low and contemptible; for, ruffian as you are, you durst not harbour one thought of executing your execrable scheme, while you knew my brother was near enough to prevent, or revenge the insult; so that you must not only be a treacherous villain, but also a most despicable coward" (p. 408). Perry's reaction—he behaves like a madman, acting "a thousand extravagancies" (p. 409)—is, as already suggested, a physiological manifestation of frustrated erotic desire; excessive desire, unfulfilled, causes a response equally excessive. As we know, this is not the first time Perry has responded in this way to sexual disappointment. But only Emilia, whom at last he realizes he has truly loved all along, is able to have any meaningful impact upon him. The other important objects of Perry's desire—Mrs. Hornbeck, the fair Fleming, and, late in the novel, the nymph of the road—are too insubstantial in his consciousness to affect him much when his efforts to conquer and possess them fail. Emilia, however, is a real presence for him, in time more and more like Roderick Random's Narcissa, and the long (and often interrupted) process of his reformation actually begins with her assertion of a confident selfhood that will not permit him to defile her.

And what is it that Emilia represents? what is it that makes her image (she is conventionally beautiful) and her presence (she is both magnetic and strong) so effectual in finally arresting Perry's helter-skelter adventurer's progress? Like all of Smollett's heroines she is drawn from the traditions of romance, and so she is an emblem of purity, the embodiment of moral idealism, the promise of stability, certitude, and quiet joy. In a typical manifestation of Smollett's dualistic practice in his novels, she is the bright and lovely opposite of the world's dark, teeming, and frequently ugly—or grotesque—manifestations of a principle of disorder. The lesson of the novel seems to be that unbridled desire (sexual, but also social) leads inevitably to excess, which in turn leaves one subject to the rule of Chance, which works from a principle of excess. What is needed is restraint, self-discipline, an effective yearning for balance in both conduct and feeling. John McAllister has suggested that Emilia provides the impetus for Perry to develop those traits—in fact, the only impetus. As a desired woman who withholds her body she rejects the im-

portunities of excessive passion, discrediting them and implicitly offering instead the attraction of marriage, an institution within which desire may be
both liberated and regulated.[33] It is only when, languishing in prison, Perry
comes to the recognition that he has nothing—"Of all his ample fortune,"
the narrator observes, "nothing now remained but his wardrobe" (p. 680)—
that he ceases to desire anything, including Emilia, for he now despairs of
having her even on her own terms. At this point his author judges him worthy
of redemption and sets into quick motion the resolution by which it is
brought about. Order and clarity emerge, even in the structure of the story,
which now goes in a straight line toward its last page. Emilia inherits a fortune
from a late uncle; Gamaliel Pickle dies intestate, and his riches become his
son's; released from prison with a renewed sense of life's possibilities, Perry is
now all "temperance," "affability," and "moderation" (p. 770); Emilia accepts
him, they marry, and at last they leave the vexing world behind them, arriving
at Perry's ancestral home "amidst the acclamations of the whole parish"
(p. 781). Perry the dispossessed wanderer is now a country gentleman; the
sexual adventurer, driven to predatory habits by excessive desire, is now a
happy husband to his beloved Emilia, with whom—such is the presumption—he will live quietly (and chastely) forever after. And there are no more
pranks.

   In narrative line and subject matter, as we know by the end (if not sooner),
Peregrine Pickle is a kind of "rake's progress." Smollett clearly took Hogarth's
great—and still popular—serial work as one of his models when writing the
novel. That it ends happily does not make it any less Hogarthian, as the whole
accumulated weight of its many separate and structurally equivalent episodes
comes to rest upon the moment of illumination when the hero acknowledges
the error of his ways, and the meaning of those ways comes into clear relief.
That the novel lacks the compression and focus of Tom Rakewell's pictured
story, or of Smollett's own *Roderick Random,* does not make it a total failure as
an experiment with narrative construction—eclectic, panoramic, restlessly
energetic and fertile in its inventiveness over a vast number of pages. The
problems of the work are many, as I argued at the outset of this chapter; one
can only wish that Smollett had restrained his own compulsions, which gave
rise to the frequent tedium of Perry's failure to restrain his. But, impatient as
the reader may become with the novel—its undifferentiated sprawl, its cease-

less practical joking, its piling of episode upon trivial episode—it is impossible not to like it for its great character portraits (Trunnion, Grizzle, Hatchway and Pipes, Crabtree) and its stunning tableau scenes (there are many more of them than I have been able to discuss). As an exercise in spatial form it is only a limited success, but its finest moments are such as many novelists, of Smollett's generation or any other, would be glad to claim for their own. These Smollett was surely aware of; just as surely, his awareness fed the rancor he felt at those who mocked his achievement and (so he fancied) sought to consign it to the shadows of obscurity.

He may have been aware of the work's failings, too. He was altogether silent on this point, so far as we know, but his next novel furnishes a clue to his judgment, for in it he returns to the kind of compression sustained throughout his very first. *The Adventures of Ferdinand Count Fathom,* at less than half the length of *Peregrine Pickle,* is Smollett's most unusual performance: a dense, tightly conceived, flawed but still compelling study of a consummate villain, not merely a rake but a criminal, whose exploits occasioned narrative experiments more radical and daring than anything he had ever attempted before. It is a better novel than *Peregrine Pickle,* more disciplined and more carefully crafted, though it offers fewer of the comic delights always associated with Smollett—for this reason more than any other it has always been underrated by those who have bothered to take it up. Indeed, *Ferdinand Count Fathom* is quite a remarkable work in its way, a tour de force of writing against the grain of convention. It has long needed to be rescued from the misunderstanding of its readers so that it might be properly valued. The chapter that follows is my attempt to make the rescue.

CHAPTER 3

Ferdinand Count Fathom

"On the whole," observed Ralph Griffiths in the very earliest review of *The Adventures of Ferdinand Count Fathom* ever to be published, Tobias Smollett's third novel is

> a work of a mixed character, compounded of various and unequal parts. It abounds on the one hand with affecting incidents, with animated descriptions, and alternate scenes of melting grief, tenderness and joy; diversified with some few exhibitions of a humorous kind. On the other hand . . . there are some extravagant excursions of the author's fancy, with certain improbable stories . . . marvelous adventures, and little incongruities; all which seem to be indications of the performance being hastily, nay and carelessly composed. Yet, with whatever crudities it may be chargeable,—with all its imperfections, we may venture to pronounce that the work has still merit enough to compensate with the discerning reader for its defects: it carries with it strong marks of genius in the author, and demonstrations of his great proficiency in the study of mankind.[1]

Griffiths's less than enthusiastic recommendation of the new story by the author of *Roderick Random* and *Peregrine Pickle* may help to account for its commercial failure.[2] But there were possibly other reasons. The effects of Smollett's attacks on important contemporaries in his controversial second novel were surely not forgotten by the time his new work came out, and the memory of the unpleasant paper war in which he had embroiled himself must have lingered also. In addition, Smollett had angered a number of powerful people with his *Essay on the External Use of Water* (March 1752), an attack on the Bath Corporation and its opportunistic promotion of the curative powers of the resort city's sulfuric waters. He had also embarrassed himself and tarnished his personal reputation by publicly thrashing Peter Gordon and his landlord Edward Groom in November 1752, and then suffering through a protracted lawsuit that cost him twenty pounds in damages—Gordon, a former associate, owed him money which he refused to pay, and so Smollett ambushed him, with Groom, in Westminster and dealt with him in a summary way.

Whatever the reasons, and there were surely a great many, *Ferdinand Count Fathom* fell all but stillborn from the press. Griffiths's review was followed by no others, and the only further contemporary commentary was lukewarm—in three letters to her friend Mrs. Dewes, Mary Granville Delany mentioned the novel three times, but managed to praise it for nothing more than being "well intended" and concluded that Smollett was not to be named "in a day with our good friend Richardson."[3] In retrospect the review by Griffiths turns out to have been crucial, for he actually set boundaries for discussion of *Ferdinand Count Fathom* from which it has scarcely yet escaped. The important terms of his evaluation—Smollett's "little incongruities" and other signs of hasty or careless composition, as not quite balanced by those "strong marks" of his "genius" or even by his admittedly impressive "proficiency in the study of mankind"—anticipate what a majority of critics since have said in estimating the work as a novelistic achievement. Its narrative is ineptly plotted and structured, say its detractors. Furthermore, while Smollett loudly condemns the conventional moralistic posturing of other fiction-writers in his dedication and opening chapter, he weakly resorts to the same mannerisms in the contrivances of his own resolution; he awkwardly mixes Gothic melodrama with picaresque satire and fails to define and then sustain any meaningful moral framework, while his irregularities of tone and diction confuse the reader. But of course the story does contain some fine episodes, some ingenious strokes of satiric attack on contemporary institutions, and some delightful caricatures and comic portraits. Such are the commonplaces to be found in criticism of this novel, from Griffiths to George Saintsbury to Paul-Gabriel Boucé, who charitably excuses the work's "clumsy" technical structure and points instead to the excellence of its "thematic structure," as though the two things could ever be entirely separated.[4] And while recent attempts to recuperate the novel have found much in it to admire, they have only rarely addressed—much less sought to overcome—the niggling reservations that have haunted it since the time of its first appearance.[5]

Ferdinand Count Fathom is not a great novel or an unrecognized masterpiece, and it certainly is not Smollett's finest achievement. But, when it has not simply been neglected altogether, the work has been unjustly blamed for faults of which it is not always guilty. Actually, it has suffered from almost inevitable comparison with Henry Fielding's somewhat earlier masterpiece of ironic rogue biography, *The Life of Mr. Jonathan Wild the Great* (1743). *Ferdinand Count Fathom* represents a failed attempt to repeat the effects of *Jonathan Wild,* so goes one familiar line of argument, but it lacks both the consistency of vision and the fidelity to principles of organic composition and structure that distinguish Fielding's triumphant narrative. There are indeed many similarities between these two works; hence the comparisons. In the last analysis, however, the differences are far more important. Smollett, like Fielding with *Wild,* may have conceived Fathom as an inversion of the conventional hero and, additionally, as a variation upon the picaro and the criminal, both familiar fixtures in early eighteenth-century popular narrative; but he certainly did not set out to make him either the subject or the object of irony. Instead, he deliberately projected him—without any irony whatsoever—as a negative exemplar, launching him rough-and-tumble into the same chaotic reality he had imagined for his first two novels, creating as a result yet another crazy, erratic, fragmented narrative texture—and one with a power to disturb cozy reader sensibilities that leaves Fielding's clever contrivances looking rather tame. The usual comparisons with *Jonathan Wild* are beside the point, for they obscure and thus devalue the particular effects Smollett managed in *Ferdinand Count Fathom,* which is a clear-eyed, straight-ahead confrontation with the nature of evil as expressed in a human figure of obsessive villainy and insinuating charm who flourishes in the midst of the modern world's instabilities and, by his sinister and extremely disruptive presence, threatens to make them worse. One suspects that the critical tendency to see Smollett's work as an inept imitation of Fielding's is simply another manifestation of the tired old complaint that, as a novelist, he was unable to match his rival's skills as the architect of well-ordered narrative constructions. I hope I have managed by now to set this silly and misleading notion fully aside, but it might be well here to recall Damian Grant's convincing argument that, in literature as in all the arts, Smollett valued natural genius above the solemn proprieties of taste, spirit and exuberance above the conventional precepts of artful composition, strength and fertility of invention above the lesser attributes of mere shapeliness.[6]

Perhaps it is a sign of Smollett's lack of interest in elaborate formal theories of art that he left so few statements of his own poetics of fiction. What he did say on the subject is not, however, as even one of his most enthusiastic readers has suggested, "almost irrelevant."[7] It was in the dedication "To Doctor ******" preceding the first chapter of *Ferdinand Count Fathom* that he set down his only extended remarks on the subject of narrative form, and these remarks are altogether crucial to our understanding of the stories he told. "A Novel," Smollett observed,

> is a large diffused picture, comprehending the characters of life, disposed in different groupes, and exhibited in various attitudes, for the purposes of an uniform plan, and general occurrence, to which every individual figure is subservient. But this plan cannot be executed with propriety, probability or success, without a principal personage to attract the attention, unite the incidents, unwind the clue of the labyrinth, and at last close the scene by virtue of his own importance. (p. 4)

This paragraph is frequently cited in histories of the novel and in studies of Smollett as an interesting delineation of things important to the novelist's craft; but it is almost as often dismissed out of hand as merely conventional, or as inconsistent with its author's own practice in his fictions. Alan Dugald McKillop, in his discussion of Smollett in *The Early Masters of English Fiction,* provided—now thirty years ago—the first major exception to this general rule. McKillop had read Smollett's remarks very shrewdly, and what he said about them goes straight to the truth of what they really mean.

It is true, McKillop acknowledged, that Smollett never shows much interest at all in the development of "an uniform plan"—in raising this issue he was indeed simply echoing convention; but otherwise his statement reveals essential clues to his sense of craft. The "first sentence" of the important paragraph in question, McKillop noted, "uses the analogy of painting, the second the analogy of dramatic plotting." One ought to remember, he went on, that in Smollett's time the word *group,* when used in a context of aesthetics, "was still largely a painter's term. In practice Smollett paid more attention to the 'groups' and the 'various attitudes' of his 'diffused picture' than to the rigorous organizing of his story around a 'principal personage' and the unwindings of a plot."[8] It is thus clear, McKillop concluded, that Smollett conceived of the forms of effective narrative composition quite broadly, according to the principles of dramatic painting. It is surprising that until quite recently no one has actively pursued the lead McKillop threw out in his early revisionist analysis of Smollett's remarks, though it has at last begun to have at least some effect on critical assessments of his works, including *Ferdinand Count Fathom.*[9] It should be obvious by now that it has provided the foundation of my approach in this book.

Interestingly, Smollett delayed his one major theoretical statement about fiction until the occasion of his third novel. Perhaps he was explaining what he had already done in *Roderick Random* and *Peregrine Pickle* as much as he was accounting for what the reader was about to find in his new narrative. In any case the statement was for him—and it is for his readers and critics—a useful retrospective view. In *Ferdinand Count Fathom* the narrative principles he outlined certainly manifest themselves in the extreme, allowing for the patterned display of opposing characters arranged into various groups representing consummate villainy and heroic virtue, and likewise permitting the strategic opposition of incidents and their settings. Episodes directly or indirectly dramatizing the ideal values of natural love, for example, are set against contrary ones showing the sordid, cruel villainies of Fathom the seducer and fortune-hunter. Oftentimes Smollett develops these same tensions within a single episode, occasionally by the ingenious device of placing the language of sentimental love in the mouth of his thoroughly reprobate protagonist. Other patterns set dark and mysterious scenes of Gothic melodrama in the forest or the graveyard against exposition of the sometimes absurdly "rational" surfaces of life in sophisticated town society. Even the twin plots of Fathom and Renaldo/Monimia, which come together in significant ways as the villain preys horribly upon the gullible innocence of the others, actually diverge radically so as to be in a critical sense separate and opposed. The latter plot finally supersedes the former in the second volume, and Fathom himself is simply displaced for about one hundred pages before the reader is allowed at last to see him completely forlorn and repentant as the novel arrives at its conclusion.[10]

By such means Smollett imposes a broad thematic structure upon his narrative and achieves the disposition of his characters into their "various attitudes." His intention to give a center to his composition in the manner of the painter, who deliberately draws the viewer's eye to the dominant features of his canvas, is apparent from his comment in the dedication upon the moral function of his story as it is made bold in the principal characters of Fathom and Renaldo. He purposefully "raised up a virtuous character," he says, "in opposition to the adventurer, with a view to amuse the fancy, engage the affection, and form a striking contrast which might heighten the expression, and give a *Relief* to the moral of the whole" (p. 5). With this claim Smollett makes it clear that the analogy of painting was a most congenial one for him, and this is—of course—the reason why his novels are best read with close attention to their pictorial qualities. I have already argued in earlier pages the importance of understanding his adoption of a Hogarthian narrative strategy, with its emphasis on a peculiar combination of the static and the dynamic by which spatial form disrupts expectations of linearity while simultaneously developing a continuous serial narrative whose meaning is clear only at the end, when it is at last possible to assimilate the cumulative effects of individual dramatic episodes—or pictures—and their abundant assortment of character portraits and tableaux. I shall not repeat the argument here. *Ferdinand Count Fathom* is pictorial in all the same ways we observed in *Roderick Random* and *Peregrine Pickle*. If it is less intensely visual in certain respects than those novels generally are, it is because Smollett allowed his third-person narrator to maintain still greater detachment than he permitted in *Peregrine Pickle,* thus promoting his work's thematic concern with evil and good as both abstract and actual forces. Fathom, with all his elusive talent for disguises, is less fully seen than either of his predecessors, even the autobiographical Roderick who is unable to observe himself, while Renaldo and Monimia are Smollett's typical renderings of idealized moral heroism. But the focus in *Ferdinand Count Fathom* is sharp, and the range of vision so well defined as to promote the compression of effect *Peregrine Pickle* lacks. Fathom is a traveler whose story, like Roderick's and Perry's, takes him over a considerable geographical expanse; but attention is always directed to his victims, to his consorts in crime, and to the details of his exploits—to externals, in other words, which are typically presented with a flourishing of the verbal painter's brush.

The narrative texture of *Ferdinand Count Fathom* features numerous elaborate anachronisms, many more than we find in any of Smollett's other novels and thus of much greater consequence to our understanding of his strategy with the factual materials he appropriated as a means of providing contextual relevance for the story he wished to tell. Because of their number and frequency, Smollett's anachronisms in this novel constitute his most extensive experiment with relations between fiction and the real world it purports to represent. Interestingly, they may be partially explained by the analogy of painting he develops in the dedication, and conversely they help to clarify the importance of that analogy to his compositional methods. It therefore seems appropriate to pause here for discussion of them before going on to consider the actual effects—structural and interpretive—they help to create. Indeed, we may learn a good deal about Smollett the novelist from a close look at his anachronic habits in *Ferdinand Count Fathom*.

Because the novel is so little read, it may be helpful first to outline and then comment generally upon a few of the details of its plotting. Fathom, the bastard son of a whoring, gin-swilling English camp follower during the War of the Spanish Succession (1702–13), is born in 1711 aboard a wagon as it rumbles across the border between Holland and Flanders. He is from the outset a nobody and a native of no country in particular. Not long after this inauspicious beginning his enterprising mother marries for the sixth time, and the child takes the name of his new stepfather, a German soldier. When the elder Fathom dies in action during the campaign of the Austrians against the Turks (1716–18), both mother and son are taken under the protection of a Hungarian colonel, Count Melvil, whose life Mrs. Fathom had saved in hope of some reward. Melvil continues his care of the boy after his mother is killed in an act of plunder. Fathom receives his education in the home of the count, where he becomes companion to the virtuous and gullible young Renaldo Melvil. Later, when they are old enough, the lads travel together to Vienna for two years to finish their education, from whence they are summoned to join the command of Count Melvil at the outset of the War of the Polish Succession (1733–35).

From this point the action fairly tumbles forward in a succession of energetic episodes. The two youths part ways when the cowardly Fathom deserts the army and begins a course of adventures for which the secret debaucheries and deceptions of his earlier years, carried out in the Melvil household, had prepared him admirably. His adventures take him to Paris and finally to several cities in England where he assumes the false title of count, dazzles all company by his brilliance, exercises his sexual powers upon virginal maidens and frustrated middle-aged ladies, shifts as necessary to practice the charlatan's arts of medicine and music, and finally is exposed and imprisoned. While he is locked up Fathom hardly languishes, for his attention is kept by a gallery of remarkable eccentrics, his fellow prisoners. At length he is released following the sudden reappearance of Renaldo, who then introduces his old friend to his beloved Monimia; and Fathom, driven by lust for this unexampled girl, very nearly destroys the two lovers in a successful attempt to part them so as to be free to feed his own appetite. Renaldo sets off to Vienna to reclaim his dead father's estate; and Monimia, it is thought, dies for loss of him and for fear of Fathom. Despite his resulting disappointment, Smollett's resilient villain now thrives again for a while, then stumbles once more, and is thrown into prison a second time. There he stays until the return of Renaldo, who finds Monimia alive and marries her. By a lucky accident, the two of them discover their former tormentor in a deplorable state of misery, poverty, and painful repentance, and they relieve him kindly.

In the course of all these frenzied movements and surprising reversals and discoveries, Fathom's countless crimes—swindles, robberies, murder, and seductions—mark him as the complete villain, hideously deformed in his moral character. An array of other wicked characters, many of whom appear only fleetingly, confirms our understanding of Fathom as he meets them one after another and either gulls them or is gulled by them. This darker dimension of the fictional world is strategically set off by the presence of Renaldo, Monimia, and the several other amazingly good characters. The progress of the plot is erratic; indeed, it is hardly a progress at all in any usual sense of the term. The two main story lines twice diverge significantly, but somewhat awkwardly, before coming together in the end. Fathom's travels take him to numerous places, many of them more than once—Vienna, Paris, London, Bath, Bristol Springs, Tunbridge Wells; but there is little development of the visual details of these places and no real logic to justify the passage from place to place except that of incessant motion, by which Fathom's villainy spreads it-self with such variety and effect.

Ronald Paulson has usefully suggested that the gradual increase in the seri-ousness of Fathom's seductions or attempted seductions of innocent young girls constitutes at least part of one important progression in the novel's ar-ticulation of an overall moral point of view.[11] But, after all, it is Smollett's jux-tapositions—of opposing story lines, of characters, of scenes and episodes, of varied attitudes toward life, love, and virtue—and his manipulations of the "facts" of his imaginary world that determine the texture of his work, define its shape, and establish its meaning as "picture." The order Smollett imposes, such as it is, reflects the principles of his Hogarthian assumptions about the nature of narrative. There is no illusion that the novel simply mirrors life as it is—except insofar as life is a very scattered affair, short on causal relations and, in its vexing uncertainty, altogether lacking in the ordinary logic that imagines it as meaningfully sequential and linear. It is instead, like a Hogarth series, an act of interpretation. And we may say further that *Ferdinand Count Fathom* is both an emblem of the diffuseness Smollett speaks of in his dedica-tion and an exercise in the kind of narrative economy, typical of spatial form, by which everything seems to happen almost simultaneously, as in a painting.

The peculiarities of Smollett's anachronistic uses of some of the facts of re-cent and contemporary history in *Ferdinand Count Fathom* make it clear that his imagination worked with unusual creativity and purpose upon the materials of his knowledge and observation, transforming them into the products of invention by recreating them, and then integrating them into the overall fictional fabric. The novel begins by establishing the impression that it will synchronize its hero-villain's adventures with the important episodes of his-tory as it unfolded in the early years of the eighteenth century. Fathom is born in 1711, "the last year of the renowned Marlborough's command" (p. 9), not long before the Treaty of Utrecht (1713) brought an end to the long War of the Spanish Succession; he is "in the sixth year of his age" (p. 14) when his mother follows the Austrian army into its bloody campaign against the Turks. When he is about twenty-two years old, Fathom finds himself on a battlefield again, this time following Renaldo Melvil into service as a soldier during the War of the Polish Succession; shortly he deserts the Austrian army only to stumble into a garrison of the French enemy where he is pressed into military service once more (chapters 18–19).

Clearly, part of Smollett's intent in these early episodes is to expose Fathom, and reveal his cowardice and villainy, by implied comparison of his character to that of the great general who led the Austrians in all of these campaigns, Prince Eugene of Savoy. Eugene and his old ally Marlborough were everywhere celebrated as the greatest military geniuses of their day, and both were objects of almost reverential admiration among the English people over a period of many years.[12] Through the first eighteen or so chapters of his novel Smollett alludes regularly to great battles in which Eugene achieved extraordinary victories against overwhelming odds. Fathom's character receives part of its definition from this pattern of allusions, as any alert reader of Smollett's day would have instantly understood, and one has the sense that this imaginary villain's life is to be enacted against a rigorously authentic background of actual events in the world.

Indeed, this is almost what happens for the remainder of the novel. But in chapter 29 Smollett, who is possibly improvising to some extent, drops the illusion of chronological precision and begins to disrupt any expectation of lockstep connections between the real world and the fictional one. While traveling incognito from Canterbury to London, following his arrival for the first time upon English soil, Fathom suffers the mortification of being mistaken for the Young Pretender, Prince Charles Edward Stuart, lately vanished in the aftermath of the unsuccessful Jacobite Rebellion of 1745–46. By the most generous calculation of the passage of time in the narrative to this point, the date cannot be later than 1735 or 1736, or some ten years before the 'Forty-Five. Fathom is now about twenty-four or twenty-five years old, but the Stuart prince (born in 1720) is at most fifteen or sixteen. Smollett could not have been unconscious of this wrenching of time as he wrote, but he did not trouble himself about it because the anachronistic juxtaposing of the historical and fictional characters served a rhetorical and thematic purpose. After all, when *Ferdinand Count Fathom* was published in 1753, the Jacobite Rebellion, though some years in the past, was still a subject capable of provoking strong feelings.

The fellow-traveler who accuses Fathom is himself a knave, and a fool as well, but there is a certain ironic justice in the implied comparison between the prince and Smollett's bogus count. Each is an arch-criminal, each doomed to failure in the undertakings dearest to his heart; the historical fact of the unsuccessful Jacobite Rebellion anticipates Fathom's own eventual undoing and collapse. The young Stuart wanted to overrun England and reclaim its throne for his family, while Fathom, upon landing at Deal after long dreams of successful plundering in this rich and verdant isle, imagined himself a second conquering Caesar (chapter 27). But Charles Edward, despite state offenses which prompted the government to offer a reward of thirty thousand pounds for his capture, appealed to the popular imagination as a figure of some real gallantry and glamor; whereas Fathom, who pursues his fantasies of power and glory in a different sphere, is only a dangerously charming, talented adventurer in sordidness whose threat to the happiness and safety of individual people is much greater than that posed by the prince himself.

Such an episode as this one brings the fictional world into a most striking connection with the real. At the very least it certifies the novelist's understanding of the act of creation as an exertion of the imagination upon the materials of actual life, but not bound by any rigid principles of literalness. There are numerous other anachronisms of a similar kind in the novel, however, and these need to be identified in some detail before any attempt is made to assess the final importance of what such habits may reveal about Smollett's approach to narrative composition. In chapters 39–42, when Fathom finds himself in prison for the first time, he meets an array of historical characters whose interest to the public dates from the late 1740s and early 1750s, though the fictional time must be 1738–39, when Smollett's adventurer is twenty-seven or twenty-eight years old. The first of these characters is Theodore de Neuhoff, "king of C—rs—ca" (p. 184), who at the time of the publication of *Ferdinand Count Fathom* had been languishing in the King's Bench Prison for debtors since 1749.[13] The deposed Corsican monarch had traveled about Europe for a decade attempting to raise money enough to restore his power and preserve the liberty of his island people; he fell into debt while in England and suffered the humiliation of imprisonment when the Pelham government steadfastly refused him any assistance. Theodore became something of a popular cause, and several writers besides Smollett (one of them was Horace Walpole[14]) pled his case before the public, but such efforts were useless.

In Smollett's novelistic representation this king nobly sustains himself as a regal personage, though he is brought low in the world. The picture given of him is touchingly comic: "instead of a crown, his majesty wore a woolen night-cap," but despite the many horrid cruelties of his circumstances and environment, "there was an air of dignity in his deportment, and a nice physiognomist would have perceived something majestic in the features of his countenance" (p. 187). Smollett's introduction of Theodore occasions repetition of long-familiar charges against Whig leaders of ruthless pragmatism in their policies toward former allies and heartless indifference in their characteristic attitudes to human suffering among the disadvantaged or broken-hearted. But the sympathetic portrait of Theodore also reflects seriously upon Fathom as an unscrupulous schemer for wealth, power, and false dignity who preys upon the weak so as to gratify his rapacious appetites. Whereas Theodore represents true majesty and natural nobility of character and spirit, Fathom is a despicable false count, a fraud in every respect of manner, appearance, and expression.

In the same concentrated prison episode, Smollett indulges in other portraits or allusions that depend for their full effect upon his first readers' awareness of events and controversies from the ten or so years immediately preceding the publication of the novel. One portrait displays the buffoonish Sir Mungo Barebones, a figure interesting in his own right as a comic creation, and certainly one of the novel's memorable caricatures. Smollett's description of him is worth quoting at some length:

> being naturally of a meagre habit, he was by indigence and hard study wore almost to the bone, and so bended towards the earth, that in walking, his body described at least 150 degrees of a circle. The want of stockings and shoes he supplied with a jockey straight boot and an half jack. His thighs and middles were cased in a monstrous pair of brown trunk breeches, . . . his shirt retained no signs of its original colour, his body was shrouded in an old greasy tattered plaid night-gown; a blue and white handkerchief surrounded his head, and his looks betokened that immense load of care, which he had voluntarily incurred for the eternal salvation of sinners. (p. 189)

Sir Mungo actually serves Smollett as the vehicle for an attack on the followers of the Yorkshire-born mathematician John Hutchinson (1674–1737), who had argued in a variety of curious tracts and discourses that the Hebrew word *Elohim* was the repository of all God's promises for the redemption of mankind, the Pentateuch the source of all other truth and knowledge, and Newton's physics therefore an exercise in ignorance and a sacrilege.[15] The disciples of this self-proclaimed theologian, whom Smollett exposes in his novel as sadly deranged and silly, had published his collected works in 1748–49, causing a storm of controversy. The fictional Sir Mungo, like the real-life Hutchinson, is an absurdity, a foolish projector in what he considers the good cause of truth, and his obsession has destroyed him. He had once "appeared in the great world" and borne "divers offices of dignity and trust, with universal applause"; but his "evil genius" had "fairly disordered his brain" and left him "incapable of managing his temporal affairs" (p. 189). Smollett deliberately introduced this ridiculous character for his topical value, and to expose a crazed but pernicious group of quixotic doctrinarians. But Sir Mungo also contributes indirectly to our understanding of Fathom as the archetype of villainy. The two schemers share in an essentially destructive impulse to pursue recognition and power by carrying out an irreverent attack upon truth: the one quixotically and comically, by perverting scripture and denying established scientific principles; the other diabolically, by seeking to undermine the moral truth inherent in the orthodox Christian commitment to the ideals of virtue in human affairs.

One other portrait from the prison chapters deserves brief mention. Fathom encounters, in chapter 40, the strange figure of a French chevalier, an absurd personage also sadly imprisoned for debts, and quite harmlessly deranged. His apparel is multicolored, with no particular pattern to it except some vague hints of his military past; his beard hangs to his waist, his jet-black hair to his rump. A quixotic projector like Sir Mungo, though of a different stamp, this ridiculous fellow had been imprisoned in France for his crazy political plotting, and after his release had traveled to England where he met renewed opposition to similar mad schemes. He then turned to poetry and failed, sinking into debtors' prison to join the rest of the "assemblage of rarities" (p. 190) there met by Fathom. It poses no great difficulty to identify this Frenchman as a good-humored caricature of Michel Descazeaux du Halley (1710–55), whose portrait by the Swedish painter Charles Banks inspired a satirical print by James MacArdell representing him as just the kind of figure pictured in Smollett's pages.[16] Descazeaux actually wrote doggerel poetry while imprisoned in the Fleet from 1746 onward, and he was a considerable object of mirth. Smollett exploits the public's minor fascination with this original, alert to the topical value of his portrait and to its usefulness, in an entirely comic way, as a means of exposing the destructive follies of the schemer and projector.

There are other quite striking anachronisms in the novel, but of a different kind. Throughout them all Fathom and Renaldo grow only a year or two older, bringing the fictional time to about 1741 and their own ages to about thirty. In chapter 39, Fathom's fellow prisoner Captain Minikin offers his personal library for the amusement of his new acquaintance. Most of the books are modern novels published in 1750 and after, and without exception these are all tales of roguish adventuring, or love, intrigue, and seduction of maidenish innocence—the precise ingredients of Smollett's own narrative.[17] In this same chapter Smollett refers for the first time to the long War of the Austrian Succession (1740–48), inaugurating a minor pattern of repeated allusions to this European conflagration, in its various stages from beginning to end, lasting for the rest of the novel. The war, though Smollett dwells upon no details of its enormous costs in human suffering and financial sacrifice, nonetheless provides part of the context within which readers are expected to understand the actions of the characters. The allusions work by the art of suggestion. Here Smollett hints at one or more of the political leaders whose ambitions brought on the long conflict; there he drops a suggestion about the valor of the fighting men. Without making too much of this tissue of allusions we may suppose that Smollett hoped his audience would see some connection between what had recently gone forward on the battlefields, where some won glory and others sank under deserved infamy, and the power struggle of good and evil that his novel dramatizes.

In one of his most interesting maneuvers Smollett develops a rather elaborate portrait of a benevolent Jew, Joshua Manasseh. The sketching begins in chapter 47, following Fathom's apparently successful attempts to destroy the love shared by Renaldo and Monimia and to separate the two so that he can have the beautiful virgin for himself. In addition to his other miseries, Renaldo, as Fathom knows, has spent his little store of money rescuing his old friend from prison, so that he cannot even return to his home and reclaim his

inheritance and estate from a rapacious stepfather. No one will assist him, neither former friends nor the several disreputable usurers he approaches. This
latter frustration baffles even Fathom. When at last Melvil goes desperately to
Joshua with his melancholy story and a request for a loan, the old Jew weeps
from the goodness of his heart and immediately provides what is needed.
From that point on he becomes one of Smollett's principal exemplars of unaffected virtue, and he proves crucially instrumental to the welfare and final
happiness of Renaldo and Monimia. Joshua is not a portrait drawn after the
example of any actual person, but his presence unmistakably registers the
great public controversy generated by a proposal in Parliament for passage of
a Jewish Naturalization Act; the Act finally was approved in May 1753, less
than three months after the publication of *Ferdinand Count Fathom*.[18] With the
portrait of Joshua, Smollett avoided anachronism, but introduced an imaginative footnote to actual contemporary history; his representation of a benevolent Jew was doubtless a genuine humanitarian gesture on his part, while it
also added in an obvious way to the topical interest of his novel. To the modern reader the principal value of the portrait resides in the rhetorical effect
created by the implied comparison between Fathom, Renaldo's supposed
friend, and Joshua himself, the inheritor of the so-called curse of Anti-Christ
whom the young Melvil initially stereotypes as a member of a race lying under
"the general reproach of nations, as a people dead to virtue and benevolence,
and wholly devoted to avarice, fraud, and extortion" (p. 224). Ironically, of
course, Renaldo's description actually fits the tribe of villains to whom
Fathom belongs, and not the "descendants of Judah."

A few additional minor anachronisms occur in *Ferdinand Count Fathom*,
some hinting of haste and carelessness, the "little incongruities" Ralph Griffiths speaks of in his review. The modern reader may actually overlook most
of these, since the facts of mid-eighteenth-century English and European history have been largely obscured by time, except to the eyes of a relatively few
specialists. In any event it is not because of any supposed wanderings of authorial attention that Smollett's third novel has been judged his weakest, or his
most awkwardly constructed. The evidence of historical inconsistencies, once
recognized and gathered, might be expected to lend support to the case
against the book. But in fact quite the reverse is true. It hardly matters at
all whether the violations of chronology in Smollett's historical allusions in

Ferdinand Count Fathom were deliberate, though they are so blatant that they could scarcely have been accidental.

During the journeyman years that followed publication of the novel, its author proved himself a capable historian, respectful toward the march of events through time and sensitive to the importance of causality in the progress of human affairs. He obviously did not regard history as something static, its episodes interchangeable or susceptible to rearrangement without damage to the meaning and truth of the whole. As chapter 1 of *Ferdinand Count Fathom* makes plain, Smollett thought the historian's calling a high one indeed, bound in practice by the principles of truth itself to avoid partiality or distortion of any kind. Some years later, in a letter to his friend William Huggins, he remarked even more emphatically upon this same seriousness of purpose: "I look upon the Historian who espouses a Faction, who strains Incidents or willfully suppresses any Circumstances of Importance that may tend to the Information of the Reader, as the worst of Prostitutes."[19] But a novel is a work of the imagination, a rendering of some artistic vision of the elusive meaning of the events that history books only record. A novel may be a "true history," as eighteenth-century storytellers were fond of saying, but it is a kind of poetic history, presumably truer than whatever real facts an author may choose to incorporate into the fabric of his or her invention. The novelist, in other words, is at liberty to reorder what is gleaned by observation, and to recreate it in making a fictional world. This is surely obvious, and it is as applicable to Fielding or Richardson or Sterne or Walter Scott as to Smollett. To the author of *Ferdinand Count Fathom,* the imaginary facts (episodes) of a novel, like the true facts of historical narrative, begin to take on their fullest meaning only when they are felt individually—directly and with intensity, through sensitive knowledge or through natural responses to their significance and their power to affect. Ultimately, of course, for understanding of such meaning to be complete, the same facts must also be seen collectively, through a process of accumulation, within the context of some larger configuration intelligibly revealing the essential truths about human nature and human behavior in society. But the novelist may invent the configuration, whereas the historian must abide by other, more rigid principles of form and truthfulness.

The analogy of painting Smollett develops in the dedication to *Ferdinand*

Count Fathom comes naturally to a writer who thinks as he did about the historical and imaginary materials of his art. There is no particular intrinsic value to unraveling his ingenious twistings of historical facts or topical allusions as he weaves them into the textures of his novelistic compositions. But his manner of doing so suggests something extremely important about his understanding of the relationship between the real world and his fictional recreations of it. For Smollett the artist it is the crucial individual moments of history that are most to be valued, for they reveal human character in relief against the inevitably blurred background of busy and relentless sequence. And thus, in appropriating historical fact for his fictional uses, Smollett often casually disregards the laws of time and process, adapting what he borrows only as it best contributes to the composition of his overall picture.

The composition is often highly theatrical, in *Ferdinand Count Fathom* as in Smollett's other novels; it is no accident that, as he writes about the principles of narrative, he develops twin analogies of painting *and* of drama. In *Ferdinand Count Fathom* the drama is an especially important part of the whole eclectic mix, as the rogue protagonist's travels are punctuated by carefully staged scenes or series of scenes adding up to self-contained dramatic constructions. Like Richardson's Lovelace, Fathom is something of a playwright, and many of the theatrical contrivances are his own—the episode of his collusion with the Melvils' servant Teresa to seduce Renaldo's sister, for example (chapters 8–10); the elaborate deceptions practiced upon the jeweler's wife, and his daughter Wilhelmina (chapters 12–17); the attempted seduction of Celinda by use of the "magic" of the Aeolian harp (chapter 34); and so on. Fathom is a consummate actor, which is why he proves able to mask himself so effectively, hiding his real nature from Count Melvil, Renaldo, Monimia, and indeed almost everyone else, whether in military camps, at gaming houses, or among the fashionable men and women met in assembly rooms. In speaking the language of love and passion he relies heavily upon the diction and mannerisms made familiar by heroic tragedy and sentimental comedy; he is extraordinarily adept at costume and equally adept at affecting the air and address of all kinds of people, from the soldier, to the nobleman, to the musician, to the professional man of medicine. For Fathom the devices of stage drama provide the means for fulfillment of what the narrator early refers to as his "most insidious principle of self-love" (p. 22). Chameleon-like, he is able to become whatever is required for the success of any scheme. He thus perverts the ideals of the drama as a literary form, as a form of art whose purpose—like that of all art, as Smollett believed—is to tell the truth.

Because he writes from a position of genuine detachment in *Ferdinand Count Fathom,* Smollett is able to use his third-person narrator with great efficiency to expose his hero-villain's theatrical contrivances for what they are—by simply describing them as they evolve, allowing his readers to see what Fathom's assorted victims cannot. Important additional contrivances help to provide a framework within which Fathom's perverse theatricalism may be understood. Allusion is one of these contrivances. The name Monimia is drawn from Thomas Otway's verse tragedy *The Orphan* (1680), a play Smollett greatly admired and no doubt saw on the stage, as it was regularly performed in London theaters throughout the first half of the eighteenth century; the Renaldo/Monimia subplot echoes the story of Otway's heroine, especially the crisis she undergoes when she is caught between the two brothers Castalio and Polydore as—disastrously—they compete for her love. The graveyard scenes of Gothic melodrama in chapters 62 and 63, when Renaldo visits the tomb of the supposedly dead Monimia, are adapted from another popular play, Congreve's *Mourning Bride* (1697).[20] And Fathom is with some regularity placed specifically into a context of dramatic allusion that directly illuminates his character; sometimes he closely resembles a usurping villain in one of Shakespeare's historical plays, and in chapter 45 his manipulations of Renaldo echo Iago's dealings with Othello.[21]

The juxtapositions of context and action always expose Fathom as a false dramatist, while they likewise promote a true vision—specifically a moral vision—both of the world and of art. The drama is thus for Smollett more than just a parallel narrative form to be exploited for tricks of staging, characterization, and language. But it is that too, for he frequently sets up scenes as though they were written for a play. The arrival of Sir Stentor Stile in chapter 24, and his encounter with his old neighbor, Sir Giles Squirrel, is presented like a moment in a Restoration comedy, while these two characters—who later turn out to be even more skillful swindlers than Fathom—are memorable caricatures based upon the conventional stage figures of the dandy and the bumpkin. The prison episode opens (in chapter 39) with the "hoarse and dreadful" offstage voice of the keeper bellowing out orders for the inmates' evening meal: "You, Bess Beetle, score a couple of fresh eggs, a pennyworth of butter, and half a pint of mountain" (p. 182)—the harangue goes on until most of the gallery of eccentrics Fathom is about to meet have been named. Here Smollett borrows a playwright's stratagem to set up what is surely his novel's most successful exercise in pictorialism, as the episode is a tour de force in both verbal caricature and in the representation of a comic tableau. The king, the captain and an Irish major, the foolish projector, the crazed political schemer, and now the criminal Fathom make up a world in miniature— as the friendly Captain Minikin tells Fathom, "this place, Sir, is quite a *microcosm*" (p. 184). Significantly, it is a fallen world, its dreams of power and glory all in a state of collapse, dreamy yet absurd.

I have already hinted at numerous details of Smollett's descriptions of the prison episode's "assemblage of rarities," but his portrait of Minikin is so delightfully exuberant that the temptation to quote it at some length is irresistible; the description is, besides, typical of his way of proceeding with his presentation of all of the prison inmates. The captain, says the narrator,

> was a person equally remarkable for his extraordinary figure and address; his age seemed to border upon forty, his stature amounted to five feet, his visage was long, meagre and weather-beaten, and his aspect, though not quite rueful, exhibited a certain formality, which was the result of care and conscious importance. He was very little encumbered with flesh and blood; yet, what body he had, was well proportioned, his limbs were elegantly turned, and by his carriage he was well intitled to that compliment which we pay to any person, when we say he has very much the air of a gentleman. There was also an evident singularity in his dress, which tho' intended as an improvement, appeared to be an extravagant exaggeration of the mode, and at once evinced him an original to the discerning eyes of our adventurer. . . . The captain's peculiarities were not confined to his external appearance; for his voice resembled the sound of a bassoon, or the aggregate hum of a whole bee-hive, and his discourse was almost nothing else than a series of quotations from the English poets, interlarded with French phrases, which he retained for their significance, on the recommendation of his friends, being himself unacquainted with that or any other outlandish tongue. (p. 183)

There is an equally fine moment just a few pages later when Fathom, at Minikin's suggestion, peeks through the keyhole of the Corsican monarch's apartment door, through which he has already heard the sound of "an human voice imitating the noise of a drum." Told that the king and his advisor Major Macleaver (whom he has promoted to general) "were employed in landing troops upon the Genoese territory," he then looks at the scene within and sees "the sovereign and his minister," their motions accompanied "by beat of drum," maneuvering mussel and oyster shells into battle against a line of marching gray peas, which they soon "put in confusion" as they "took possession of their ground" (p. 187). One cannot help wondering whether Sterne had read this scene when he imagined Uncle Toby and Corporal Trim constructing their fortifications.

This entire episode exhibits Smollett the comic genius at his best with pictorial representation, and particularly with character portraiture. There are other finely drawn caricatures in the novel—Sir Stentor and Sir Giles, for example. The former, especially memorable, is all decked out "in the exact uniform of an English jockey" when he first appears to Fathom's view in the earlier Paris episode; his "leathern cap, cut bob, fustian frock, flannel waistcoat, buff breeches, hunting-boots and whip" perfectly adorn his crude person, while he announces his arrival with a "smack of his whip, as equalled the explosion of an ordinary cohorn," and a bellowing of his foxhunter's voice— "By your leave, Gentlevolks, I hope there's no offence, in an honest plain Englishman's coming with money in his pocket, to taste a bit of your Vrench frigasee and ragooze" (p. 100). Like Pallet and the physician in *Peregrine Pickle,* Sir Stentor and Sir Giles serve to mock the boorishness of British travelers, but they are also crooks, and they are thus evidence that England is not precisely the paradisal "land of promise, flowing with milk and honey" (p. 77) that Fathom has imagined himself plundering with unimpeded success.

There are relatively few grotesques in the novel, by comparison with *Peregrine Pickle* and especially *Roderick Random,* though the old madam in the Paris bagnio scene of chapter 23 is a strikingly effective one. This

> venerable priestess, a personage turned of seventy, . . . seemed to exercise the
> functions of her calling, in despight of the most cruel ravages of time: for age
> had bent her into the form of a Turkish bow: her head was agitated by the palsy,
> like the leaf of the poplar-tree, her hair fell down in scanty parcels, as white as
> the driven snow: her face was not simply wrinkled, but ploughed into innumer-
> able furrows: her jaw could not boast of one remaining tooth; one eye distilled a
> large quantity of rheum, by virtue of the fiery edge that surrounded it, the other

was altogether extinguished, and she had lost her nose in the course of her min-
istration. (p. 93)

The hero-villain himself, despite the disguise of his pretty appearances, is the
principal grotesque in *Ferdinand Count Fathom*. Clearly, Smollett wanted awareness of Fathom's true character, in all its hidden ugliness, to grow without distraction until finally, when he is entirely undone, he is seen fully—by Renaldo
and Monimia, and by the reader—in a condition that signifies the gruesome
moral consequences of his evil conduct. The details of the description of him
at this moment are very precise. We are told that he was "stretched almost
naked upon straw, insensible, convulsed, and seemingly in the grasp of death.
He was wore to the bone either by famine or distemper; his face was overshadowed with hair and filth; his eyes were sunk, glazed and distorted; his
nostrils dilated; his lips covered with a black slough, and his complexion faded
into a pale clay-colour, tending to a yellow hue: in a word, the extremity of
indigence, squalor and distress, could not be more feelingly represented"
(p. 347). This is a powerful evocation of horror and degradation, in intensity
equal to the description of the "fifty miserable distempered wretches"
Roderick Random discovers below deck in the *Thunder* and matched in
Ferdinand Count Fathom only by the Gothic effects of terror Smollett achieves
in his graphic account of Fathom's reactions to his discovery of the corpse in
chapter 21.

By making most of the aberrant characters in *Ferdinand Count Fathom* caricatures instead of grotesques—that is, figures of comedy rather than fierce
satire—Smollett manages a kind of counterpoint that locates even the novel's
villains closer to the ideals represented by Renaldo and Monimia than to
Fathom and the example of his deeper and totally obsessive wickedness.
There are plenty of villains—sharpers, thieves, murderers; and there are numerous targets of strong satire—pettifogging lawyers, medical quacks, avaricious merchants, corrupt noblemen, the English social disease of gambling.
But Fathom himself is the ultimate villain, the ultimate object of his author's
scorn; despite his attractiveness, perhaps (like Milton's Satan) even more because of it, he is insidiously dangerous and must be reviled, exposed, destroyed, and—the strongest blow against his character—in the end utterly
transformed by Melvil's forgiveness. Smollett's strategy is, so to speak, to

keep Fathom morally separate from all the other characters in the novel so there can be no mistaking the meaning of who and what he is. He is no mere picaro or charming rogue.

I do not mean to suggest that *Ferdinand Count Fathom* is a lightsome book except for the presence of its hero-villain. It certainly is not that. On balance, it is the very darkest of all of Smollett's novels. But still there are enough fine comic moments and equally fine comic portraits to make it seem strange that neither Rowlandson nor Cruikshank, Smollett's greatest illustrators, ever drew scenes or characters from the work. Possibly they did not find its eccentrics and other human oddities so appealing as those of the other novels. It is just as likely that *Ferdinand Count Fathom*'s comparative lack of popularity discouraged publishers from commissioning illustrations. Those that were prepared—by Thomas Stothard and his disciple Luke Clennell—are altogether without distinction, very disappointing for their failure to catch anything of the energy to be found in the scenes selected.[22]

It is too bad that Hogarth did not illustrate the work, as his hand would have been the surest of all—better even than that of Rowlandson, who was most effective as an illustrator with scenes of high comedy. It could almost be said that Smollett was at his most Hogarthian in *Ferdinand Count Fathom*. Quite apart from the serial structure and spatial form of the novel, the contrapuntal and alternating plots repeat Hogarth's strategy in *Industry and Idleness* (1747), and with many of the same dramatic and thematic effects. Robert Etheridge Moore has observed, rightly I think, that as a narrative *Ferdinand Count Fathom* is more closely modeled on *The Rake's Progress* than any of Smollett's other novels,[23] and he has further suggested several specific parallels between its story and additional works by Hogarth. The scene in chapter 36, Moore says (p. 165), when Fathom is found in bed with Mrs. Trapwell at a Covent Garden bagnio, directly echoes the great bagnio scene (5) of *Marriage à la Mode,* which shows the aftermath of a duel in which Lady Squander's lover, the rake Silvertongue, has killed her husband; the situation (assignation, discovery) is similar, and so the parallel is at least plausible, though there are few specific corresponding details. Moore has also noted (p. 171) that the image of Fathom's mother carrying him on her back in a knapsack and suckling him with gin (chapter 2) is borrowed directly from a detail (the parodic "Good Samaritan" grouping) of Hogarth's *March to Finchley* (1750). In this instance he is more than plausible. Certainly the print was recent enough to have been in Smollett's mind's eye as he began his novel, and it was very popular; his description of Fathom's mother would fit Hogarth's figure almost equally well.

There are other parallels of this kind, some direct and others indirect. The drinking scene in chapter 24, when Sir Stentor and Sir Giles are setting Fathom up to take him at play, ends with Sir Giles "sunk down upon the floor, in a state of temporary annihilation" (p. 104); the echo of *Midnight Modern Conversation*[24] is so clear as almost to constitute an explicit allusion. The same evening continues with a spectacle that seems to have been inspired in part by scene 6 of *The Rake's Progress,* which shows Tom Rakewell, all his money lost at the tables, cursing his fate as the gaming house goes up in flames. The scene is crowded, unlike Smollett's which is spare, but the use of shadowing obscures all figures but Tom, other despairing gamblers, and the several sharpers present, giving a concentrated poignancy to the whole. Smollett focuses exclusively on Fathom and Sir Stentor, thus highlighting the unscrupulousness of both; before dawn he adjourns them to the isolation of the former's lodgings, where the episode ends in a moment of stark drama: instead of raising his arm to curse his fate, a devastated Fathom shrinks from "a most intolerable sneer" directed at him by his triumphant antagonist (p. 106). Here it is not the specific details of Hogarth's vivid scene that Smollett repeats, but its intensity and admonitory power.

Fathom's career as adventurer leads him repeatedly into arresting scenes comparable to those just described. As he travels, it is the spaces he enters and the people he encounters within them that mark the stages of his movement; no principle governs his progress except that of movement itself, though his passage from the Continent to England occurs because he has long dreamed of visiting his native land, in his mind so ripe for the exercise of his talents. Fathom shows even less capacity for growth and change than Peregrine Pickle until the circumstances provoking his final reformation finally overwhelm him, and so he is unable to distinguish among the moments of his experience, which seem altogether equivalent; he simply shifts from one place or enterprise to another as necessity demands, always seeking fulfillment of his obsessive desire to conquer and possess. The spatial form of his story is thus generated by his very nature, or such is the illusion Smollett projects. Interestingly, however, Smollett subtly imposes a kind of symmetry upon

William Hogarth, *A Rake's Progress,* Scene 6 (1735).
(By courtesy of the Trustees of Sir John Soane's Museum.)

Fathom's story by a tactic unlike any he had ever used before. The first volume of the novel develops an upward dramatic movement, as the hero-villain's career follows an overall trajectory of ascendancy and success; but with the Trapwell episode at the outset of volume 2 a long, slow decline begins, ending with the total collapse not only of all his schemes but of his very character, even his body. Like Hogarth, who makes Tom Rakewell's desperate marriage (scene 5 of 8) the pivotal moment in his story, Smollett all but announces to his reader the comparable turn of direction in his narrative— Mrs. Trapwell's *"allurements,"* proclaims the heading to chapter 36, subject Fathom to *"a new vicissitude of fortune"* (p. 169). Superficially at least, *Ferdinand Count Fathom* is more elegantly shaped than either *Peregrine Pickle* or *Roderick Random.* Could Smollett have been nodding in the direction of Fielding and his fellow proponents of organic regularity in literary form?

In truth, this is an idle—if irresistible—question, for even if we could answer it with any certainty we would say little of importance about *Ferdinand
Count Fathom* and how it really functions as a narrative. Its gesture toward
shapeliness is of no particular significance, since it is the novel's character portraits and tableaux that give it its particular texture and, ultimately, both its essential structure and its meaning. Smollett's readers must *see* the turbulent, disturbed world of Fathom's experience in order to understand his place within
it—or, as the novel's ending actually urges, his place *out* of it. And see it we
do. I have already marked many of the character portraits as worthy of attention, and some of the tableau scenes; I should like to turn now to a few additional examples of the latter. Nothing else in the novel quite equals the prison
episode as a pictorial rendering of a social group, but there are numerous
other striking instances of this kind of verbal sketching. Smollett was fond of
stagecoach scenes, as we have seen in *Roderick Random* and *Peregrine Pickle,* and
in *Ferdinand Count Fathom* he gives us another. The coach that carries Fathom
from Canterbury to London (chapters 28–30) also carries an assortment of
character types, most of them eccentrics. A funny picture begins the scene,
one created more by simile than by overt description. Because the coach is already crowded when Fathom boards, he is obliged to "insinuate himself side-
long between a corpulent quaker and a fat Wapping-landlady, in which attitude he stuck fast, like a thin quarto between two voluminous dictionaries on
a book-seller's shelf" (p. 129). As the scene proceeds, the almost staccato
repartee between the two hefty passengers on either side of him turns hostile
and bawdy, further establishing their characters by emphasizing their personal
styles: when the "jolly dame" observes that the silent Fathom (whom she
takes for a Frenchman) will soon be "better acquainted with a buttock of English beef," the Quaker (who is the beef in question) responds, "Yes, verily, . . .
but the swine's fat will be all on one side" (p. 129)—and so on. The lady also
attacks a scrawny merchant, who surprisingly proves himself her match in
invective—and who, it turns out, is a smuggler and petty thief; it is he who,
hoping for a reward, later fingers Fathom as the Young Pretender (chapter 30). The other characters (besides Fathom, who is only an observer) sit
silently; one is a barber, the merchant's accomplice; the other is a virginal
young girl named Elenor, whom Fathom will shortly seduce and toss away.

The same assemblage of character types becomes part of the next scene, when Fathom is taken before a magistrate under the pall of the suspicion cast upon him by the merchant-smuggler. The trial that follows is a farce, like that of Roderick Random aboard the *Thunder,* as the magistrate is an ignorant fool—a bumpkin whose crude manner and inelegant language make him an anticipation of Justice Gobble in *Sir Launcelot Greaves.* When the scene shifts again to the coach, the smuggler is no longer of the party (he has been exposed and arrested); and while the Quaker and the Wapping landlady engage in close conversation about what they have just witnessed, Fathom launches a campaign to conquer the fair Elenor. Soon the focus has shifted altogether away from the high-spirited representation of a low-life tableau and toward Fathom as moral criminal. By the end of chapter 30 he has made his conquest. Smollett's language here is significant: "she submitted to his desire; not with the reluctance of a vanquished people, but with all the transports of a joyful city, that opens its gates to receive a darling prince" (p. 142). The episode is now much less visual than at its outset, allowing for the abstracted distance necessary to the effectiveness of the kind of summary judgment just quoted. The trial in the preceding chapter may have been a travesty, and Smollett's account of it a satire on the ineptitude of country justice; but in a moral sense the magistrate actually miscarried in acquitting Fathom, the conquering "darling prince" who, one chapter later, will cheerfully leave Elenor thoroughly debauched, addicted to drugs, and "bereft of her reason" (p. 146).

No account of the visual effects in *Ferdinand Count Fathom* could possibly be even remotely satisfactory without some attention to the Gothic episodes— the first in English fiction. Thomas R. Preston has made the point that these episodes—in the forest (chapters 20 and 21) and the graveyard (chapters 62 and 63)—directly fulfill Smollett's intention, stated in the dedication, to introduce "a deep impression of terror" into his narrative to enforce its moral purpose of confirming readers in the "pursuit of morality and virtue" by providing a deterrent "from the practice of vice" (p. 5).[25] I have already alluded to the gloom of the moment during the first of these episodes when Fathom finds the dead body, exchanges places with it, and thus saves his life. The earlier portion of that same episode, when, as night falls, he is caught in the midst of a violent storm, is still more gloomy and displays Smollett in a rare instance of almost symbolic representation. Fathom, deserted by his guide, feels a heavy oppression in the "silence and solitude" of the obscure place where he has lost himself, while the "indistinct images of the trees" that appear "on every side" of him "disturb his fancy, and raise strange phantoms in his imagination." Suddenly the storm bursts—lightning, deafening thunder, torrential rain—and leaves him "almost quite overcome," as the narrator observes that "so many concuring circumstances of danger and distress, might have appalled the most undaunted breast" (p. 83). Though hardly able to "set fear at defiance," Fathom resolves to "disentangle himself from the mazes of the wood"; he traverses the "unknown forest" through "a succession of groves, and bogs, and thorns and brakes" (pp. 83, 84) until at last he arrives at the lonely cottage where, when he ascends the ladder to his garret chamber, he endures a scene of criminality and death during which he is himself almost murdered.

The episode is so powerful and effective because it places the villain Fathom alone in a moral wilderness, his natural habitat, and exposes the horror that abides there. The parallel episode in chapters 62 and 63 plays an exact reversal upon those effects. Whereas Fathom wanders in the regions of obscurity and death, Renaldo enters the place where Monimia is supposedly buried only to find in its gloom that she actually lives. "The uncommon darkness of the night, the solemn silence, and lonely situation of the place" make the parallel apparent, and on his first night there Renaldo sinks despairingly to the ground, oppressed by "the noisy wind that whistles through these vaulted caves of death" (pp. 312, 314). On the second evening, however, in the equal gloom of the midnight hour, "something strange and supernatural" occurs: out of the darkness appears "the figure of a woman arrayed in white, with a veil that covered her face, and flowed down upon her back and shoulders" (p. 318). This "phantome," at first thought by Renaldo to be a ghost, is the living Monimia. The episode, begun in an atmosphere of death, ends in an affirmation of life. The contrivance by which Smollett engineers this reversal—the collusion between Madame Clement and Monimia's physician—may be just a bit too clever, and the staging of Renaldo's discovery overly melodramatic. But the rhetorical point of the episode and its earlier counterpart is clear and forceful: from villainy flows the horror of hideous death, and from virtue flows life, though the latter may have to pass the threat of destruction before its redemptive power can be fully expressed.

Renaldo and Monimia are abstracted figures who, as versions of the conventional idealized hero and heroine, are seen only in vague outlines; they are never fully bodied. In the graveyard episode the arisen Monimia is a "phantome," but earlier, when she is first introduced (in chapter 43), she is little more—"her stature was tall," we are told, "her motion graceful; . . . in short, every feature was elegantly perfect; and the harmony of the whole ravishing and delightful" (p. 200). Like Roderick Random's Narcissa, she is no more than an "amiable apparition." Renaldo is never really described at all, except early on (in chapter 10), and then only by comparison with Fathom: the two "were certainly, in all respects, the reverse of each other. Renaldo, under a total defect of exterior cultivation, possessed a most excellent understanding, with every virtue that dignifies the human heart; while the other, beneath a most agreeable outside, with an inaptitude and aversion to letters, concealed an amazing fund of villainy and ingratitude" (p. 42). Here Smollett makes it clear that he is content to allow Renaldo's moral beauty to suffice for the conjuring of his picture. Fathom he further characterizes by attributing to him some very Hobbesian reflections on human character and conduct, adding to the effect of contrast. This youthful villain, we learn, was already "fully persuaded, that the sons of nature preyed upon one another, and such was the end and condition of their being"; virtually all of the "principal figures of life" resemble "the savage tyrants of the wood," and as Fathom concludes that he is himself most like the "wily fox," he dedicates himself to "practising a thousand crafty ambuscades for the destruction of the ignorant and unwary" by the "continual exercise of that gift of deceiving, with which he knew himself endued to an unrivalled degree" (pp. 42–43).

Deceit, duplicity, disguise, imposture—these constitute Fathom's way of acting out his wicked impulses in the world. The point Smollett wishes to make with his hero-villain is obvious: evil is a fact of human existence; it needs nothing to motivate it into action (Fathom has no motive except pure desire), but just *is;* it is most dangerous when concealed behind the appearances of virtue. Only the novel's other crooks and con artists are generally able to see what Fathom is by penetrating his disguises; for most of the novel Renaldo and Monimia do not see him at all because his posturing blocks their vision. The reader understands him only because the narrator is explicit about the facts of his disguises, but, beyond the allusion to the Volponian fox, never permits any clear view of the flesh-and-blood person behind his many masks—until the end, when they have all been stripped away. Fathom is, then, as much an abstraction as Renaldo and Monimia, and Smollett's rhetorical strategy—dualistic, contrapuntal, almost Manichean in its implications— is the more powerful because this is so. As Aileen Douglas has observed, Fathom is an "oddly immaterial hero, . . . seemingly unconfined by his physicality."[26] For the first time as a novelist, Smollett has projected evil as in a condition of complete equivalency with transcendent moral idealism. This is why Fathom is such a disturbing character. Strong enough almost to devastate the world, and smart enough to cover his nature from view, he is subject to none of the reductive treatment accorded the grotesques in Smollett's fiction; and he is the more dangerous as a result of his invisibility, for what cannot be seen cannot be combated, or even averted. Fathom is the instrument of Smollett's most intensive exploration of the theme of duplicity that runs through all of his novels, which invariably castigate the world for its falseness, emphasizing the moral imperative of truth-telling. We have seen how this theme is played out in *Peregrine Pickle,* which even makes truthfulness in artistic expression a major issue. In *Ferdinand Count Fathom* Smollett concentrates the worst of the world's duplicity in his protagonist, whose credo is neatly summed up by his cohort Ratchkali in words specifically concerning England and its capital city but, by extension, applicable to all places. This land, says Ratchkali, is "the paradise of artists of our profession," while the "metropolis" of London "is a vast masquerade, in which a man of stratagem may wear a thousand different disguises, without danger of detection" (pp. 144, 145). London—city of deceiving appearances, image of the modern world—is another moral wilderness where, unlike the forest of the earlier Gothic episode, Fathom may feel completely at home. This is what Ratchkali knows, and his words are very important as an estimate both of Fathom and of the world of fraudulence and corruption to which he naturally belongs.

The spatial form of *Ferdinand Count Fathom* is perfectly suited to its display of predatory evil, which is always active and on the move—and is besides a force for disorder. As Fathom's erratic career takes him through and past scene after scene of perfidy and destruction, a comprehensive picture of his life and its meaning develops gradually until the providential resolution— which begins in chapter 56, with the reflectiveness into which Fathom is provoked by an avalanche of crises—makes it complete by drawing final attention to the real moral center of things signified by the collapse of evil energy and the triumph of Renaldo and Monimia. Here is the fulfillment of the "*Relief* to the moral of the whole" promised in the dedication. Once again Smollett closes a novel with the stuff of myth and fable, but in *Ferdinand Count Fathom* the instruments by which he achieves resolution are actually quite substantial. The old Jew Joshua Manasseh introduces a truly effectual force of benevolence into the world of deceitful cruelty Fathom has created for himself, helping to unmake it; Madame Clement uses a "stratagem" (p. 322) of her own to defeat the master strategist Fathom (Smollett's irony here is blatant), causing Monimia to feign her death—the death of innocence, so to speak—as a means of escaping him and thus ensuring that her reappearance will occur as a transforming renewal, a symbolic resurrection of all she represents. Smollett is a little heavy on the melodrama, but what he does makes for a resolution more satisfying than that found in either *Roderick Random* or *Peregrine Pickle*. The scene when Renaldo and Monimia, now married and ascendant, confront the fallen Fathom is actually moving and powerful, really quite unforgettable—especially because it is the first time the two of them, his principal victims, have ever seen him clearly. Fathom's sincere remorse redeems him, certified as it is by his genuine suffering and the faithful love of his former conquest Elenor, now his wife; and the forgiveness he receives seems both morally just and dramatically appropriate.

Smollett's experiments in *Ferdinand Count Fathom*—with double plotting and a contrapuntal variation upon spatial form, with character, with relations between history and fiction, with the rhetorical and symbolic effects of scenes of Gothic gloom—are not always perfectly successful, but they mark his novel as something unusual both in his own career and among the many other works of popular fiction published during the middle years of the eighteenth century. The so-called failings of the novel enumerated by its critics—erratic structure, inconsistencies of tone, inept plotting, excessive moral posturing—are not always failings at all, but consequences of its experiments. *Ferdinand Count Fathom* is a daring attempt to escape the limitations of novelistic convention as defined by Richardson, Fielding, and by Smollett himself in his first two narratives. Something is amiss when Smollett's departures from convention are rejected or even scorned, while immoderate praise is heaped upon those of his much more outrageously unconventional contemporary Sterne.

Ferdinand Count Fathom is not the masterpiece that *Tristram Shandy* is, but in its lesser way it is an equally original and extremely interesting work—ingeniously conceived, ably crafted, and altogether compelling as an elaborated study of the criminal life. Properly accepted for precisely the kind of novel it sets out to be, it will more than repay the efforts of the most exacting reader, while also shedding light on the art of its unorthodox maverick of an author, whose works—even his finest—have never been highly enough valued or widely enough enjoyed.

CHAPTER 4

Sir Launcelot Greaves

The Adventures of Sir Launcelot Greaves is the first work by an important English novelist to have been written specifically for serial publication. As Smollett laid plans to commence with *The British Magazine, or Monthly Repository for Gentlemen and Ladies,* he seems to have decided that sales might be helped by inclusion of a new novel within its pages during the early months of its run. It is unclear just when he began composing the story of his English Quixote, but by January 1760 enough of the narrative was completed for the opening chapter to appear in the inaugural number of the *British Magazine*. He kept writing, probably month by month, until the last installment was printed in the number for December 1761.

Smollett's idea for promoting his new periodical venture proved a good one, as all indications are that *Sir Launcelot Greaves*—known widely to be his though published with no hint of his authorship—did indeed enhance the magazine's circulation in a market already glutted with similar monthly miscellanies. The fortunes of the *British Magazine* were further enhanced by Smollett's numerous other contributions—verses, essays, and possibly some historical pieces—and by the participation of several talented men besides himself, among them Samuel Derrick and Oliver Goldsmith. From the beginning, the *British Magazine* maintained an overall level of quality exceeding that of its many competitors, and this was an attraction in itself that surely drew readers to the monthly episodes of knightly adventures. If the novel helped to promote the magazine, the magazine also helped to promote the novel. Neither was hurt by Goldsmith's very public support, expressed in a clever essay, "The Description of a Wow-Wow in the Country," published in the *Public Ledger* for 16 February 1760. Goldsmith's account of a tittle-tattle occasion descending into boring contentiousness ends brightly with his story of the sudden appearance of an Oxford scholar who reads aloud from *Sir Launcelot Greaves* "to the entire satisfaction of the audience," whose members then— the "sensible part of the company," at least—"give orders for the *British Magazine*." Smollett must have enjoyed this puff immensely, and he surely appreciated it from a colleague of Goldsmith's standing.

It is impossible to say how Smollett's new novel might have fared in the marketplace without the benefit of its innovative mode of initial publication. It was not widely praised, even during its serial run; few contemporaries followed the lead of Goldsmith's puff, and commentary of any kind was scarce. About three months after the last installment appeared in the *British Magazine,* Smollett allowed John Coote to publish a complete version of the novel in two volumes, and in this form *Sir Launcelot Greaves* was an abject commercial failure. Possibly it had already exhausted the limited audience for yet another—if strikingly original—imitation of *Don Quixote,* previously exploited by a host of contemporary writers, most successfully by Fielding in *Joseph Andrews* and by Charlotte Lennox in *The Female Quixote*. In any case no new English edition of *Sir Launcelot Greaves* was printed prior to Smollett's death in 1771, though there were at least three Irish editions (in 1762, 1763, and 1767). A second English edition (called "new" by its publisher, George Robinson) at last appeared in 1774. The novel was then reprinted as many as a dozen times through the 1790s, but it was never very popular with the early audience for prose fiction; indeed, among all of Smollett's novels, only *Ferdinand Count Fathom* attracted fewer eighteenth-century readers.

The initial reception of *Sir Launcelot Greaves* must have been a severe disappointment for Smollett. It is no wonder that he once more—as he had for most of the 1750s, following similar disappointments with *Peregrine Pickle* and *Ferdinand Count Fathom*—left off fiction-writing and, throughout virtually all of what proved to be the last decade of his life, devoted his attention to other projects. He was astonishingly productive during this time. The *Briton,* the *Continuation* of the *Complete History,* the *Travels,* the edition of Voltaire, the *Present State,* and the *Adventures of an Atom* are simply the most important of the many works he completed prior to the appearance of *Humphry Clinker* in the year of his death. Most of these efforts were lucrative, and on the whole they enabled Smollett to add greatly to his stature as a member of the community of letters. We may only speculate as to what it was that prompted him to turn to fiction again after three disappointments in a row and so much success in other forms. Possibly he was simply worn out by all the varied and relentless activity, which consumed more energy than he had to give during this period of seriously declining health, and so for renewal he resorted to his first love as a writer. Maybe he no longer cared so much about commercial and critical success when, as a man who knew he was dying, he decided to spend his last couple of years shaping assorted notes, sketches, and drafts into a finished new novel.[1] By this time he had already given up all other literary projects, and there can be no doubt that *Humphry Clinker* was a great and singleminded labor of restoration and of love—love for life itself, so exuberantly celebrated in its pages, but also for the novelist's vital art, so splendidly exemplified by the five story-telling correspondents in this most eclectic of all important eighteenth-century fictional narratives. If *Humphry Clinker* is the record of Matt Bramble's quest for health and happiness through discovery and appreciation of his most fundamental identity in the world, then it is also testimony to Smollett's acknowledgment of and joy in his most basic identity as a writer.

One of the old commonplaces about *Sir Launcelot Greaves* is that, after the indignation and ferocious satiric energy of the three novels of his youth, it represents a mellowing of Smollett's character as a man and as a writer and thus anticipates *Humphry Clinker*. Quite apart from the prejudicial effect of such a notion, which discourages a fair reading of *Sir Launcelot Greaves,* it betrays ignorance of some of the more important work completed after it, work that no informed reader would ever describe as mellow. The *Briton* engaged Smollett in bitter controversy on behalf of Lord Bute's administration; his nastiness was bested by that of his chief antagonist John Wilkes in the *North Briton,* but it was full of heat and was by no means simply a matter of skillful rhetorical posturing. What made Smollett give up this venture into political journalism after only eight months was not a fit of sweet temper but weariness with the futility of all such endeavors and furious disappointment at Bute's failure to reward him adequately for his efforts.[2] Smollett is less rancorous in the *Travels,* but this work's frequent splenetic outbursts—besides providing much of its real charm—provoked a mischievous Laurence Sterne to dub his rival the "learned Smelfungus."[3] The *Adventures of an Atom,* a wickedly satiric attack on the conduct of English politics from the late 1750s through the mid-1760s, outdoes Swift in vitriol and is Smollett at his *least* mellow; it was the last work he published before turning his hand to *Humphry Clinker.* The purpose here is not simply to suggest that Smollett remained angry and irascible to the end, though to some degree he did (Matt Bramble himself is evidence enough that this is so), but to point out the irrelevancy and misguidedness of the old commonplace. Certainly *Humphry Clinker* is a gentler work than any of its author's other novels, and it is also more reflective—not surprising, since it was written by a dying man. But nothing is gained for it or for *Sir Launcelot Greaves* by seeing them as stages of a journey into mellowness during Smollett's last years, and in fact this perspective obscures the real meaning of both novels, diminishing them. *Sir Launcelot Greaves* in particular has suffered from being read as though it were little more than a prelude to the masterpiece that followed it. The truth is that neither novel is soft-hearted, and neither blinks at the harshness, the violence, or the contemptible folly of most human activity as Smollett understood it.

Sir Launcelot Greaves actually represents yet another experiment for Smollett—with serial form, of course, but also with the challenge of portraying nearly perfected goodness in action at the very center of a narrative. This novel is in fact a kind of reversal upon *Ferdinand Count Fathom* and its story of a thoroughgoing villain. It is Smollett's least subjective character study, for it focuses hardly at all upon its hero's felt responses to the world, but rather upon his quite predictable behavior within it. Greaves is, after all, an idealized idealist, a version of the Quixote figure whose supposed madness defines his character but is not madness at all except when viewed in light of the world's real madness—its corruption and brutality, its insane departures from the standard of morality and conduct embodied in the hero. Greaves *looks* like a madman, of course, wearing his ancestral armor and accompanied by his odd squire Crabshaw, and in the strictest sense he is as much an aberrant character as Fathom. But his deviation from a norm of appearance and conduct is much more than just eccentricity; it is an indictment of that norm, just as Fathom's criminality is an affirmation of the idealism it seeks to undermine and destroy.

Unlike Fathom, whom Smollett carefully delineates as a close study in radical

Thomas Rowlandson, Sir Launcelot Greaves and Timothy Crabshaw (1790).
(From the private collection of the author.)

deviance, Greaves is more a device than a fully imagined personage; in all his uncompromising righteousness, he makes possible the novel's intense scrutiny of the public world, which he judges and sometimes improves by the force of his example but from which—unlike Roderick, Perry, and Fathom—he is entirely separate. Interestingly, Smollett manages to maintain his hero's focus upon the public world without developing the same kinds of close connections between history and fiction that we have observed in his earlier novels. Few of the characters in *Sir Launcelot Greaves* are drawn from life; historical allusions are much scarcer than is usual for Smollett, and there are no glaring instances of the anachronistic uses of the factual by which he elsewhere engages in the creation of provocatively atemporal conjunctions between the real and the imagined. It might be said that *Sir Launcelot Greaves* is a reflection *upon,* rather than *of,* the real. Even when he is at his most precise in his representations of English culture and its institutions in this novel, Smollett preserves a distanced and generalized manner that allows him to avoid particularities while enforcing the broadest moral values. The idealized Greaves is the perfect device for making this manner work effectively.

If Fathom is all but invisible, Greaves is "physically conspicuous," as Aileen Douglas has observed, and always in a context that is "insistently public and communal."[4] He is himself not a divided character, and in this he resembles Fathom, but his presence—and that of the virtuous Aurelia, his female counterpart, whom he loves and pursues—throws the rest of the world into relief, revealing a deep division, and the drama of conflict Smollett plays out through the narrative prevents all possibility of reconciliation. The world simply cannot be recreated so as to take on the attributes of the hero who exposes and rebukes it. The ending of the story in most respects closely resembles the endings we have seen in Smollett's other novels. There is the same retreat to the mythic environs of the ancestral estate, where thousands congregate to celebrate the joyous union of the hero and heroine and the happy new order their marriage signifies. But in *Roderick Random, Peregrine Pickle,* and *Ferdinand Count Fathom* the ending is preceded by a transformation, a sign that, if the hero must leave the world behind, at least the part of it that he represents has been redeemed. In *Sir Launcelot Greaves* there is no such redemption, despite the marriages and other happy turns with which the novel concludes. The hero, of course, requires no redemption, and though he leaves parts of the world better than he found them (the madhouse, for example, and the community of Justice Gobble's victims), nothing whatsoever is so completely transformed as to coincide with the moral idealism he embodies. Oddly, this novel of idealized and constant virtue triumphant is Smollett's darkest—"much darker" even, says Douglas, than that other important mid-century contemplation of the moral authority of virtue in a public arena, Fielding's *Amelia* (p. 122).

Sir Launcelot Greaves is still more urgent in its concern with the conflict between the virtuous character and a wicked world than any of Smollett's other novels. Practically all of its episodes turn upon that conflict, once Greaves is introduced, and they do so in a way that places the hero in a directly oppositional relation to whatever he encounters. The strategy broadly resembles that of *Ferdinand Count Fathom,* but the reversal of roles—in the one novel, evil seeks to dominate and eradicate goodness, and in the other, goodness seeks to preserve itself by overcoming the evil that endangers it—all but forces the narrative into a frequently heavy-handed didacticism. *Sir Launcelot Greaves,* despite some fine character portraits and delightful comic moments, is burdened by a discursive manner that fails to generate the kind of imaginative energy we associate with Smollett. The voluble Tom Clarke requires most of three chapters to introduce and establish the character of Greaves as a young man so good that he grew up to make all his neighbors believe "the golden age was revived in Yorkshire" (p. 61), and then launched himself into knight errantry determined to preserve innocence and to earn the hand of the fair Aurelia by righting wrongs and thus spreading the influence of his golden age idealism everywhere. This last he is never really able to do, but the attempt occasions numerous long harangues, some of them in Greaves's own voice.

There are no surprises among the subjects of these; for the most part they are the standard stock in trade of the eighteenth-century social satirist. Chapters 3, 9, and 10 take up the failings of the English election system; in chapters 11 and 12, and again in chapter 17, the focus is upon the corruptions of justice; chapters 20 and 21 turn to conditions in prisons, and chapters 23 and 24 expose the sufferings of those who have been unjustly confined in asylums for the insane. Greaves is often insistently loquacious. In chapter 12 he lectures Justice Gobble, assuming his role of judge and investing it with the authority of a confident moralist: "if such a despicable reptile shall annoy man-

kind with impunity," he declaims, "if such a contemptible miscreant shall
have it in his power to do such deeds of inhumanity and oppression, what
avails the law?" (p. 136). In chapter 23, locked in his asylum apartment, he
reflects silently, and at length, upon the abridgement of English liberty endured by those who, like himself, have been subjected to the barbarism of imprisonment in a private madhouse. "How little reason have we to boast of the
blessings enjoyed by the British subject," he muses, "if he holds them on such
a precarious tenure." He goes on then to some unfavorable comparisons with
"the Bastile in France, and the Inquisition in Portugal" (pp. 232, 233). Such
moments as these are usually full of passion, and it seems clear that Greaves is
almost always either the voice or the instrument of his author's indignation.
But the manner is most often preachy rather than dramatic, polemical rather
than novelistic; Smollett the crusading controversialist gets in the way of
Smollett the storyteller. Surely this is a major reason why *Sir Launcelot Greaves*
was such a limited success among its earliest readers, and it is certainly a reason why readers of later generations have liked it so little.

   Despite its problems and limitations, the novel—like *Ferdinand Count
Fathom* before it—possesses virtues and strengths that have regularly been
overlooked. To some extent its failure to please has resulted from the failure
of its readers to recognize and respond to its very real attractions, which have
been obscured because the novel is in so many ways a departure from Smollett's usual rambunctious manner. *Hard Times,* by his greatest nineteenth-
century admirer, suffered a similar fate among several generations of readers,
and for some of the same reasons—it was un-Dickensian, so ran the usual
complaint against it. Dickens's novel was recovered and successfully proclaimed a masterpiece half-a-century ago by F. R. Leavis;[5] *Sir Launcelot Greaves*
is no masterpiece, but it has long been denied the kind of attention to its particular excellence that would reclaim it as a significant achievement. The process of reclamation has begun in the work of Paul-Gabriel Boucé, Aileen
Douglas, and John Skinner, who, in their extended studies of the novel, have
treated it with greater respect than it has typically enjoyed at the hands of
critics.[6] I should like to continue that process in the remaining pages of this
chapter.

   Sir Launcelot Greaves is Smollett's shortest novel by far, and, notwithstanding
its discursiveness, it is also his most tightly compressed and carefully disci-

plined.[7] Overall the work shows a remarkable restraint. The number of episodes is small for a story by Smollett, but each is conducted with a precise economy. The third-person narrator, though a real presence, rarely becomes intrusive—even more rarely than in *Ferdinand Count Fathom;* instead, the voices and actions of the characters are allowed to carry the story entirely, while the reader—with the narrator—is positioned simply to observe them as they do so. There are few pranks; the most egregious is the joke played upon Captain Crowe in chapters 6 and 7, as he readies himself for his career in knight errantry and is obliged by Clarke, Ferret, and Fillet to imitate Greaves's solemn ritual of an all-night vigil in a church, where they terrify him with the appearance of a pair of ancestral ghosts. The novel is full of violence, but it is generally more verbal than physical (though Greaves does engage in the occasional fight, and though he gives Crabshaw a couple of good drubbings for ineptitude or folly); more episodes turn upon the effects of moral violence— the sufferings of society's victims—than upon thrashings and head-bashings. The result of all this restraint is that *Sir Launcelot Greaves* operates at lower energy than Smollett's other novels, and at a reduced decibel level. But there is no total loss of imaginative power; on the contrary, the novel's effects are in some ways intensified by the discipline Smollett imposed upon their creation.

No doubt the publication of his novel in serial form forced upon Smollett the need to rein himself in, to control his instinct to improvise and sprawl out as he wrote. As Robert D. Mayo has observed, after the first few monthly installments—each of them a chapter—he grew very skillful at producing copy for each new installment that was just long enough for the development of a scene or episode and that closed with a hook intended to make his readers want to buy the next installment.[8] The first seven chapters are of uneven length (the third is about 5,000 words, the sixth about 1,800), but following the somewhat awkwardly distended "history" of Greaves given in the voice of Tom Clarke, who spreads it out over chapters 3, 4, and 5, Smollett "found his stride," says Mayo, "and thereafter the monthly parts seldom varied more than a page from the archetypal length of 3400 words, now firmly fixed in his mind" (p. 281). As a result *Sir Launcelot Greaves* very early develops a regular, rhythmic movement unusual for a novel by Smollett. Mayo's calculations belie Sir Walter Scott's curiously sneering description of Smollett's habits with the composition of the monthly installments. When "post-time drew near,"

Scott wrote, "he used to retire for half an hour or an hour to prepare the necessary quantity of *copy,* as it is technically called in the printing-house, which
he never gave himself the trouble to correct, or even to read over."[9] John
Valdimir Price has successfully challenged Scott's description as inaccurate,
reckless, and damaging to the novel's reputation because it had a long-term
effect of discouraging thoughtful critical assessments of it.[10] Scott was on the
whole a Smollett partisan, but it seems clear that careless reading of *Sir
Launcelot Greaves* led him to the wholly unfounded conclusion that its composition was altogether haphazard. Smollett, like Dickens after him, no doubt
did frequently find himself writing an installment against a printer's deadline;
but there is no evidence that he was so cavalier about it as Scott imagined.

Certain other effects in the novel, besides its relative brevity and its rhythmic movement, also seem to have resulted largely from its mode of publication. *Sir Launcelot Greaves* departs from the comprehensive biographical form
of Smollett's first three stories, devoting its main plot line to the span of just a
few months in the adult life of its hero. (Much the same kind of thing would
occur in *Humphry Clinker*—a novel that also profited, in the tight structuring
of its individual letters, from the particular discipline Smollett developed
while writing the monthly installments of *Sir Launcelot Greaves.*) The time
frame of the action covers only the period from the October evening when
Greaves makes his appearance in the opening episode until his marriage and
return to Greavesbury-hall, apparently in the following spring, as "Chapter
the Last" concludes; the details of his earlier years—his childhood and adolescence, his education and travels—are all enclosed within Tom Clarke's in-
set history, which, despite its extended interruption of the fledgling plot's forward progress, still allows Greaves and his quest to hold the center of the
novel's stage. Taken together, chapters 1 and 2 make for one of the great
opening sequences in all of English fiction; Smollett's decision to begin with
the comic scene at the Black Lion Inn surely arose from his desire to make the
first installments of his novel—and the magazine in which they appeared—
flash unforgettably upon the consciousness of his readers, catching their permanent interest in the knight errant whose appearance on a stormy night so
startles the assembled company. Once this beginning had been made, biographical background was of necessity subordinated to present dramatic action, and Smollett went on in further installments to maintain the centrality of

that action with a concentration of focus he did not even attempt in *Roderick Random, Peregrine Pickle,* or *Ferdinand Count Fathom.*

In these earlier novels, biographical form is an important part of the eclectic mix Smollett strove to achieve. If its importance is diminished in *Sir Launcelot Greaves,* that is consistent with this novel's generally constricted range of generic types, or rather with its almost minimalist exploitation of most of the narrative kinds it appropriates. Roderick, Perry, and Fathom all bear resemblances to the central figure of popular rogue and criminal narratives, though to differing degrees; there is no hint of the rogue or picaro, and certainly nothing of the criminal, in the character of Greaves. There are parallels with the travel book, as the action takes Smollett's principals from place to place—Greaves is always in motion, pursuing both Aurelia and continued opportunities to do good, while Aurelia is on the run from her tyrannical uncle and, later, from the rejected suitor Sycamore; but people and events are on display, not locales or customs, while the geographical "map" of the story is sharply limited. The entire action takes place along the Great Western Road and in London, "the metropolis, that vast labyrinth" (p. 158), to which it leads.

As a vehicle for exposure of failed and corrupt institutions, with Greaves as its primary device and voice, the novel borrows its spirit—and frequently its didactic urgency—from the traditions of formal satire; the darkness of its vision, described above, suggests that it is really the closest of all Smollett's novels to those traditions, and especially to the bitterness and intolerance of Juvenalian satire. The most obvious formal generic affinity displayed in *Sir Launcelot Greaves* is, of course, with *Don Quixote.* But Smollett's novel is not merely a slavish imitation. Its satirical edge is sharper than its model's, and there is little of the Cervantean affection for and tolerance of flawed human nature. Greaves, like his prototype in Cervantes, is an idealist, but—after the opening scene at the Black Lion—hardly a comic figure. He is acutely conscious of the contemporary world in which he lives; his idealism may be madness in a context of folly and wickedness, but he is himself not mad at all. His words to a skeptical Ferret in chapter 2 set the record straight on this matter almost before the story has even gotten underway. "I am neither an affected imitator of Don Quixote," he says, "nor, as I trust in heaven, visited by that spirit of lunacy so admirably displayed in the fictitious character exhibited by

the inimitable Cervantes. I have not yet encountered a windmill for a giant,"
he continues, "nor mistaken this public house for a magnificent castle. . . . I
see and distinguish objects as they are discerned and described by other men.
I reason without prejudice, can endure contradiction, and, as the company
perceives, even bear impertinent censure without passion or resentment."
Greaves, it is clear, dons his ancestral armor not as the result of some crazed
confusion about his identity, but as a symbolic act proclaiming his intention to
do all he can to defeat evil and return the world to an old sense of the right,
the good, and the true. "I quarrel with none but the foes of virtue and decorum," he protests in closing his harangue to Ferret, "against whom I have de-
clared perpetual war, and them I will every where attack as the natural enemies of mankind" (p. 50).

John Skinner has argued convincingly that, far from simply mimicking Cervantes in *Sir Launcelot Greaves,* Smollett actually recuperates the kind of romance sensibility that Cervantes mocks—not the conventions of romance,
and not its absurd confusion of the real with the magical and the marvelous
(which Smollett scorns at such length in the preface to *Roderick Random*), but
its celebration of pure virtue, its enactment of the triumph of moral idealism
in the stories of its heroes and heroines, and its exaltation of romantic love as
the highest expression of all that is worth striving for in human life. Romance,
Skinner concludes, is at the generic center of *Sir Launcelot Greaves,* and it is a
stronger center than anything comparable we may find in Smollett's other
novels.[11] This view of the novel is upheld, I believe, in the otherwise comic
scene (in chapter 13) when Greaves instructs Captain Crowe in the rudiments
of knight-errantry. He strikes a somber note as he turns to the subject of love.
"He that does not believe that love is an infallible pilot, must not embark on
the voyage of chivalry; for, next to the protection of Heaven, it is from love
that the knight derives all his prowess and glory. . . . A knight without a mistress is a meer non-entity, or at least a monster in nature, a pilot without compass, a ship without rudder, and must be driven to and fro upon the waves of
discomfiture and disgrace" (p. 144). At one level such advice, rendered to a
half-cracked old salt and would-be knight like Crowe (and almost in his own
vernacular too), is ludicrous; but at a more fundamental level what Greaves
says is simply a straightforward definition of what drives him—and his story,
which would not be happening at all but for his beloved Aurelia. The ending

of the story only confirms the validity of the hero's remarks to the Captain. It also confirms the validity of the romance as narrative model. The model is Smollett's; it cannot be Greaves's own, as there is no hint that he has even read any romances. Here Smollett is an illusionist; the romance pattern is unmistakable, but the heroism of Greaves the knight errant seems to spring from nowhere except his own innate goodness.

Romance, at least in the works Smollett knew—from medieval romances of chivalry to seventeenth-century French heroic romances and their English imitations [12]—was essentially a discursive mode, and this may help to explain the manner in which the narrative of *Sir Launcelot Greaves* is conducted. But if this novel is Smollett's most discursive, it is also—in a structural sense, at least—his most precisely Hogarthian. By the time of the novel's composition Hogarth was nearing the end of his long and distinguished career (he died in 1764), and despite the controversy generated by his *Analysis of Beauty*—published in the same year as *Ferdinand Count Fathom* (1753) and greeted with loud and continuing jeers from the artistic establishment because of its challenge to the notion that the arts ought to be governed by fixed "rules" [13]—he was more than ever the dominant painter of his age. The argument of the *Analysis* surely appealed to Smollett, maverick that he was himself; and in any case he had spent the last several years in an increasingly intense preoccupation with the graphic arts. It was during this period that, apparently more than satisfied with the frontispieces furnished by Francis Hayman for the second edition of *Roderick Random,* he asked the same artist to provide twenty-eight illustrations for his translation of *Don Quixote,* published at last (after a long delay of almost six years) in 1755; it is very likely that he closely supervised Hayman's work on these illustrations. In the same decade of the 1750s Smollett also arranged for illustration of others of his works, including the *Complete History* (also by Hayman). [14] Meanwhile, in 1756 he launched the series of features in the *Critical Review* that brought so much attention to the achievement of contemporary artists—Hogarth, of course, but also Joseph Wilton, Thomas Frye, and others. [15] And as he conceived the notion of publishing *Sir Launcelot Greaves* serially in his new *British Magazine,* he asked the illustrator Anthony Walker for a pair of drawings to be included in its pages.

It should not be surprising, then, that the tight structure of this novel, written as it was in a context of Smollett's extended period of heightened interest

Anthony Walker, Sir Launcelot Greaves & his Squire, Timothy Crabshaw (1760).
(Reproduced, with permission, from the private collection of James G. Basker.)

in the arts, depends almost entirely on the sequential presentation of pictorial vignettes. The great model is still Hogarth the serial artist—"the inimitable Hogarth" Smollett calls him once again, in chapter 12 (p. 133); and, apart from the fumbling Tom Clarke's long wandering over the subject of the hero's previous life, the movement of the narrative through chapters of almost equal length—each is either a completed episode, or a distinctive scene contributing to an episode of more than one scene—gives it a rhythmic feeling and a deliberate equivalency of visual effects that is emphatically Hogarthian in the manner of its progression. Very likely this was all to some extent accidental, a consequence of serial publication. But at the same time the serial mode and its structural requirements must have come more or less naturally to Smollett, given his instincts as a storyteller who always proceeded spatially, by creating a succession of visual episodes. And the overall structural effect he achieved in *Sir Launcelot Greaves* must have pleased him, for—as I have already suggested—it was one that he would strive for again, with even greater effect, in the letters of *Humphry Clinker.*

Smollett is nowhere more successfully pictorial in *Sir Launcelot Greaves* than in the opening chapters introducing the principal characters as they gather at the Black Lion. The scene as a whole not only makes for a splendid beginning to the novel, but it is also its funniest and most inherently comic—even Greaves is briefly projected as a comic presence when he is first described at the outset of the second chapter. The novel is never this funny again; it is only rarely funny at all, and, though a comedy in the strict modal sense, there are few repetitions of the high spirits that greet the reader in the first dozen pages or so. Smollett's technique in the initial paragraph of chapter 1 is cinematic, as he skillfully moves the reader's eye from the outdoor scene along "the great northern road from York to London" where four unnamed travelers are pelted by a rainstorm, to the kitchen of the inn where they retreat for shelter, quickly noting particular details of its floor ("paved with red bricks") and furnishings ("three or four Windsor chairs," "shining plates of pewter and copper sauce-pans nicely scoured") and then precisely placing the travelers within it—three sitting over a "bowl of rumbo," the fourth alone "at the opposite side of the chimney" near "another groupe" composed of the landlady, her two daughters, and "a country lad, who served both as waiter and ostler" (p. 39).

The next long paragraph introduces and characterizes each of the travelers: Fillet the kindly surgeon, Captain Crowe the curmudgeonly seaman, Tom Clarke (Crowe's nephew) the talkative young attorney, and Ferret the weaselly misanthrope. The one real caricature, Captain Crowe, is not so much described as anatomized by reference to his eccentric style of speaking in a sailor's lingo so broken and full of "abrupt transitions" that its meaning "was not easy to decypher" (p. 40). Ferret, a grotesque (and a cartoon rendering of Smollett's literary and political enemy, John Shebbeare[16]), is more precisely pictured: he "looked as if he wanted to shrink within himself, from the impertinence of society. He wore a black periwig as straight as the pinions of a raven, and this was covered with an hat flapped, and fastened to his head by a speckled handkerchief tied under his chin. He was wrapped in a great coat of brown frize, under which he seemed to conceal a small bundle" (p. 40). Following this description, and for most of the remainder of the chapter, Smollett simply allows his travelers to speak, further revealing themselves. Fillet confirms the first impression that he is a solid and sturdy man, as predictable as he is kindly. Clarke speaks a landlubber's version of his uncle's disjointed nautical style, but still he manages to expose both his good heart and his awakened libidinous interest in Dolly, one of the landlady's daughters—he is "somewhat libertine in his amours," we are told when he is first introduced (p. 40). In a tour de force, Smollett gives Crowe the big verbal moment: "Look ye here, brother," he says in response to Fillet's expression of concern about his horse-weary rear end, "—look ye here—mind these poor crippled joints: two fingers on the starboard, and three on the larboard hand: crooked, d'ye see, like the knees of a bilander.—I'll tell you what, brother, you seem to be a—ship deep laden—rich cargoe—current setting into the bay—hard gale—lee-shore—all hands in the boat—tow round the headland—self pulling for dear blood, against the whole crew" (p. 42). And on he goes, his language as mangled as his poor body. This portion of the episode concludes with an exchange between Ferret (precise of speech, but mean-spirited) and Tom (voluble, imprecise, and obsessed with the language of the law) that turns upon scatological references and ends with a focus upon Dolly and her plump, desirable flesh. "I seize Dolly *in tail*," says Tom in lawyer's speech as the exchange concludes (p. 43).

We have seen instances of this same combination of visual representation and characterization by style in Smollett's other novels, but rarely are they carried off to equal effect. Smollett follows these flourishes with another, different in kind but equally striking, as he draws his first chapter to a close. Tom's rhapsody upon Dolly is "interrupted by a noise that alarmed the whole company" (p. 43). A "storm of wind" howling about the house makes the darkness of the night still more fearsome than it was before, accentuating the "horrour of divers loud screams" that penetrate the noise outside (pp. 43–44). The superstitions of Crowe and Tom rise to a pitch of the highest fear: as Ferret remonstrates against them for trembling at the imagined "visitation of spirits, ghosts, and goblins," his "lecture" is "suddenly suspended by a violent knocking at the door, which threatened the whole house with immediate demolition" (pp. 44–45). Crowe, Fillet, and the ostler position themselves for defense, Tom retreats to safety with the ladies, Ferret prudently withdraws "into an adjoining pantry." And the author announces that his reader must "wait with patience for the next chapter, in which he will see the cause of this disturbance explained much to his comfort and edification" (p. 45).

Dickens was never better than this at hooking his audience. The mock-Gothic effects contribute both to the high comedy of the chapter—was Smollett perhaps spoofing the melodrama of the first of the Gothic episodes in his own *Ferdinand Count Fathom* (chapters 20 and 21)?—and to the suspenseful anticipation with which it concludes. The same effects are renewed as the second chapter begins: the door flies open with the third in a series of "dreadful shocks," and in stalks an "apparition" that strikes "fear and trepidation" into the assembled company. It is Greaves himself, dressed in his armor and bearing on his shoulders the body of a man who appears "to have been drowned, and fished up from the bottom of the neighbouring river" (p. 46). After a brief speech in high style (the comic incongruity is exquisite), Greaves lays down his burden, and we gain our first sight of his ridiculous squire, Timothy Crabshaw. Smollett lavishes on the description of Crabshaw the kind of precise visual detail we associate with the presentation of his greatest eccentrics and caricatures—he has a "thick, squat, and brawny" body, a "prominent belly," a low and "remarkably convex" forehead, with eyes like those of a "Hampshire porker," a nose like "a tennis-ball" in shape and "a mulberry" in color, an upper jaw "furnished with two long white sharp-pointed teeth or fangs," and a "peaked and incurvated chin" whose length joins with his "impending forehead" to "form in profile" the "exact resemblance of a moon in the first quarter" (p. 47).

Given all the analogies to the inanimate, this portrait comes very close to the grotesque, which it avoids only because the scene is so quintessentially a comic one. Everything up to this point—the whole of chapter 1 and the elements of chapter 2 just outlined—is in preparation for the moment of calm (after Crabshaw has been drained of the water in his belly) when Greaves is at last properly seen without the furor of the storm and the crisis of his squire's near drowning to distract from a right view of his appearance. "His age did not seem to exceed thirty," we are told; "he was tall, and seemingly robust; his face long and oval, his nose aquiline, his mouth furnished with a set of elegant teeth white as the drifted snow; his complexion clear, and his aspect noble" (p. 49). In these and all other details—flowing chestnut hair, shining eyes, and stately manner—he is the exact opposite of Crabshaw, and the contrasting descriptions are certainly intended to emphasize Greaves as the picture of an ideal, the hero of a romance. Following the description of him, Greaves proclaims his knight errantry and, during a long and sometimes heated exchange with Ferret, provides—in a passage already quoted ("I am neither an affected imitator of Don Quixote, nor . . . visited by that spirit of lunacy so admirably displayed . . . by the inimitable Cervantes. . . . I quarrel with none but the foes of virtue and decorum")—a clear rationale for his decision to take up such a lonely quest in a corrupt world. The chapter closes with the novel's mood now moderated (though Captain Crowe, near the very end, gets in a few more disjointed words), and the reader learns that, in the next, Tom will furnish the history of the intriguing Sir Launcelot, who—it happens—is his godfather.

Taken together, Smollett's first two chapters are a brilliant tableau, for they perfectly capture the whole range of characters—Aurelia excepted—who are the novel's principals. Almost self-contained, they nevertheless anticipate the story that is to come—its spatial form, for stories of knights errant are always episodic, and its visual method, which will yield other vignettes. Elsewhere Smollett is not always so graphic or so successful, but he does manage a good many moments that are uncommonly fine. Among the best are the two election scenes (in chapter 3, and in chapters 9 and 10), both of them recalling Hogarth's popular series of four election pictures, painted a few years earlier, in 1753 and 1754, and then issued as prints between 1755 and 1758. If

Smollett anticipated the first of these pictures, *An Election Entertainment,* in *Peregrine Pickle,* in *Sir Launcelot Greaves* he makes almost an explicit allusion to the entire series.[17]

The election scene in chapter 3 is quite brief, and it serves mainly to set Greaves into direct opposition with Anthony Darnel, Aurelia's uncle and guardian, who is represented as so corrupt that he does not hesitate to attempt buying the parliamentary seat formerly held by his late brother (Aurelia's father) and now contested by Sir Everhard Greaves, Launcelot's father. In this scene, unlike the more extended episode a few chapters later, Smollett makes no issue of party conflict, focusing instead upon personalities: Darnel is the disreputable political manipulator who "flattered and caressed the women, feasted the electors, hired mobs, made processions, and scattered about his money" (p. 62); Sir Everhard is the honorable candidate, and his advocate Sir Launcelot is the reluctant orator whose eloquence so sways the assembled crowd that Darnel slinks away with his hangers-on and concedes the election to his opponent. The happy outcome of this episode is not repeated in the second one, which occurs later in the sequence of the story, after it has darkened. The first election scene is described by Tom Clarke as part of his history of the hero, and is crucial to the shift which causes Greaves to turn knight errant—he is smitten with the matchless Aurelia, but her outraged uncle hurries her away to keep them apart; the effect is such that Greaves's world, once so full of brightness and hope, now seems utterly fallen and corrupt, and so he dons his armor and sets off to find Aurelia and bring about a restoration of beauty, light, and love.

From this point forward Smollett's focus is on the world's corruptions as Greaves witnesses them. Nothing in the novel so forcefully clarifies this focus as the second election episode. Unlike the first, whose potential for the triumph of wickedness Greaves is able to overcome, the second ends badly. Greaves once again speaks eloquently, denouncing the two miscreant candidates Sir Valentine Quickset (a Tory) and Mr. Isaac Vanderpelft (a Whig) as no more than "the opposite extremes of the ignorant clown and the designing courtier" (p. 114), but he is shouted down by the hostile crowd and supplanted by the mountebank Ferret, who repeats many of the same sentiments, but in scurrilous tones, while hawking an "Elixir of Long Life" guaranteed to keep all his listeners alive until they shall have seen their country "ruined"

(p. 117). Ferret outrageously—and very effectively—mocks one kind of quackery by cynically proclaiming another, and even Greaves cannot help "owning within himself" that the misanthrope has "mixed some melancholy truths with his scurrility" (p. 118). The whole episode has a nightmare quality about it, and what it portends is the utter failure of the rule of law—a failure elsewhere contemplated in the episode featuring the trading Justice Gobble (chapters 11 and 12) and in the scenes at the King's Bench Prison (chapters 20 and 21) and the madhouse (chapters 23 and 24).[18]

That the issue of elections and the law deeply troubled Smollett is made clear by what he wrote at about the same time in the *Continuation* to his *Complete History of England,* where he said of the political spectacles of the 1750s:

> The scenes of corruption, perjury, riot, and intemperance, which every election
> for a member of parliament had lately produced, were now grown so infamously
> open and intolerable . . . that the fundamentals of the constitution seemed to
> shake, and the very essence of parliaments to be in danger.[19]

These are precisely the sentiments expressed by Hogarth in his election pictures, which—with their representations of teeming crowds of grotesques absurdly engaged in what is nothing more or less than ritual debauchery—were designed to be a scathing commentary on the disgraceful parliamentary contests leading up to the General Election of 1754. Both of Smollett's election scenes evoke Hogarth, the second more emphatically because it is darker and also more extensively developed. There are few exact parallels, though both Smollett and Hogarth use color motifs (blue for Tories, orange for Whigs) and familiar slogans for the two parties—Smollett's Tories carry banners proclaiming "LIBERTY AND THE LANDED INTEREST" and "NO FOREIGN CONNECTIONS,—OLD ENGLAND FOR EVER," to which the Whig contingent responds by crying out "NO SLAVERY,—NO POPISH PRETENDER," while brandishing their own bannered slogan, "LIBERTY OF CONSCIENCE AND THE PROTESTANT SUCCESSION" (pp. 108–9). William Gaunt has observed that the election scenes drawn by Smollett and Hogarth are "close in exuberance" if not in precise correspondences; it might even be said, Gaunt remarks further, "that the novel illustrated the picture."[20] It might just as well be said the other way around, for Smollett fills his two scenes, the second especially, with ominous noises of crowds and a relentless verbal energy sug-

William Hogarth, *The Polling* (1753–54).
(By courtesy of the Trustees of Sir John Soane's Museum.)

gesting almost orgiastic violence, but with few precise visual details, and so it seems clear that he expected his readers' memory of the Hogarth pictures to provide additional texture, tone, and graphic clarity. Here he practiced as a pictorial novelist who deliberately exploited the possibilities of intertextual reference to create a comprehensive effect.[21]

It may be worth pausing here to note that the parallels between Smollett's election scenes and those by Hogarth provide a revealing—because extreme—instance of how the spatial form employed by each actually works. Hogarth's four paintings are a continuous narrative serially presented; issued as prints over a four-year period, they carried out a sequence of enforced stop-action effects—both time and space were literally suspended between one print and the next. The monthly installments of *Sir Launcelot Greaves* enforced an identically radical version of spatial form upon the novel; each chapter, including those devoted to the election episodes, was a completed

William Hogarth, *Chairing the Member* (1753–54).
(By courtesy of the Trustees of Sir John Soane's Museum.)

narrative unit divided by both space and time from the next unit. Because this
form came so naturally to both Hogarth and Smollett, the question of just
how much time or space might separate the individual pictures in any series
they created seems to have troubled them not at all. The compositional principle was the same no matter what. And it was this principle that allowed
them to look at a particular moment of experience with eyes so intensely focused, so free from concern with what came before or was to come after it,
that they were able to penetrate surface appearances and to represent reality
with extraordinary authenticity as perpetually startling and visually disorienting—startling because the truth of what they saw was usually hidden from
view, visually disorienting because that truth took unexpected physical shapes
in unexpected configural relationships with each other and with the entire
imaginative context.

Damian Grant, in his consideration of Smollett's scenes and characters, has made the same point in a different way. Grant is interested not specifically in a compositional principle but in a principle of comic style, yet what he says is well worth repeating here. "The comic imagination," he remarks, "operates on life as a prism does on light: it —'analyses' experience, reduces it to its constituent parts, which will then appear either grotesque or absurd."[22] This was a conscious process for Smollett, says Grant, and surely it was equally conscious for Hogarth—for both, it was a matter of assuming a particular visual style for a particular picture concerned with a particular subject; but since their individual pictures gather to produce a completed narrative, the operation of the comic imagination as Grant describes it was also crucial to the overall form each sought to create in every composition. For each, style generated form. The consciousness of this entire process for Smollett is readily apparent in the Justice Gobble episode, which follows only two chapters after the second election scene and, in its portrait of judicial corruption taken to a truly grotesque extreme, furthers the novel's developing concern with the collapse of the law and with the inhuman suffering caused by that collapse.

Greaves himself goes before Gobble a sufferer, falsely accused by Ferret of disturbing the public peace by his knight errantry and thrown into the very same jail where he had just found Tom Clarke, also falsely accused, and where he had discovered Crabshaw undergoing the humiliation of being "fairly set in the stocks, surrounded by a mob of people" (p. 122). Upon inquiring among his fellow prisoners about the character of the justice who had committed these outrages against decency and fairness, he is met with recitations of woe by four of Gobble's most wounded victims, one of them a kinswoman of Greaves whose treatment by the magistrate has "deprived her of her reason" (p. 129). Greaves, weeping, is—like the reader—prepared to encounter a monster when he is conducted to Gobble's house. He meets not one monster but two, the justice and his wife: "Mr Gobble sat in judgment, with a crimson velvet night cap on his head; and on his right hand appeared his lady, puffed up with the pride and insolence of her husband's office, fat, frowzy, and not over-clean, well stricken in years, without the least vestige of an agreeable feature, having a rubicond nose, ferret eyes, and imperious aspect." The wife disposed of thus summarily, Smollett's narrator turns to some final details of the justice's appearance. He is "a little, affected, pert prig, who endeavoured to solemnize his countenance by assuming an air of consequence, in which pride, impudence, and folly were strangely blended" (p. 130).

From these scant visual details—with his crimson cap he looks vaguely like a turkey—emerges a picture of just the sort of absurd personage who would speak in the way Gobble does, mangling—gobbling—the language as he mangles the law. He is no comic figure like Captain Crowe and Tom Clarke, whose linguistic eccentricities only betray their good-natured and quite harmlessly obsessive ways of being. Gobble, both ignorant and malicious, is also self-interested, and he has the power to act out all his perverse impulses. More than anything, it is the conflict between the impartial precision of the law and his deliberate practice of blurring it that makes him seem sinister. It is not by accident that Smollett characterizes him principally by his style. "The laws of this land," Gobble begins as the supposed criminal Greaves stands before him, "has provided—I says, as how provision is made by the laws of this here land, in reverence to delinquems and manefactors, whereby the king's peace is upholden by we magistrates, who represent his majesty's person, better than in e'er a contagious nation under the sun: but, howsomever, that there king's peace, and this here magistrate's authority, cannot be adequably and identically upheld, if so be as how criminals escapes unpunished" (pp. 130–31). And so on. Sir Launcelot's "solemn and deliberate reply" to this ridiculous harangue (p. 131) discomposes Gobble, but not as much as the later discovery that he is a gentleman of property, indeed a baronet. The justice's absurd and dangerous pretentiousness now gives way to the silliness of his groveling before such grandeur, and his reduction is completed by the narrator's observation that his "terror and compunction" "seemed to produce" in him "the same unsavoury effects that are so humorously delineated by the inimitable Hogarth in the print of Felix on his tribunal, done in the Dutch stile" (p. 133). The reference is to Hogarth's "Paul Before Felix Burlesqued" (1751), a parody of Rembrandt issued as a subscription ticket for the engraving of his grand historical work on the same subject (1748). The reference embeds a telling scatological joke, for in the burlesque Felix, the judge, appears to be emptying his bowels. Certainly none of Smollett's first readers could have doubted either the intent or the tone of this conclusion to his hero's encounter with

William Hogarth, *Paul Before Felix Burlesqued* (Engraving, 1751).
(Copyright British Museum.)

Gobble; the allusion to Hogarth was not so much for purposes of clarification as for the sake of a good laugh. The laughter is itself reductive.

The grim Gobble episode, a typical Smollett tableau providing a comprehensive analysis (to borrow Grant's term) of failed justice, thus ends on a note of severe judgment accentuated by high good humor. And the conditions created by Gobble's malfeasance seem to be relieved, as at least some of his victims are brought once again to happiness by Greaves's intervention. Gobble, collapsed into nothing by Smollett's scatological joke, is ground into dust by Greaves himself with the words of reproach quoted earlier. If there were "no human institution to take cognizance of such atrocious crimes" as yours, he says, "I would listen to the dictates of eternal Justice, and, arming myself with the right of nature, exterminate such villains from the face of the earth!" (p. 136). It would seem that, with such a threat of divine vengeance hanging over the world as represented by Gobble, justice would somehow prevail in human affairs. And indeed in some quarters it does seem to do so—the second episode involving a magistrate and a courtroom (chapter 17) concludes with the wise Mr. Elmy citing the litigious farmer Prickle with contempt for his refusal to give up a frivolous suit against Captain Crowe and Tom Clarke.

But it does not prevail in all quarters, or even many. Almost immediately upon his arrival in London at the beginning of chapter 20, Greaves goes to the King's Bench Prison in search of Aurelia, whom he fears her uncle may have caused to be confined there. Though Smollett describes the prison as a surprisingly pleasant place, where "the voice of misery never complains" (p. 205), it is still home to sufferers who have been unjustly treated. The King's Bench buildings were new at the time this description was written,[23] as Smollett was well aware, for he was himself there, serving a sentence for libel, from late November 1760 until the end of the following February.[24] He represents living conditions at the new prison as much less harsh than those at the older Fleet and the Marshalsea, where scenes in *Roderick Random, Peregrine Pickle,* and *Ferdinand Count Fathom* are set. But still the King's Bench buildings are, as the headings to chapters 20 and 21 proclaim, the "MANSIONS OF THE DAMNED," where live "THE CHILDREN OF WRETCHEDNESS" (pp. 203, 210). As in the world outside, there is much strife and great unhappiness. In an interesting echo of Captain Minikin's words to the hero in chapter 39 of *Ferdinand Count Fathom,* Greaves's conductor Mr. Felton characterizes the little universe of the King's Bench as "this microcosm or republic in miniature" (p. 206). Broken into the Crabclaw and Tapley factions, each struggling for a meaningless ascendancy, it is populated by such as Captain and Mrs. Clewlin, whose formerly flourishing lives (they remind us of Fielding's Billy and Amelia Booth) have collapsed into squalor and physical degeneracy as the result of a father's cruelty and the irruption of smallpox in the prison, which broke their hearts by killing their child. The picture of life in this microcosm is finally not a pretty one.

Smollett makes his prison episode extremely effective both as drama and as social commentary by developing it over two chapters in a pattern of falling action and modulating tones. Chapter 20, after starting off by representing the King's Bench as a bright and airy place, moves on to the comedy of the boxing match by which Crabclaw and Tapley are to settle between them the issue of supremacy once and for all. The former, an ill-tempered doctor, is unexceptional in appearance, but filled with "a mixture of rage and disdain"; the latter, a brewer, is pictured as "large, raw-boned, and round as a but of beer, but very fat, unwieldy, short-winded and phlegmatic" (pp. 207–8). Not surprisingly, the brewer wins the match by simply falling on his opponent and nearly smothering him. The Clewlins are participants in this comic moment, serving as seconds to the combatants. But when the focus turns directly to them in chapter 21, the tone shifts from the exuberant to the melancholy and sentimental, as Mr. Felton tells their sad story to a curious Greaves. The hero weeps, but apparently feels he can do nothing to rescue them from the lowness into which they have fallen. He knows he cannot recreate the world, not even this little part of it. Other stories of misery and suffering follow, and though Greaves lays out five guineas to relieve one family, all those he meets or hears of in the prison are finally left in their distress. As a parting gesture of compassion he kindly offers a bank note of twenty pounds "to be distributed in charities among the objects of the place" (p. 217). But the very language here is telling. Like the *Thunder*'s miserable sailors and the Marshalsea's wretched prisoners in *Roderick Random,* the inhabitants of the King's Bench as seen in *Sir Launcelot Greaves* are reduced to nothing—they are *objects,* nearly spiritless and all but deprived of their humanity. The picture of this "microcosm" as it emerges from Felton's narrative, and in the final brief scene when one of the sufferers appears before Greaves, is a dark one indeed. And its darkness is emphasized all the more by the movement of the complete episode from the laughable spectacle of the boxing match between the doctor and the brewer to the painful images of abject misery and hopelessness.

In his next—and final—major episode Smollett joins the recurring issue of the failure of the law with another important theme of his novel as he sends his hero to the private madhouse where, at last, he finds Aurelia. It is his rival Sycamore who has contrived at his confinement there, while Aurelia is the victim of her uncle's last desperate measure to bend her to his will. From the very beginning of his career in knight errantry Greaves has been thought mad, like his prototype Don Quixote. Though he knows his own heart and the merit of his purpose, he clearly acknowledges early on that the world might be expected to see him as crazed. Of the apparently disordered Captain Crowe and his ludicrous appearance as knight errant—a parody of himself—he says, "madness and honesty are not incompatible—indeed I feel it by experience" (p. 98). Shortly thereafter he asks his own squire, Crabshaw, "do you really think I am mad?" (p. 102), and then goes on to explain that he is not, for he has suffered no "privation" of "reason itself" (p. 103). Others do not share Greaves's sanguine view of his mental health. After the favorable conclusion of his encounter with Justice Gobble, he is "more and more persuaded that a knight-errant's profession might be exercised, even in England, to the advantage of the community"; but Tom Clarke, anxious about his uncle's increasing derangement as he persists in imitating Greaves, thinks differently—and Smollett's narrator seems to have entered into an alliance with him: "not without good reason," we are told, Clarke had "laid it down as a maxim, that knight-errantry and madness were synonimous terms; and that madness, though exhibited in the most advantageous and agreeable light, could not change its nature, but must continue a perversion of sense to the end of the chapter" (p. 142).

Clarke is wrong, of course, insofar as his remark touches upon the matter of the hero's behavior. His appearance is eccentric, an aberration, but it is only an expression of the new purpose of his life—to preserve innocence and right the wrongs he perceives with eyes that are always clear. Only a cynical world could think him mad. If the madhouse seems almost an inevitable destination for him, and it does, it is only because the world is as corrupt as it is cynical, and it is wholly unable to bear the consequences of his campaign against it. Greaves actually lays down his armor, discarding the visible symbolic sign of his profession, after he defeats the bogus "knight of the griffin," but he does not leave off the practice of knight errantry, for his very next adventure takes him to the King's Bench, where he weeps at Felton's stories of manifold distresses. Immediately afterward Sycamore, the defeated knight who had thought he could "eclipse his rival even in his own lunatic sphere" (p. 187), has Greaves arrested and carried to the madhouse because he fears that his goodness will prevail with Aurelia and wants him out of the way. The simple ingenuity of this contrivance convicts the world of perverseness while also getting the hero into the place where he appears to belong with a minimum of dramatic fuss on Smollett's part. That Aurelia—the idealized heroine, perfect in innocence, exalted in her virtue—is also there only underscores the conviction. She too has been thought mad—or, rather, her uncle had earlier lodged a charge of lunacy against her when she refused to accede to his wishes and marry Sycamore. Somehow it seems completely appropriate that Greaves and Aurelia should discover each other in so wretched a place. When they do, the novel makes its darkest and most emphatic statement about the inversion of values, the depravity and corruption, that has closed about them and almost destroyed both their chance for happiness together and the very meaning of who they are as moral agents.

The madhouse is another microcosm, like the prison. Its inhabitants include, in the words of the incorrigibly mean-spirited (and drunken) poet Dick Distich, "fathers kidnapped by their children, wives confined by their husbands, gentlemen of fortune sequestered by their relations, and innocent persons immured by the malice of their adversaries" (p. 231). Only Distich is at all visually portrayed; Smollett otherwise conducts the major business of representing the miserable sufferers in the place by their speech, which is appropriately disjointed, delusional, frenzied, and in some cases even violent. Greaves first realizes where he is when he overhears snatches of this speech through the walls of his locked apartment—one voice is that of the "king" of Prussia, another is that of a religious fanatic, and there are still other crazed voices heard from a "mathematician," an "alchemist," a "pope" of Rome, and a fox-hunting squire (pp. 228–29). This moment is a verbal tour de force, more powerful than any picture could possibly be simply because derangement is much more effectively presented to the ear than to the eye. The eccentricities of what is heard are so far beyond the similar quirks of Captain Crowe's language as to put his particular oddity in clear perspective, as is also the case with the peculiarity—to the world, at any rate—of Greaves's exalted knightly style. For the voices heard from the inmates of the madhouse are the voices of true insanity, whereas the speech of Crowe and Greaves only reveals their goodness of heart—comically obsessive in the one, righteous and purposefully right in the other.

The truly sinister characters in the madhouse episode are Shackle, the unseen but powerful keeper, "a ruffian, capable of undertaking the darkest schemes of villainy" (p. 231), and the doctor whom Greaves rebukes both for his incompetence and for his disreputable part in Shackle's corrupt business of confining people illegally for profit. Significantly, Smollett represents the doctor's speech as no less disjointed and deranged than that of the inmates Greaves has overheard. "O! sir," he replies when the hero asks for a diagnosis

of his disorder, it "is a—kind of a—sir, —'tis very common in this country—a sort of a . . . not absolute madness—no—not madness—you have
heard, no doubt, of what is called a weakness of the nerves, sir." He continues
at length in this vein, leaving no doubt as to which man is insane. Greaves
himself reflects that "it was very hard that one man should not dare to ask the
most ordinary question without being reputed mad, while another should talk
nonsense by the hour, and yet be esteemed as an oracle" (p. 230). It is frustration with the absurdity and the injustice of what has happened to him that
provokes the long soliloquy during which Greaves, totally isolated and seemingly helpless, speaks to himself of the illusory "blessings enjoyed by the
British subject" (p. 232) whose life may be ruined by arbitrary confinement in
"such a prison" as "a private mad-house . . . , under the direction of a ruffian"
and worse than "the Bastile in France" or "the Inquisition in Portugal"
(p. 233).

With his lucky release at the hands of Tom Clarke and Captain Crowe,
Greaves is free to rescue Aurelia, punish Sycamore, prosecute Shackle, and
prepare for the happy ending to his story. It is difficult to gauge the full effect
of his knight errantry; he has righted some wrongs, relieved a number of distressed souls, and found the woman he loves. But he clearly has not rid the
world of all its trading justices; the King's Bench still encloses misery within
its walls; Shackle's madhouse may be shut down, but it is only one among
many; cruel guardians still tyrannize over their innocent wards. As I observed
in the earlier pages of this discussion, nothing really changes much; there is no
transformation of any kind. The final chapter of the novel simply rushes
Greaves and Aurelia away into their bliss, while also joining Tom Clarke with
Dolly Cowslip (after the mystery of her birth is removed) and restoring Captain Crowe to the inheritance he thought he had lost—to the crooked agency
of Ferret, as it turns out. In a repetition of the conclusions to *Roderick Random,*
Peregrine Pickle, and *Ferdinand Count Fathom,* the world is simply left behind, totally displaced by the joy that sets in after all the principals retreat from it to
the paradisal country. Once again Smollett resorts to the satirist's strategy of
repudiating what is and playing out a fantasy of what might be if goodness
were always rewarded as it ought to be. But by categorically denying to the
world any hope of transformation or redemption, *Sir Launcelot Greaves* places
even greater emphasis upon the mythic, upon the fable of virtue triumphant,

than the three earlier novels; for, if its vision is darker than theirs, and it is, then its ending is made all the more bright by the contrast it represents.

This effect is in large measure a result of the way in which Greaves and Aurelia are presented throughout the narrative. Greaves is physically a strong presence always, as I suggested earlier—from the moment of his initial appearance in chapter 2, through the description of him as an ideal figure almost immediately thereafter, to his active movement across the landscape of the novel and the drama of its successive episodes. But, other than in the opening scene at the Black Lion, he is never so vivid a *visual* presence as other characters—Crowe, Crabshaw, Ferret, Gobble and his wife, even Sycamore in his ridiculous get-up as Polydore, the knight of the griffin. As he always does with his unequivocally good characters, Smollett keeps the portrait of his hero at the level of an abstraction. In this respect Greaves is more like Renaldo, in *Ferdinand Count Fathom,* than he is like Roderick Random or Peregrine Pickle. And, also like Renaldo, he doubles the image of the woman he loves instead of having to move toward it, as Roderick and Perry do in their relations to Narcissa and Emilia. Aurelia is even more an abstraction than Greaves. Like the Quixote's Dulcinea, she is rarely seen—until the final chapter, when the hero is at last able to contemplate her beauty. Interestingly, instead of rhapsodizing upon her physical attributes, he is struck by her "good sense," her "virtue," her "vigour of mind," and a heart "frank, generous, and open; susceptible of the most tender impressions; glowing with a keen sense of honour, and melting with humanity" (p. 249). Deprived of her presence earlier, Greaves has only been able to think of her as an apparition, the beloved idea that inspires his knight-errantry. At one point when their paths cross she is masked and cannot be recognized at all (p. 149). On the occasion of their most important meeting in chapter 15, the narrator avoids precise descriptive detail, remarking of her only that she "shone with all the fabled graces of nymph or goddess," and of him that he matched her in amiability and in the beauty, elegance, and expressiveness of his features (p. 159). Throughout, Aurelia is the all but invisible reflection of Greaves's idealized self-construction as a quixotic hero, a presence he believes in even if he cannot see her—as he also believes in himself.

Greaves himself is fully bodied in the novel, but not when he is with her. We often see him, in his armor or out, engaged with an adversary in talk or battle, his manly figure completely visible; but in Aurelia's presence he merges with her into the generalized indistinctness of an idea. The obvious purpose of this strategy is to place virtue as an active but abstract conception into a dialectical opposition with the real, which is concrete, often making the latter so bizarre or twisted that it takes on the attributes of the *sur*real. The same effect is enhanced by the tense narrative relation between the seemingly erratic course of the hero's adventures—they take him wherever Aurelia and the troubles of others lead—and the regularity of the chapter divisions, with their repetition, eventually over almost equal numbers of words and pages, of rising action, falling action, and hook. The formal symmetry of the novel, already noted as most unusual for Smollett, is aligned directly with the principle of order embodied in the hero and heroine; its texture renders the disorder of experience, set off and made all the more vexing and threatening because it is enclosed by a structure with which it is in conflict. I observed earlier that *Sir Launcelot Greaves* is the most Hogarthian of all of Smollett's novels. This is so because its particular narrative tension most nearly duplicates the tension Hogarth always managed to create in his own serial narratives, each proceeding from one picture to another of the same size and shape, and then to another, every picture containing its own narrative of disorder and disruption and all of them accumulating to create the significance of a whole complex story. It is its Hogarthian tension, more than anything else, that is the source of the strange power of *Sir Launcelot Greaves*—and it is indeed a powerful novel, notwithstanding its sometimes annoying discursiveness and other flaws.

Even the ending works. It is much more appropriate dramatically and thematically than the endings to *Roderick Random, Peregrine Pickle,* and *Ferdinand Count Fathom,* and it is far less problematical because its tones of festivity and celebration are perfectly consistent with the high and always unequivocal nobility of the novel's central figure. It does not have to superimpose itself upon the story that precedes it. If Greaves is a reinvention of Don Quixote as a romance hero, then he takes on a stature that is doubly mythic. For the Quixote was already a fabled character in the minds of eighteenth-century British readers, a phenomenon Smollett was altogether willing to exploit; and a romance hero is always mythic. As the tangible embodiment of an abstract and quixotic idea of human virtue, Greaves acts out a fantasy of conflict met by unwavering resolve, of moral danger overcome by righteousness and wisdom. Such a fantasy can have no other than a perfect ending in affirmation for the hero and the reward of happiness in marriage to a heroine who, by mirroring him, is also of mythic stature.

The resolution to the story of Smollett's English Quixote has often been dismissed as a thoughtless contrivance, conventional and stale, weak and unsatisfying. This seems to me manifestly unfair, and of a piece with the general critical tendency over the years, already lamented in the earlier pages of this chapter, to misread and thus underestimate the work as a whole. *Sir Launcelot Greaves* is admittedly not Smollett's best novel, and finally it is not even among his most compelling—interesting, powerful, and skillful though it may be. But, like *Ferdinand Count Fathom,* it has always merited more praise than it has received from readers whose numbers have always been fewer than it has deserved. As I hope I have shown, its delights are real and its strengths are considerable. But this is all beginning to sound like special pleading—something that, in my introduction, I promised to avoid in this book. I shall resist the temptation to continue it so that I may turn now to the one novel by Smollett that needs no pleading at all, as it provides on every page the kind of substantive enjoyment that has always accumulated admirers and their praise—the last completed work of his life, and unquestionably a masterpiece by any standard, *The Expedition of Humphry Clinker.*

CHAPTER 5

Humphry Clinker

The relatively short step from the serial form of *Sir Launcelot Greaves* to the epistolary form of *Humphry Clinker* seems to have been an easy one for Smollett to take. It was surely made easier than it might have been otherwise by some of the work in which he engaged during the decade that separated the two novels. In the *Travels through France and Italy,* published at about the halfway point of that decade, he attempted the letter narrative for the first time, and with great success. The persona of this work writes with a distinctive voice, and to no identifiable correspondent, with the effect that, as the sole registering consciousness, he is able to keep the focus about equally divided between the objects of his observation and his always precise and extremely idiosyncratic responses to them. Smollett's traveler is more than just a dry run for the character of Matthew Bramble, but, as many of his readers have noticed over the years, the two bear close resemblances to one another in temperament and in their expressive styles.[1] By writing the *Travels* Smollett admirably prepared himself for the more ambitious fictional narrative of the peripatetic principals of *Humphry Clinker,* not just for the character of Matt but for the other four correspondents as well, each of them a distinctive voice in his or her own right and all of them engaged in negotiating the relations between private consciousness and the public environment in which the itinerant life must be lived.

Just two years after the *Travels* appeared, Smollett began issuing the weekly six-penny numbers of *The Present State of All Nations.* The first number was published in late June 1768, and while the work was projected from the beginning for collection into a multi-volume set (the set was printed in eight volumes, 1768–69), with goodly portions of it probably written by other hands, a careful reading of the sections known certainly to be Smollett's—the more than 400 pages of the first three volumes devoted to England and Scotland—reveals a rhythm of natural breaks in the narrative movement suggesting that he attempted to make each of the individual weekly installments close in such a way as to pique audience interest in the next one—as he had done with the monthly installments of *Sir Launcelot Greaves*.[2] Louis L. Martz has shown conclusively that Smollett's work on the *Present State* was crucial in the background of his treatment of England and Scotland in *Humphry Clinker*,[3] but without hinting at any formal connection between the two works. Yet there does seem to have been such a connection, real and important if minor, as the experience of writing the *Present State* surely helped Smollett meet the challenge of sustaining a continuous narrative in *Humphry Clinker* while making each of its letters a thing complete in itself. This connection deserves notice in any consideration of the novel's genesis. The same might be said for Smollett's journalistic efforts—his continued work on the *Critical Review* through the year 1763, his numerous essay contributions to the *British Magazine,* and his weekly labors on the *Briton;* this work, too, enforced a kind of formal constraint, along with the habit of attending to the need for brevity, clear focus, and frequent closure.

All of these projects, together with the composition of *Sir Launcelot Greaves,* taught Smollett how to write in such a manner as to make *Humphry Clinker* truly a triumphant example of the eighteenth-century novel in letters. From them he learned a new way of disciplining his natural tendency to write episodically, pictorially, spatially. No other novelist of Smollett's time, not even Richardson, was able to generate a comparable range of particularized voices and styles in an epistolary work of such compression and such insistent dramatic, emotional, and moral tension between the realms of private and public experience. If each of *Humphry Clinker*'s eighty-two letters is a discrete and self-contained unit, each is also deeply personal, a little drama of energetic feeling and action. Many letters are remarkable for a visual precision so striking that it momentarily suspends all forward motion both within the individual letter and within the larger narrative of which it is a part. We have seen this effect in others of Smollett's novels, but not always with the same intensity, which is to say that *Humphry Clinker* represents no lessening of Smollett's fidelity to a Hogarthian model.

The epistolary mode is reflective, since a letter is a private communication written in a condition of isolation, and yet it is outwardly directed too. By writing, the author of a letter seeks to take possession of his or her audience—the public beyond the self—by contriving to manipulate it into understanding. But the form engages necessarily in a paradox, for the letter-writer is also at risk of being owned by the public world, which is the provocation for private expression and, to a great extent, its determinant as well. That is to say, a letter arises from the need to account for and (usually) to justify personal action and feeling, and so it not only gives shape to the remembered facts of private experience but also articulates the letter-writer's response to those facts in a way that seems appropriate for a particular intended audience. A letter is not, as readers of epistolary fiction used to say (especially about the letters in the novels of Richardson, who promoted this view himself), a spontaneous utterance, a gesture of "writing to the moment," but a construction of events and of the self in relation to them. Smollett clearly understood this, but he varied the usual dynamic of epistolarity by allowing us almost no knowledge of the effects the letters sent by his five correspondents have upon their recipients—we see no answers to any of them, and only very occasionally is there even the slightest hint that an answer to a letter has been received. The public world Smollett's characters address in *Humphry Clinker* is essentially that of the reader, who receives *all* of their letters and is obliged to put together the fragments of the narrative—the letters themselves, in all their variety of voices and sensibilities—so as to grasp the novel's overriding, comprehensive conception of moral and social reality. The five separate sequences of letters develop as sustained personal narratives, yet these narratives overlap, and none is complete without all of the others—we cannot fully understand Matt's narrative without Jery's, or Jery's without Matt's, or Lydia's without those of both her uncle and her brother; and so forth. Something like this is also true of the central parallel narratives in *Clarissa*—the heroine's narrative, and Lovelace's. But Smollett, in a work much less prolix, achieves a far greater complication of interlinking effects by imagining more than twice as many primary correspondents; and, unlike Richardson, he places their sepa-

rate stories into complementary rather than competing relations with one another, which is why they are able to move so credibly toward the novel's har-
monious ending.

This point requires elaboration. Richardson's novel, as it endlessly refines
and clarifies its letter-writers' perceptions, deals in absolutes—Clarissa and
Lovelace see themselves, each other, and the world in ways that are altogether
opposite, and there is never any possibility that their two sets of perceptions might be brought together. Smollett deals not in absolutes but in rela-
tivities and ambiguities, and in the end reconciliation among alternative
perceptions—most importantly those figuring in the letters of Matt, Jery,
and Lydia—proves not only possible but inevitable. The contrast between
Humphry Clinker and *Clarissa* is of course not merely a matter of technique;
and besides, the issue is not whether one novel is better than the other because of its particular conception of character or its rendering of voice and
perception. The two works are simply different. *Clarissa* is a prose tragedy dramatizing the chaotic and disastrous results of a conflict between two specific
absolutes of good and evil; it is thus necessarily all about the inexorable process by which the total isolation of its primary correspondents deepens into
the grim reality of death. *Humphry Clinker* is a comedy, and it therefore quite
naturally resolves its ambiguities into clarity, the initial disorder and alterity of
its multiple voices into order and oneness. But as a novel in letters it has always been seen to pale by comparison with *Clarissa,* when in fact it is fully as
remarkable an achievement in its own separate way. If in this brief and very
general consideration of the two works together I have wished to describe
Richardson's practice as a way of highlighting Smollett's, I have also wished to
claim for *Humphry Clinker* the kind of recognition that is its due. The eighteenth century produced not just one genuine masterpiece of epistolary fiction, but two.

All of Smollett's novels are comedies, of course, in the purest modal sense,
but they all strain themselves over a tension created by the strong satiric
impulses that drive them. *Roderick Random, Peregrine Pickle, Ferdinand Count
Fathom,* and *Sir Launcelot Greaves* end with that tension unresolved as their heroes and heroines very deliberately retreat from a world they have altogether
repudiated and come to rest in a mythic rural paradise. It is understandable
that so many critics, from Ronald Paulson to John Skinner, have arrived at the

conclusion that these novels are really satires with comic endings that ring false because they are imposed arbitrarily—and with a hurry that adds to the impression that they are forced.[4] It should be clear by now that I do not agree with this stock assessment. Smollett cared nothing about consistency of form or mode. His first four novels are satiric narratives that shift and give way to comedy, but their satiric vision of the world is never actually yielded up or modulated into the comic; it is simply displaced, like the world itself. *Humphry Clinker* is different. I want to save extended discussion of this novel's ending to later pages, for the reconciliation there enacted cannot be adequately accounted for without careful consideration of what precedes it. But here it is worth pausing briefly to describe the way in which Smollett develops his novel's tension between the modes of satire and comedy before finally resolving it.

Both modes are given strong and explicit expression from the opening pages of the novel. Matt's voice is the satiric one, and it is the first voice heard, in the very first letter. Irritated, constipated, gouty, Matt immediately announces that he is "distressed in mind and body" (p. 7)—he is from the beginning a "risible misanthrope," in the words of Thomas R. Preston,[5] poised to lash out at the world. In the fourth letter Jery's comic voice is heard for the first time. "I have got into a family of originals," he writes (p. 10), establishing his position as observer and preparing himself to be perpetually amused as the family journey proceeds. If Jery is "a pert jackanapes" at this point, full—as Matt says—of "college-petulance and self-conceit" (p. 13), that will gradually change as he grows more and more fond of his irascible uncle and love-bitten sister. Matt flails about in later letters, agitated by astonishment and sometimes outrage at what he witnesses, while Jery maintains his balance. Life is a "farce," he writes from Bath, "which I am determined to enjoy as long as I can," adding that the "follies, that move my uncle's spleen, excite my laughter" (p. 48). It is Jery who, as the novel arrives at its festive conclusion in multiple weddings and clarified personal relationships, makes the definitive statement about it: "The comedy is near a close," he says, and "the curtain is ready to drop" (p. 330). Throughout, the *idea* of life as comedy guides all of his responses to the world, while in an epistemological sense the model of comedy as a literary form provides a presiding metaphor that helps him both to understand what he observes as more fit for mirth than scorn and, progressively, to move from smug detachment to sympathetic engagement. With Jery, all of the other correspondents progress from the isolation signified in their early letters, written in radically different tones and often from contradictory perceptions, to a heightened sense of community and a capacity to rejoice in one another; this is true even of the linguistic and emotional outsiders Tabitha and Winifred, whose malapropisms and limited sensibilities initially set them far apart from their fellow travelers. This progression affirms the rightness of Jery's understanding of life, which prevails unequivocally at the end. Tabby and Win yield passively to the inevitability of it; Lydia's romance fantasy is finally fulfilled and coincides with it; most importantly, Matt abandons satire in favor of it. It was surely by no accident that Smollett gave the greatest number of letters in the novel (fifty-five of the total) to the two characters who most clearly articulate the competing modes of seeing and knowing that create its primary tension. Those by the comic writer Jery, we may note, outnumber those by his uncle the satirist.[6]

In a seminal essay published more than thirty years ago, Sheridan Baker called *Humphry Clinker* a comic romance, arguing that it develops a burlesque of romance as one way of promoting its own comic vision.[7] Baker's argument quite rightly remains essentially unchallenged, though I believe the term *burlesque* is too strong as a description of what Smollett does with romance in his novel. Certainly there are burlesque elements. Clinker—poor and ragged, bumbling, foolish—is in most respects the absurd inverse of a romance hero. His very name plays a joke upon romance convention, and a scatological one at that: "Humphry" echoes with romance associations, but suffers reduction both by a deliberate misspelling and by a corollary association with the proverbial "to dine with Duke Humphrey"—that is, to dine in poverty; "Clinker" directly undercuts the attenuated romance associations of "Humphry"—by its sound, of course, but even more because in the eighteenth century it was the name for a blacksmith's cinder (appropriately enough, as Humphry was bred to the forge as a farrier) and also a slang term for a specimen of human excrement. Smollett's titular "hero" does not even appear until the novel is well underway, and when he does come on the scene his posteriors are bare, signaling—even before we are told his name—his role as a device for spoofing the very idea of exalted heroism as embodied in romance. But, as Win Jenkins notices, the skin he exposes is "as fair as Alabaster" (p. 78), a sure indication—straight from romance convention—that he is not what he seems to be. Despite his fumbling and bumbling, Clinker possesses a natural simplicity of heart and nobility of character and thus, as Baker and others have frequently noted, he embodies the values that help in the end to draw the Bramble family together in a union of spirit and human feeling. Smollett even gives him his own birth-mystery plot, for he is revealed to be Bramble's natural son, the offspring of one of the amours of his college days at Oxford. Transformed into Matthew Loyd, he fully assumes the role—if not quite the stature—of a romance hero.

Humphry Clinker is the best evidence that Smollett's version of romance is comic, not burlesque, for the transformation that elevates him socially and gives him a new identity is, in moral terms, not a radical one; it is not at all the stuff of farce, the extravagance of which is essential to the distortions of burlesque, for it expresses recognition of Clinker's genuine merit. Transformation of just this kind is a principal motif of the novel's strategy of allowing its central characters to recreate themselves by writing down, in their letters, the process of their interaction with one another and the world. They are all transformed in the end. A second birth-mystery plot, this one treated not at all comically, confirms the importance of this motif, as Wilson becomes George Dennison, bringing Lydia's visionary romance to a happy conclusion and thus both validating and authenticating it; the story of Lydia and Dennison is a story of romance made "real," and it works because Lydia has grown from a giddy girl, the prototype of Sheridan's Lydia Languish[8]—"she has got a languishing eye," Matt says of her in his first letter, "and reads romances" (p. 13)—into a young woman of refined feeling. *Humphry Clinker* does partake of the spirit of Cervantes; both Clinker and Lismahago are versions of the Quixote figure, and the latter is actually introduced (p. 182) with a conspicuous reference to the way in which he resembles the ridiculous Spanish knight. In other words, Smollett's last novel stops far short of repeating the recuperative adaptation of romance carried out in *Sir Launcelot Greaves*. Instead, it spoofs the same form as a way of reducing it to its essentials, a set of enduring values—benevolence of spirit, clarity of understanding and integrity of action, faithfulness to friends, family, and ideals, love and its redemptive power—that serve to focus the moral vision promoted in the novel as a whole.

Romance, important as it is in *Humphry Clinker,* is only one ingredient in a remarkably eclectic mix. The novel is almost a Bakhtinian carnival of the crossing, superimposing, and interlinking of generic forms. As an example of the quite common eighteenth-century practice of joining the travel narrative and the story in letters it shows exceptional originality, for—even more than the semi-fictional *Travels through France and Italy*—it maintains a delicate balance between observers and observed, always interesting the reader in the former at least as much as in the latter.[9] It is in addition a "historical" or "biographical" study of a set of quite ordinary people, it is a narrative anatomy of contemporary society, and it is a fable of passage through the world of experience—for Matt especially, in B. L. Reid's descriptive phrase, it is a "healing journey."[10] *Humphry Clinker* even throws in elements of the criminal narrative with its introduction of the highwayman Martin and its comic episode of Clinker's arrest, trial, and imprisonment. As I have said elsewhere, "one suspects that Smollett, in projecting what he must have known would be his last book, sought to join in a kind of definitive, paradigmatic form the many assorted attractions of the new and developing art of the novel as practiced by his seminal generation of writers."[11] By so doing, and by so effectively merging the narrative kinds he adopted, he created a new novelistic hybrid, in the process also achieving what Robert Folkenflik has praised as a surprising "unity in variety."[12] In the preceding chapter I suggested that, for Smollett, *Humphry Clinker* was a celebration of the novel as a form. Certainly it seems to have been just that. Possibly it was meant to answer Sterne, as Sterne had answered Richardson, Fielding, and Smollett himself in his so-called anti-novel *Tristram Shandy,* with an affirmation of nearly every accessible narrative possibility in a kind of pro-novel tour de force. Whether or not this is so, the public had never seen anything like *Humphry Clinker* when it appeared. The story of its warm reception has been too often told to require repetition here.[13] It is enough to observe that reviewers raved about its originality, private readers laughed about it in their correspondence, essayists praised it as a triumph, and booksellers all over the British Isles issued some two dozen editions of it before 1800. Smollett, dead in Italy before he could ever have known his novel was a hit with critics and public alike, was sadly deprived of the acceptance and acclaim he had spent a lifetime wishing for and deserving. We can only speculate that he must somehow have known his last novel was his best work, and that his final days were gladdened by that knowledge.

Smollett's readers were drawn to *Humphry Clinker* not only by the many attractions I have been outlining over the last several pages, but also—no doubt—by the way in which the novel weaves an intricate pattern of historical references into its multi-form texture. *Humphry Clinker* is, in fact, the most historically grounded of all Smollett's novels. This should not be surprising, as he devoted perhaps the greatest share of his time and energy to historical writing during the decade preceding the novel's publication—he completed all work on his *Continuation* of the *Complete History,* brought the *Modern Part* of the massive *Universal History* to a conclusion,[14] supervised and contributed to the *Present State,* and wrote his amazing historical satire, the *Adventures of an Atom.* History, past and contemporary, enters all of Smollett's novels, as we have seen, but it is at the very center of *Humphry Clinker,* giving the work a topical value unusual even for Smollett. The world so closely observed by the Bramble family traveling party is a world of real people and real places, so precisely represented that, as its details accumulate, the boundary between fiction and nonfiction seriously blurs. There is less uncertainty—less experimentation, too—in *Humphry Clinker*'s management of the relations between the historical and the imagined than in Smollett's other novels; the stop-action effects of individual episodes frequently seem to freeze historical moments in time, emphasizing the precedence of the spatial over the temporal, but otherwise time is less a relative conception than it is in, say, *Roderick Random;* instead, it is a particularizing one. The letters are dated (the first is written on the second day of April, the last on the twentieth day of November), and though there are minor chronological inaccuracies,[15] on the whole they display Smollett's great care to place them credibly within a clearly defined temporal framework; even the intervals between them (varying from three or four days to a few weeks) are consistent both with the circumstances prompting them (a scene observed and impulsively described; a response to a letter received; the fulfillment of a promise to continue with a subject started in an earlier letter, not yet answered) and with what we know about the speed of the post during the period when the novel's action takes place.

That period is clearly the mid-1760s, between 1763 and 1768, when the architecture of the younger John Wood was continuing the transformation of

the city of Bath begun by his father, when Methodism and religious enthusiasm were flourishing as they had never done before, when the treaty of 1763
that concluded the Seven Years' War was still controversial, like the principal
figures in its negotiation—Pitt and Bute, both now out of office but not out
of the public consciousness.[16] There are few of those tricks with historical
time and the historical event Smollett played so interestingly in *Ferdinand
Count Fathom* and the other novels of his youth, when he was obviously ex-
perimenting with the ways in which fiction could interpret the real by recreating its defining temporal moments. Anachronisms do occur, but generally not
as the result of a shuffling of chronology; instead, Smollett engages in something like a warping of time by which he is able to make actual relics of the
past appear in the novel's present. Thus he introduces the superannuated actor James Quin, for example, whom Matt greets as an old friend in Bath, but
whom Smollett had blasted in *Roderick Random* for his part in keeping *The Regicide* off the stage—Smollett was very likely making amends by portraying his
former enemy as a jolly soul, mellowed by age and claret and full of the good
humor that makes for entertaining company; and we meet the duke of Newcastle, long out of power but still holding his daily levee, the object of
Smollett's wrathful contempt for many years and the butt of ferociously exco-
riating jokes in the *Adventures of an Atom,* now presented as a ridiculous old
man who cannot even remember the names of his onetime political allies and
does not know that Cape Breton is an island.

In *Humphry Clinker,* Smollett's focus is emphatically upon the recognizably
present world in which he and his readers lived. As he develops that focus, he
admirably exploits all the possibilities of the travel format. His evocations of
place are, so far as can be determined, painstakingly accurate. The cities described in the letters, particularly those of Matt and Jery, exactly catch what
those cities—Bath, London, Edinburgh, Glasgow, and the rest—would have
seemed at the time to visitors of differing sensibilities; the travelers stop at
real inns, some of them still standing; the descriptions of the Scottish landscape and its culture, though obviously a nostalgic indulgence for Smollett,
are drawn very largely from his historical account in the *Present State.*[17] His
method throughout is comprehensive. He allows his travelers to circle around
every place to which he takes them, presenting different views and perspec-
tives in their separate letters, until the place itself—including the people en-

countered in it—is seen whole. The reader who follows those letters, page after page, is made to feel almost as though he or she were taking the same journey, while seeing the sights with the eyes of others. Smollett's earliest readers
could have taken the same journey; it still can be done now, though many of
the places have changed as time has passed and buildings have disappeared—
indeed it has been done, by the editor of the Georgia *Humphry Clinker,*
Thomas R. Preston.

The travel narrative, then, is the medium for the historicism of *Humphry
Clinker.* But it is much more than that. It provides the dominant ordering
principle for the novel's structure, the circular pattern of its movement from
beginning to end, as the characters progress from Gloucester, at the Welsh
border, across the south of England through Bristol and Bath to London,
then north to Scotland, and finally south again in a path toward their home.
The journey occasions all the letters, and the letters are in turn the medium
through which the characters reveal themselves to us as they record the effects their journey has upon them. Their individual letters particularize those
effects, allowing the reader to observe them unseen, with the stolen intimacy
of a voyeur—as though all of the letters had been intercepted before reaching
their destinations and then spread out for secret perusal, leaving the authors
with their defenses down. The great success of *Humphry Clinker* as a set of
character studies depends absolutely upon this stolen intimacy, which—this
is the strategy—catches the letter-writers in attitudes and postures not intended to be seen by anyone except those whom they address.

And of course it is the novel's characters, caught in this way, who provide
its greatest charm as they detail the places and scenes in which they find themselves. Smollett is never more vivid in transmitting felt reality than he is in almost every letter of *Humphry Clinker.* Only *Roderick Random,* with its autobiographical voice, renders the world with comparable urgency; but *Roderick
Random,* because it features only one voice, lacks both the variety and the
range of *Humphry Clinker*—though it must be said, too, that *Humphry Clinker*
lacks the singleminded ferocity of Roderick's frequently anguished story.
Comparisons of this kind between the two novels finally do not mean much,
since they are such different works, except as a way of highlighting the power
each has to project individual sensibilities. *Roderick Random,* even to a reader
who knew nothing of its author or his career, would seem to be a novel writ-

ten from the perspective of youth—it is not just singleminded and self-absorbed in its expressions of indignation against a hostile and unpredictable universe, but absolutely certain of the justice of its own self-righteousness. Smollett punishes Roderick for his excesses before redeeming him and sending him into the bliss of marriage and rural retirement, but does not moderate his own uncompromising position before the world his novel scourges and finally rejects. If *Humphry Clinker* seems a more mature and balanced work, that is because it acknowledges the need for accommodation so as to achieve the equilibrium necessary for happiness *in* the world. Indeed, *Humphry Clinker* is the first of Smollett's novels to do so. It is, as I have already suggested, the only one in which a comic vision prevails from the first page to the last. How odd, too, and touching, since the enactment of this gesture of accommodation occurred just as Smollett himself was about to leave the world forever.

With the exception of the eponymous hero, a noble simpleton, all of the principals in *Humphry Clinker* suffer from an internal division of sensibilities—though to varying degrees, of course. The accommodations with which their separate stories conclude bring an end to internal conflict and signify their triumph over it. As we know, the issue of the fragmented self was a constant one for Smollett, both as a man and as a writer, and it is an interesting fact of his life and career that he was most emphatic about it in his first and last novels, which are also the two works from his entire canon that came most directly from his personal experience—in an earlier chapter I touched on the autobiographical elements of *Roderick Random,* and it is widely accepted that the irascible but tender-hearted Matt Bramble is a self-portrait (though not an exact one) of his author.[18] Our sense of the issue's especially crucial importance in these two works arises largely from their personally expressive modes, the autobiographical narrative and the letter, but the modes themselves may well have been chosen because they *are* so intensely personal. At the risk of appearing to psychoanalyze Smollett, it is worth observing that *Roderick Random* and *Humphry Clinker* very probably gave outlet to strongly felt needs at critical times in his life—in the case of the former work, for articulation of a definition of the self as isolated in a brutal, unfeeling world that dashes the hopes of youth; in the case of the latter, for reflection upon the journey of life as, most properly, a passage from alienation to communal engagement, a quest for the personal fulfillment that comes only with the balancing of high principles and affectionate, amused tolerance for the imperfections of human society.

But I do not mean to suggest that *Humphry Clinker* sentimentalizes its characters or its plot of conflict leading to reconciliation. On the contrary: because of the multiple voices it represents the fragmentation of experience even more completely than *Roderick Random* is able to do with its single voice, and it never blinks from the task.[19] From the outset *Humphry Clinker* establishes both the internal tension that divides the characters within themselves and the external conflict that separates them from the world and from each other. Matt, for years, has been living the sedentary life on his Welsh estate; Jery is fresh from Oxford, full of the superior attitudes engendered in that seat of elitist isolation; Lydia, all naïveté and innocence, has been at boarding school under the watchful care of a governess who has protected her from the knowledge of anything beyond its grounds; Tabitha, always kept at arm's length by the brother with whom she has lived, is still trapped in the loneliness forced upon her by her spinster's role and by her tormenting eccentricities of personality; the servant Win, a mix of silliness and simplicity, necessarily resides at the edges of life. It is the process of their coming to know one another that leads all five correspondents to greater knowledge of and comfort in the world—and, at least in the cases of Matt, Jery, and Lydia, to greater self-knowledge and full, healthy emotional balance.

Significantly, the first letter of the novel is Matt's. "The pills are good for nothing," he writes to Dr. Lewis; "I have told you over and over, how hard I am to move" (p. 7). The hilarious implied conjunction of two defining ideas of movement—as a loosening of the bowels and as a breaking of the habits of inertia—establish instantly the nature of Matt's fundamental problem with life, the reason why he is emotionally repressed and physically cramped. We will remember that, for Smollett the physician, the attributes of the external body were signs of the interior life, and that the vital, healthy body was a body in motion. Matt is gouty and constipated because he is sedentary and irritable, but of course he is inclined to remain sedentary and irritable because he is gouty and constipated. He resists the journey he has undertaken, tolerating the idea of it only because it may help Lydia to stay out of harm's (i.e., Wilson's) way and because of the bare possibility that it may make him feel better. He resists it even more once it is underway because, as he says in his second letter, he is "surrounded with domestic vexations" (p. 13). But we also know from his earliest letters that Matt is at heart all benevolence. "Let Morgan's widow have the Alderney cow, and forty shillings to clothe her children," he instructs Dr. Lewis within a few lines of his complaint about his bowels (p. 7); his tirade about domestic vexations, which progresses through a litany of all their causes in the assorted offenses against his peace committed by the members of his family, is followed by expressions of tenderness for those in the broader community who depend on him—in response to some unwanted advice about the prudent management of his estate, he writes that he will "not begin at this time of day" to "distress" his tenants "because they are unfortunate, and cannot make regular payments" (p. 16).

Matt seems unconscious of the internal divisions he reveals in his letters, but they are obvious to the reader. And they are obvious to Jery, too. The smug young Oxonian recoils from his "so unpleasant" uncle at first—"rather than be obliged to keep him company," he says, "I'd resign all claim to the inheritance of his estate" (p. 10). But his view quickly softens as he becomes convinced that Matt suffers both from bodily pain and from "a natural excess of mental sensibility" (p. 18), and he is genuinely moved by the unaffected kindness of Matt's gift of twenty pounds to a poor widow—"the tears ran down my cheeks," he admits (p. 24). Jery's tears are, of course, the earliest sign of his own divided sensibilities. Matt is right to describe him early on as a "pert jackanapes," for he is full of himself as a worldly sophisticate in the midst of boors; but he also loves Lydia and wishes to protect her, and he grows increasingly fond of his grumpy uncle, whose character, he acknowledges, "opens and improves upon me every day. . . . He affects misanthropy, in order to conceal the sensibility of a heart, which is tender, even to a degree of weakness" (p. 29). To this shrewd assessment of Matt he adds another later on, during the extended episode at Bath: "He is splenetic with his familiars only; and not even with them, while they keep his attention employed; but when his spirits are not exerted externally, they seem to recoil and prey upon himself" (p. 48). Jery only rarely lets down his guard to display his own feelings directly, but his sensitivity to Matt is a sure sign of the tender heart he manages to conceal behind his manner of bemused detachment.

Tabitha and Win display internal divisions too, primarily through the language of their letters rather than through their actions—though Tabitha, as the novel approaches its ending, does change in ways that mark a difference from her earlier termagant's manner, as both Matt and Jery acknowledge; she is not the one-dimensional grotesque she first appears to be in their letters and in her own. She is at the outset a "fantastical animal" (p. 13), a "wildcat" (p. 15), as Matt characterizes her. Jery, in his first letter, describes her as "a maiden of forty-five, exceedingly starched, vain, and ridiculous" (p. 10); later, while at Bath, he repeats this same information and then proceeds to fill out her portrait in great detail. "In her person," he writes,

> she is tall, raw-boned, aukward, flat-chested, and stooping; her complexion is sallow and freckled; her eyes are not grey, but greenish, like those of a cat, and generally inflamed; her hair is of a sandy, or rather dusty hue; her forehead low; her nose long, sharp, and, towards the extremity, always red in cool weather; her lips skinny, her mouth extensive, her teeth straggling and loose, of various colours and conformation; and her long neck shrivelled into a thousand wrinkles—In her temper, she is proud, stiff, vain, imperious, prying, malicious, greedy, and uncharitable. (pp. 58–59)

Jery goes on at length with a history of his aunt's man-hunting escapades and an assessment of her character—"She is one of those geniuses," he concludes, "who find some diabolical enjoyment in being dreaded and detested by their fellow-creatures" (p. 59). All of what Jery says of her is true; but he, like Matt, seems unaware of the loneliness and insecurity of her dependent, marginalized position, with no friend or adherent but her wretched dog Chowder, whose spirit is as mean as his mistress's. The softening of Tabitha's character after Matt forces her to choose between himself and the dog (she loves and needs Matt more after all) suggests that Smollett was fully conscious of her plight, though he sustains her as a comic grotesque to the end. Finally, even her brother and her nephew note that she becomes positively docile, even gentle, when she is at last joined in marriage with the only fitting suitor she has ever found, and the only man who would ever have her, the equally comic (and almost equally grotesque) Obadiah Lismahago.

The truth is, of course, that such sympathetic understanding for Tabitha as the novel reveals is obscured by the power of Jery's portrait and by the hilarity of her letters. Smollett plays her almost entirely for laughs, and he consistently emphasizes more than anything else her greed, self-absorption, and general crudity of feeling—her nearly total inability, until the end, to relate to the rest of the world. The portrait itself is worthy of Hogarth; indeed, as Pamela Cantrell has argued convincingly, it was almost certainly drawn after the central figure of Hogarth's *Morning,* the first of the pictures in a famous series entitled *The Four Times of Day* (1738).[20] Hogarth's character, and Smollett's, betray the same vanity and hypocrisy (the figure in *Morning* is blithely walking to church on a cold day, wearing a fashionable dress that exposes her skinny arms and her flat, bony chest to the freezing air), while they are similarly indifferent to the world around them. Tabitha is utterly incapable of a charitable act; and Hogarth's lady, says Cantrell, only notices (and is offended by) the two lovers among the several figures who appear in her way, while she does not see the other people at all, as they are beneath her. "The lady believes she should be admired for her superiority," says Cantrell, "but in fact she is, because of her narrow view of life and lack of human compassion, less honorable than the poor people who surround her. She suffers from a skewed sense of values, in other words, valuing wealth and appearance over kindness and empathy" (p. 79).

Jery's portrait of Tabitha is Smollett at his pictorial best, and it is one of the most memorable among many fine drawings of eccentrics and comic figures in *Humphry Clinker.* The echo of Hogarth only enhances its effect for anyone who has seen the print of *Morning,* though no reader needs to know Hogarth's picture in order to appreciate Smollett's. The record of Tabitha's letters (there are six of them) creates just as fine an effect, expanding upon the portrait by giving her a medium for expression of her own character. If the overall treatment of her in the novel hints at soft places beneath her ridiculously starched facade, the letters reveal another kind of division by their extremely funny malapropisms, most of them turning upon sexual or other scatological jokes. We know from Jery and Matt that the pious, stiff, money-grubbing middle-aged maiden is a sex-starved predator eager to use her substantial fortune of four thousand pounds to ensnare any man she can. What her letters show is that her libido is even stronger than her powerful desire for the security of marriage, and that she is unconsciously fixated upon bodily functions. By simply allowing her to write, Smollett reduces her to the fundamentals of her own nature. In her very first letter she makes mention of Chowder's bowels (he has been "construpated") and instructs Mrs. Gwyllim, the housekeeper at

William Hogarth, *Morning* (Engraving, 1738).
(By permission of The Huntington Library, San Marino, California.)

Brambleton Hall, to take care that the gate is "shit every evening before dark," closing with a reference to the castration of "Dicky," one of the farm animals (p. 8). In later letters she worries about the maids, all "a-gog after the men" (p. 44), and complains to "Doctor Lews" about one of the estate employees, Roger—"Roger gets this, and Roger gets that," she writes, "but I'd have you to know, I won't be rogered at this rate by any ragmatical fellow in the kingdom" (p. 75). Still further on, having received no answer from the doctor, she declares to Mrs. Gwyllim that she will have nothing more to do with him, "though he beshits me on his bended knees," adding the admonition that she should "keep a watchfull eye over the hind Williams, who is one of his amissories, and, I believe, no better than he should be at bottom" (p. 153).

Tabitha's last two letters contain her most hilarious sexual malapropisms. As she contemplates the family's eventual return home, she sends Mrs. Gwyllim orders to "let Roger search into, and make a general clearance of the slit holes which the maids have in secret," and then passes on the news of the budding romance between Win and Clinker: The latter is "a pious young man," she says, "who has laboured exceedingly, that she may bring forth fruits of repentance. I make no doubt," she continues, "but he will take the same pains with that pert hussey Mary Jones, and all of you," concluding with a "fervent prayer" that "he may have power given to penetrate and instill his goodness, even into your most inward parts" (p. 264). Following her marriage, which is to relieve her of all responsibilities as manager of her brother's household, she writes a final letter to Mrs. Gwyllim, instructing her to "get your accunts ready for inspection, as we are coming home without further delay" (p. 336). All of Tabitha's letters betray her ignorance and ineptitude with language, their hilarity enforcing the reader's awareness of a large chasm between her social pretensions and her inelegance of character while also emphasizing comic associations between her self-absorbed obsessions with money and with sex. Both obsessions are all about possession and power. In reality Tabitha has none of the latter, which is why it is possible to feel a certain sympathy for her; and she wants nothing more than to act out the former obsession—also, perhaps, a reason for sympathy, since she has essentially nothing of her own, but even more a source of the laughter and the irritation her words and her actions excite in the reader and, as we know from their own letters, in Matt and Jery.

I have lingered over the character of Tabitha because I believe that she deserves more than she usually gets from those critics who write of her, which is
a few expressions of amusement and a word or two about her as a type of the
comic spinster. *Humphry Clinker*'s other malapropist, Winifred Jenkins, is in
the main no more than a foil to Tabitha, and so I can deal with her more
briefly.[21] Win's simple innocence, her goodness of heart, and her wide-eyed
wonder at the world into which the family journey has taken her contrasts
sharply with her mistress's deviousness, meanness, and obtuseness. Even
her vanities, by comparison with Tabitha's, seem only harmless expressions
of silliness. When Jery's foppish valet Dutton seduces her affections, then
dresses her in a ridiculously pretentious style for an evening at the theater, she
is only a charming picture of absurdity—"all of a flutter," as Jery describes
her, truly "remarkable for the frisure of her head" and for the priming and
patching of her face, "from the chin up to the eyes" (pp. 202–3). Win's letters
are a pure delight; she is the only one of the five correspondents in the novel
who seems untroubled by conflicting needs and impulses—she is altogether
unconscious as she exposes the comic opposition between her determination
to appear proper and respectable and her accidentally expressed desire for
sex. What Win does in the novel, besides providing a lot of laughs, is keep the
issue of sexuality as a primary source of healthy comic energy constantly alive.
In the end she is, with her marriage to Clinker, a proof that the fulfillment of
sexual desire can express a festive sense of oneness with what is desired—
their marriage, the last to be recorded in the novel, rings out its clearest and
purest celebratory note.

A sampling from Win's letters will suffice to illustrate her character as she
presents it. "What is life but a veil of affliction?" she writes to Mary Jones after Clinker is mistakenly arrested for robbery and sent to prison. "O Mary! the
whole family have been in such a constipation!" It was the power of Clinker's
faith (he is a "pyehouse young man"), she believes, that got him released—
with a little assistance from "Apias Korkus, who lives with the ould bailiff";
he "is, indeed, a very powerfull labourer in the Lord's vineyard," and, as she
tells Mary, she has no doubt that "all of us, will be brought" by his endeavors
"to produce blessed fruit of generation and repentance. . . . O Mary Jones,
pray without seizing for grease to prepare you for the operations of this won-
derful instrument, which, I hope, will be exorcised this winter upon you and

others at Brambleton-hall" (p. 152). "O, if I was given to tail-baring," she proclaims on a later occasion, "I have my own secrets to discover——There has been a deal of huggling and flurtation betwixt my mistress and an ould Scots officer, called Kismycago" (p. 213). The joke here, of course, is that Win's tail *was* bared when a fire in the inn at Harrowgate forced her to descend by ladder from her apartment into the arms of her rescuer Clinker, dressed only in her nightgown. The "moon shone very bright," Jery remarks in his amused description of the incident, "and a fresh breeze of wind blowing, none of Mrs. Winifred's beauties could possibly escape the view of the fortunate Clinker, whose heart was not able to withstand the united force of so many charms; at least, I am much mistaken, if he has not been her humble slave from that moment" (p. 170). It is the desire kindled on that night that enflames both Win and Clinker with the idea of marrying. As a sign that their wedding is intended as a pure comic celebration of the reconciliations with which the novel concludes, Smollett assigns Win the very last letter, which contains perhaps her most famous accidental *bon mot:* "We were yesterday," she announces proudly to Mary Jones, "three kiple chined, by the grease of God, in the holy bands of mattermoney" (p. 337).

Together with Lydia, Tabitha and Win represent Smollett's first serious attempt to give voices to important female characters in any of his novels. Tabitha and Win's are comic voices, their effects amusing and reductive. Lydia's voice is something else again, as she is an articulate young woman who breaks from the mold of silence or dismissal to be an extremely interesting, even crucial, participant in the development of a Smollett narrative. She is unlike Smollett's other heroines—Narcissa, Emilia, Monimia, Aurelia—in another way as well, for she is at the edges of the story in which she appears, though at the end her marriage to the son of her uncle's old friend Dennison (whose estate is the novel's principal emblem of civilized order) moves her to its moral center. But in the eyes of Wilson/Dennison she is very much like them, for he sees her as an apparition, an idealized figure of moral and emotional purity, the heroine of a romance. As I suggested earlier, in a certain way she *is* the heroine of a romance, just as her future husband is something of a romance hero. In the only letter he writes to her, young Dennison makes it clear that she is the idol of his imagination. When "I found myself actually in your presence," he remarks of one of their rare clandestine meetings, "when I heard you speak;—when I saw you smile; when I beheld your charming eyes turned favourably upon me; my breast was filled with such tumults of delight, as wholly deprived me of the power of utterance, and wrapt me in a delirium of joy!" (p. 17). This is just the kind of elevated language Roderick Random or Peregrine Pickle might have used in addressing Narcissa or Emilia.[22]

But Lydia is more than this, more than the idealized object of Dennison's male gaze, as he seems to know in the end—and as Matt and Jery come to know too. The reader, who has access to her letters, knows it much earlier. Give a heroine a voice, Smollett realized, and she ceases to be abstracted and apparitional. What Lydia writes shows her to be a complex person of real depth and warring sensibilities. The girl with the "languishing eye," in Matt's phrase, whose spirits are depressed because of a love she thinks she has lost, gets over her disappointment sufficiently to enter the world with a considerable enthusiasm for it. She is not flighty; as she becomes caught up in the family journey, she puts aside the romances her uncle thinks she reads and engages with the real. When she assumes her own voice, it is as distinct from the voices of Matt and Jery as her perceptions are from their perceptions.

Lydia's letters are few in number (only eleven) but sufficient to prove that she is no empty-headed simpleton. As a correspondent she displays considerable assurance and a genuine craftiness, both in language and tone, as she shifts confidently and skillfully between the circumspection necessary in the letters to her old schoolmistress Mrs. Jermyn and the candor into which she is able to relax when writing to her friend and confidante Letty Willis. She takes real delight in the scenes she witnesses at Bath and London, counteracting the outraged reactions of her uncle and the distant musings of her brother; yet she is able to grow into an awareness of her deeper self, which leads her to know, as Matt knows of himself at the end, that the great world is foolish and giddy—that it is no place for love or happiness. "I am heartily tired of this itinerant way of life," she writes in a late moment of despondency over her anxiety that she may have lost Dennison forever. It is not just despondency that makes her reflective in this way, however, but also dawning wisdom. "I am quite dizzy with a perpetual succession of objects," she continues in the same letter. "Nature never intended me for the busy world——I long for repose and solitude. . . . Unexperienced as I am in the commerce of life, I have seen enough to give me a disgust to the generality of those who carry it on—

There is such malice, treachery, and dissimulation, even among professed friends and intimate companions, as cannot fail to strike a virtuous mind with horror; and when Vice quits the stage for a moment, her place is immediately occupied by Folly, which is often too serious to excite any thing but compassion" (p. 296). Here Lydia has begun to sound very much like Matt, though without his stridency; they will both modulate their voices into tones that express full balancing of their sensibilities before the novel arrives at its last pages.

It may seem odd at first thought that Smollett, pictorial novelist that he was, chose not to render his three principals in *Humphry Clinker*—Matt, Jery, and Lydia—at all visually. They cannot observe themselves, or at least they do not, and no one of them ever describes any of the others in significant physical detail. There is no narrator to do it. Instead, all three are defined primarily by their letters, or rather by the language used in them; the definitions are amplified only by impressions of them as persons, and accounts of their conduct, found in the letters of others. I shall have more to say about this matter of language later, and shall pause here only to note that *Humphry Clinker* provides further major instances of Smollett's frequent habit of characterization by style. The emphasis in the portrayals of his three principals is decidedly on the words they write; those words are expressions of the workings of active, alert minds and highly charged feelings. Tabitha and Win are represented visually because they are conceived as having no minds, and their emotional capacities are limited, even stunted. Most of all, they have no words—or, more accurately, the words they have are unreliable because they make chaos out of the order that, properly used, language brings to the disorder of human affairs.

Surely no reader has ever had difficulty visualizing Matt and Jery and Lydia, despite the absence of precise physical description. The language is enough. Certainly it was enough for the great Rowlandson, whose illustrations of the 1790s represent them with amazing accuracy—as is clearly shown by his drawing of the scene (p. 82) when Clinker, serving at table during the family dinner at Salt Hill, spills the custard, tramples Chowder, and drops the china dish to the floor, shattering it into "a thousand pieces." Tabitha, as seen in Rowlandson's picture, is precisely the figure Jery has described earlier; but Matt, Jery, and Lydia are just right too. Hogarth, from whom Rowlandson learned his art, could not have done better. They must all have been easy

Thomas Rowlandson, Direful consequences of Clinker's aukwardness (1793).
(By permission of the University of Iowa Libraries, Iowa City.)

sketches. The central figure of Clinker, of course, is extensively described
prior to Jery's account of the dinner incident, and so Rowlandson had little to
do except copy him from the pages of the novel.

Like Lismahago, introduced some one hundred pages later, Clinker writes
no letters. But these two comic figures are important characters, almost principals. As many of Smollett's readers have observed, it is Clinker who, by the
example of his constancy and simple goodness, helps to focus the central values on which the novel finally turns—and to "expedite" their full enactment;
Lismahago, his absurdity and his cranky disputatiousness notwithstanding,
proves himself worthy of Matt's respect for his intelligence and his loyalty to
ideals of honor, and he is gladly welcomed into the Bramble family. Neither
character lacks words. Clinker, for all his simplicity, is a gifted preacher who
can move felons toward repentance and women into pious ecstasies, while
Lismahago is a compulsive talker who is never at a loss for something to say
in contradiction to what another has said to him. But, quite simply, neither is
a member of the Bramble family until the end, and so both are outside the

circle of correspondence by which Smollett's narrative is conducted. They do not observe, but are observed.

Both are triumphs of comic portraiture—they are strong Cervantean conceptions, with multiple eccentricities, fondly caricatured; in the case of Lismahago, caricature almost crosses over into the grotesque. We have seen how Clinker is first introduced with his posteriors bare; his hangdog humility and miserable poverty immediately touch Matt's heart, and he shortly takes him on as a servant. In the first of his two significant transformations in the novel, Clinker is metamorphosed from the "equally queer and pathetic" ragamuffin of his initial appearance—shabby, starving, and "about twenty years of age" as Jery describes him, "of a middling size, with bandy legs, stooping shoulders, high forehead, sandy locks, pinking eyes, flat nose, and long chin" (p. 78)—into the "smart fellow" (p. 81) seen in the Rowlandson picture. The transformation is effected by Matt's generous response to his abjectness. "Heark ye, Clinker, you are a most notorious offender"—against decency and propriety, that is, at least according to the complaints of Tabitha and the landlord of the inn at Marlborough where the party has stopped. But Matt changes the terms of his offense: "You stand convicted of sickness, hunger, wretchedness, and want. . . . Get a shirt with all convenient dispatch, that your nakedness may not henceforward give offence to travelling gentlewomen, especially maidens in years" (p. 80). With the guinea Matt places in his hand, Clinker is able to redeem his clothes from a pawnbroker so as to make the appearance he does in the dinner scene. Thereafter he is always Matt's loyal adherent, as he has penetrated the crust over the old curmudgeon's tender interior; his loyalty occasions some of the novel's funniest visual moments, as Clinker quixotically insists on rescuing his master from distresses (coaching accidents, the sea in which he is bathing) both real and imaginary.

Lismahago is an even greater achievement as a comic portrait. Still more emphatically a Cervantean figure than Clinker, he first appears (in Jery's graphic words) as a "tall, meagure figure, answering, with his horse, the description of Don Quixote mounted on Rozinante." Dressed in antiquated military garb, he tries to be graceful before the ladies who gaze upon his arrival, but crashes to the ground when the girth of his saddle gives way, loses his hat and periwig, and displays "a head-piece of various colours, patched

and plaistered in a woeful condition" (p. 182). Once he is on his feet, his head
covered again, he seems to Jery an astonishing figure indeed:

> He would have measured above six feet in height, had he stood upright; but he
> stooped very much; was very narrow in the shoulders, and very thick in the
> calves of his legs, which were cased in black spatterdashes—As for his thighs,
> they were long and slender, like those of a grasshopper; his face was, at least, half
> a yard in length, brown and shrivelled, with projecting cheek-bones, little grey
> eyes on the greenish hue, a large hook-nose, a pointed chin, a mouth from ear to
> ear, very ill furnished with teeth, and a high, narrow fore-head, well furrowed
> with wrinkles. His horse was exactly in the stile of its rider; a resurrection of dry
> bones. (p. 183)

Lismahago lives up to his picture—"this Caledonian," Jery writes of him
shortly after their first encounter, "is a self-conceited pedant, aukward, rude,
and disputacious"; he is "so addicted to wrangling, that he will cavil at the
clearest truths, and, in the pride of argumentation, attempt to reconcile con-
tradictions" (p. 185). Like all of Smollett's greatest comic characters, including
Clinker, Lismahago is defined by an obsession; because he is such a determined curmudgeon he is a perfect foil to the gentler Matt, also a man obsessed, while the hard-edged absurdity of his appearance and manner make
him just the right mate for Tabitha.

Once they have been introduced, Clinker and Lismahago remain more or
less constant presences throughout the remainder of the novel (though the
latter does disappear for most of the excursion to Scotland), frequently caught
visually in ludicrous postures, as when the prankster Sir Thomas Bullford actually composes the picture of Lismahago escaping from an imaginary fire in
the house where he has welcomed the party as his guests—"O, what a subject!——O, what *caricatura!*—O, for a Rosa, a Rembrandt, a Schalken!—
Zooks, I'll give a hundred guineas to have it painted!——what a fine descent
from the cross, or ascent to the gallows!" (p. 288). The other fine comic portraits in the novel, and there are many of them, appear only fleetingly along
the way of the Bramble family's journey, usually as figures in a tableau picture
drawn by Matt in one of his letters or, more often, by Jery. Indeed, Smollett's
Hogarthian narrative method depends upon such encounters, which give his
work its distinctive spatial form, occasioning the accumulating vignettes—

satiric, comic, sometimes sentimental—by which it creates itself into a whole. There are so many such portraits, and so many tableaux, that a few examples will have to suffice as illustration of the way the novel uses them to develop both its structure (and texture) and its major centers of thematic interest.

Jery is the most prolific portrait artist. We have already seen ample evidence of his skill in the descriptions of Tabitha, Clinker, and Lismahago; it is a skill he clearly delights in applying at every opportunity. Here is his quickly sketched picture of Sir Ulic Mackilligut, the impoverished old Irish knight who, having met the Brambles at Bath, thinks to repair his fortune by capturing the prize of Tabitha's hand in marriage. First seen in the midst of the ludicrous scene of a dancing lesson (the master is "blind of one eye, and lame of one foot"), Sir Ulic "seemed to be about the age of three-score, stooped mortally, was tall, raw-boned, hard-favoured, with a woollen night-cap on his head; and he had stript off his coat, that he might be more nimble in his motions" (p. 30). Jery is very good at the kind of economy represented in this sketch, which allows the circumstances surrounding its subject—here, the dancing lesson—to fill out a whole visual scene. Sir Ulic is a successful caricature even though he is not described in great detail; the reader can see him clearly because Jery makes it so easy to imagine his ridiculous appearance as the clumsy pupil of an equally clumsy and absurd instructor. Later, his portrait is filled out even more as his behavior makes the motive for his courtship of Tabitha increasingly clear.

Sir Ulic is only one of many such sketches in Jery's letters. Some of the others are even more quickly lined out—for example, the picture of yet another of Tabitha's suitors, the old Scottish lawyer Micklewhimmen, who feigns invalidism, captures the lady's heart, and then loses it by dashing nimbly past her and knocking her down as he escapes from the same fire that exposes Win Jenkins's beauties to the eyes of Clinker: "charity begins at hame!" (p. 170), he cries out in refusing to assist her as she also tries to escape, ironically returning one of her own favorite phrases upon her. This hypocrite later justifies his action by a casuistical argument about the supremacy of instinct over reason in times of crisis, and even Tabby sees through him. Micklewhimmen is not represented in great physical detail, but he is an "original," as Jery describes him (p. 168), and in the context of any work by Smollett this word always implies physical oddity; his eccentricity is even more a matter of comically fraudulent character and abuse of language than of appearance, and Jery perfectly captures him by developing just the right focus.

Taken all together, Jery's numerous sketches and portraits help to project an extremely graphic overall picture of a world he sees as alive with quirky people and bustling with a vital energy. A good many of his sketches occur in the midst of the big tableau scenes Jery also delights in describing. Some of these are important defining moments in the narrative as a whole, in the sense that they bring into direct view the central thematic issues that recur throughout the novel. At Bath Jery observes a quite grand and comprehensive tableau that includes all the great variety of English society, gathered there ostensibly for the benefits of the waters but actually for individual displays of presumed importance and fashionable accomplishments. It is the mixing of classes at Bath that so agitates Matt; but, as we know, what his uncle finds so troubling and so outrageous as a violation of ideal social and moral order only makes Jery laugh. "Heark ye, Lewis," Matt writes in his second letter from the city, "my misanthropy increases every day. . . . This place is the rendezvous of the diseased" (p. 46)—and he does not mean only the physically diseased. Jery looks at Bath in another way. In the opening paragraph of his own second letter from there, his comic vision at its sharpest, he displays its mixed society whole, stripping away all the pretensions that fix his uncle's eye and employing a reductive strategy by which he is able to show with perfect clarity that the world of Bath is all a spectacle of common humanity, at least as funny and absurd as it is vexing and disruptive. "Here," he says, writing first of the bathers,

> a man has daily opportunities of seeing the most remarkable characters. . . . He sees them in their natural attitudes and true colours; descended from their pedestals, and divested of their formal draperies, undisguised by art and affectation—Here we have ministers of state, judges, generals, bishops, projectors, philosophers, wits, poets, players, *chemists, fiddlers,* and *buffoons.* . . . Another entertainment, peculiar to Bath, arises from the general mixture of all degrees assembled in our public rooms, without distinction of rank or fortune. This is what my uncle reprobates, as a monstrous jumble of heterogeneous principles; a vile mob of noise and impertinence, without decency or subordination. But this chaos is to me a source of infinite amusement. (p. 47)

The spectacle of the gathered bodies in the baths and within the assembly rooms is observed here from the perspective of a comic playwright imagining crowd scenes, the members of the ensemble company of actors playing in little dramas of laughable absurdity, first out of costume and then fully garbed, their identities all so mixed up that no one can tell who is who. Jery quickly goes on to particularize the scenes by his glimpses of assorted characters who move downstage (so to speak) and come into clearer focus for him—"an antiquated Abigail, dressed in her lady's cast-clothes," mistaken "for some countess just arrived at the Bath" and led by a deceived Master of Ceremonies to the position of highest honor at the upper end of the public room as a ball night begins; a "Scotch lord," who opens the ball with "a mulatto heiress from St. Christopher's," while "the gay colonel Tinsel" dances the entire evening with "the daughter of an eminent tinman from the borough of Southwark" (p. 47). On another occasion, at the Pump Room, Jery catches sight of "a broken-winded Wapping landlady" as she pushes her fat body through "a circle of peers, to salute her brandy-merchant," who stands by a window "prop'd upon crutches"; he sees a "paralytic attorney of Shoe-Lane," shuffling his way to the bar, accidentally kicking the shins of the Lord Chancellor of England, who is at the moment taking a glass of water at the pump (p. 48). There are other characters in this comic drama, a few of them—Matt's old friend James Quin, for example—pictured and heard from in considerable detail. Jery's impulses remain consistent throughout his letters from Bath. For him the place is a site for broad observation of the panorama of human folly and pretension, and by keeping himself at a distance he is able to get at the truth about it with a real precision of comic effect.

Humphry Clinker is always reminding us that it is a travel narrative, but of a particular kind, one that emphasizes the travelers' responses to the places visited and the sights witnessed over the attractions of the places themselves. It is this emphasis that gives the representations of place their power to arrest the progression of the main narrative so completely that we almost forget the travelers have anywhere to go other than where they are. We are reminded every time they begin writing of their plans to move on that the novel's plot, its overarching structure, depends on a continuing rhythmic pattern of stopping and going, repeated for each correspondent individually and for all of them collectively. By the accumulation of multiple responses to particular places, Smollett vastly complicates both the conventions of the travel book and the Hogarthian spatial model he so much favored as a writer, superimposing several pictures upon one another in each frame or segment of his narrative series, so that, just as the entire series cannot be fully understood until all of its frames have been seen, or read, so also the individual frames, or pictures, cannot be understood until the process of superimposition is complete. The effect is like that of what used to be called trick photography, the art of merging separate captured images of the same subject into one. If we can imagine the same art practiced upon a series of subjects adding up to a whole narrative, we will have a good idea of how *Humphry Clinker* works to achieve its overall effect of unity in multiplicity. The method is very difficult, and it seems very modern; after Smollett, no novelist attempted it again until this century, when Joyce and then Faulkner adapted it almost simultaneously in *Ulysses, The Sound and the Fury,* and *As I Lay Dying.*

Jery is absolutely crucial to the method as Smollett practiced it. His comic sensibility centers him between the extremes of Matt's irritated volatility and Lydia's sentimentality. He remains thus positioned throughout the novel, even during the long Scottish section when Matt begins to enjoy greater equanimity of feeling than he has known before. In London, it is Jery who most perfectly registers the absurdity of the scene at the king's levee, where the effusive and sycophantic Barton immoderately praises all present, completely disregarding the truth about everyone. Jery delights in recording Barton's absurdity, which reaches its height with the appearance of "the old Duke of N——," who, "squeezing into the circle" of those gathered "with a busy face of importance, thrust his head into every countenance, as if he had been in search of somebody, to whom he wanted to impart something of great consequence." When Newcastle approaches Matt, he launches into a blathering of disjointed nonsense by which he is fully exposed as a fool—here is another instance of characterization by style rather than appearance, and in this case it is decidedly an exercise in *caricature* by style. "My dear friend, Mr. A——," the duke addresses Matt, whom he should remember from their former acquaintance (Matt was once in Parliament) but does not, "I am rejoiced to see you— How long have you been come from abroad?—How did you leave our good friends, the Dutch? The king of Prussia don't think of another war, ah?——

He's a great king! a great conqueror! a very great conqueror! Your Alexanders and Hannibals were nothing at all to him, sir——Corporals! drummers! dross! mere trash——Damned trash, heh?" (p. 96). The reader does not need to know that Smollett had condemned both Newcastle and the rapacious Prussian monarch, Frederick the Great, in the *Briton* and in the *Adventures of an Atom* to enjoy the joke at the duke's expense. To Barton's ecstasy in the aftermath of all this brainless silliness, Matt replies that Newcastle was "for thirty years" and should still remain "the constant and common butt of ridicule and execration"—he was "an ape in politics," notorious both for his folly and his corruption, a "venal drudge" for the disgraceful administration of Sir Robert Walpole, and an agent of faction during the years of Pitt's supremacy. The whole scene is an exquisite vignette loaded with political satire, and it is to be repeated when Matt and Jery attend the duke's own levee a few days hence.

The episode of the king's levee ends on a final note of hilarity when Jery and Matt, as they leave the scene, discover Humphry Clinker, "exalted upon a stool, with his hat in one hand, and a paper in the other, in the act of holding forth to the people" (p. 97). The juxtaposition of the two pictures—of Newcastle babbling and Clinker preaching—is no accident. Its effect is doubly reductive: the duke's nonsense is further diminished by the implied comparison with Clinker's Methodistical spoutings, while Clinker's pious words, which Jery does not repeat, are placed on a level with those just heard from the ridiculous peer. The difference is that whereas one figure is a harmless innocent, the other is a disgraceful relic of the arbitrary exercise of power who can never be thought of as harmless, absurd though he may have become in his dotage. Still, it is the duke's absurdity that most delights Jery. The account of his attendance upon the noble old fool at his own levee is dominated by a single picture of Newcastle rushing from his morning ablutions to greet the Turkish ambassador, who comes in the belief that he is paying a courtesy call upon the prime minister. All a-flutter, Newcastle bolts from his private quarters "with a shaving-cloth under his chin, his face frothed up to the eyes with soap lather" (p. 108); the ambassador takes him for a hired jester and, when disabused of this notion, remarks with astonishment (and no irony whatsoever): "Holy prophet! I don't wonder that this nation prospers, seeing it is governed by the counsel of ideots; a series of men, whom all good musselmen revere as the organs of immediate inspiration!" (p. 109). This is a moment so

Thomas Rowlandson, Turkish ambassador introduced to the Duke of N——
(1793). (By permission of the University of Iowa Libraries, Iowa City.)

hilariously pictorial that it almost cries out for the pencil of a gifted illustrator. Rowlandson obliged with a drawing that exactly renders what Jery sees and describes, perfectly revealing Newcastle's clownishness (note how he leans forward, bug-eyed, chattering and gesturing), the ambassador's bafflement, and the utter indifference of nearly everyone else in the room—to them, Newcastle is already a joke whose levee attracts them only because it is a social occasion, and they do not even bother to look at this further instance of his folly.

Jery's acute visual sense is next piqued when he attends another levee of sorts, a Sunday afternoon at the house of S——, who is of course Smollett himself. "I question," he writes, "if the whole kingdom could produce such another assemblage of originals." They are all marked by peculiarities of dress, even more by oddities of character and appearance, initially "produced by affectation, and afterwards confirmed by habit" (p. 123). One feigns blindness, another lameness, a third an aversion to the country that makes him sit with his back to the window; others affect mental distraction, stuttering, or disputatiousness. The company includes a poet, a political philosopher, a pamphleteering controversialist, and a travel writer, and their nationalities range from English to Scottish to Irish to "foreign," so that—as Jery puts it—their conversation "resembled the confusion of tongues at Babel" (p. 124). The episode as a whole is another sparkling tableau, this time of a literary society as full of absurdities as any other gathering of human types Jery has thus far seen.

His other splendid visual flourish of the London letters comes when he accompanies his aunt and Lady Griskin on a visit to Clerkenwell Prison, where Clinker is being held for robbery—only to discover the fellow "haranguing the felons in the chapel." "I never saw any thing so strongly picturesque as this congregation of felons clanking their chains," he declares, while "orator Clinker" stood, in a "transport of fervor," expatiating on "the torments of hell, denounced in scripture against evil-doers, comprehending murderers, robbers, thieves, and whoremongers. The variety of attention exhibited in the faces of these ragamuffins, formed a groupe that would not have disgraced the pencil of a Raphael. In one, it denoted admiration; in another, doubt; in a third, disdain; in a fourth, contempt; in a fifth, terror; in a sixth, derision; and in a seventh, indignation" (p. 147). The ludicrousness of the scene is heightened by Jery's mischievous comparison of it with the manner of one of Raphael's grand biblical paintings, and it is the ludicrousness itself that he so much enjoys.

After this flourish, as the family party journeys northward, Jery's comic spirit grows temporarily quieter—and with it the voice that so delights in creating ridiculous pictures through the words of his letters. It is not until their return to England, and the beginning of the Sir Thomas Bullford episode, that he reverts to his old form, in which he then continues until the novel ends. The reason for this shift is simple. The farther he gets from the centers of English society the less there is to exercise Jery's great capacity for amusement. His letters from Scotland reveal that, like his uncle, he is deeply impressed by Edinburgh and Glasgow, where he finds more to admire than to laugh at. He is also moved by the grandeur of the Scottish landscape, and likewise by the sentimental scene that takes place in a village just outside Lanerk, where an old man, reduced to street labor by his poverty, is reunited with a long-lost son;[23] this is a scene, he says, which "warmly interested the benevolent spirit of Mr. Bramble" (p. 254). But it interested Jery no less, a sign that he has moved toward a position of moderated sensibilities, as his uncle has also done in the same environment. If he returns to a comic mode later, in his final English letters, he has taken some of the edges off of it—he is not quite the same as he was before the time in Scotland. And Matt, of course, loses most of the satiric edge to his own voice. Lydia is affected too, as her desire for the excitement of the great world wanes in the serene quiet of the remote north. All three feel greater understanding of and fondness for each other. It is the visit to Scotland, then, that turns the novel toward its resolution, bringing the principal travelers—and their voices—closer together in bonds of recognition and affection.

I shall return presently to the scenes in Scotland, and their effect, particularly on Matt. He is, of course, the member of the traveling party most in need of emotional equilibrium, and he finds it there, along with his physical health. The Matt of the early letters, from Bath, London, and elsewhere in England, is not only a man divided—out of balance and out of sorts—but also a stranger in the world, fully as much an alien as any of Smollett's earlier adventuring heroes. It is not merely that he is a Welshman—though, like Roderick Random's Scottishness, his national origin certainly marks him as an outsider in English society. He is simply unable to cope with all the newness of things after many years of seclusion at idyllic Brambleton Hall, where, paradoxically, he became ill; as he realizes late in the novel, it was his sedentary life that caused all his complaints. Yet, as he begins his travels, he feels assaulted by noise, crowding, and the general frenzy of the bustling world, not to mention rotting food, stinking medicinal waters, and smelly bodies. He is a man with no skin, no defenses, and so he lashes out in a satirist's rage. In doing so he sometimes writes visually, as Jery almost always does. For example, he provides a rather precise description of Tabitha and Lady Griskin caught in a moment of conflict over the hand of Jery's friend Barton, ending with the remark that "the expression of the two faces, while they continued in this attitude, would be no bad subject for a pencil like that of the incomparable Hogarth" (p. 141). The reference to Hogarth suggests that Matt has a well-developed visual imagination, and he can do an amusing tableau scene almost as well as Jery when his splenetic impulses are displaced by a moment of joy, as when he devotes almost an entire letter from Bath—"this stew-pan of idleness and insignificance," as he calls it (p. 55)—to his encounter with a group of old

Thomas Rowlandson, *Matthew Bramble recognises some ancient Friends*
(1793). (By permission of the University of Iowa Libraries, Iowa City.)

friends, all of them now broken down, awkward, and eccentric. The letter is
such a visual tour de force that it is no wonder Rowlandson chose to illustrate
the scene it describes—a scene which, Matt says, brought him "the most
happy day I have passed these twenty years" (p. 54). These old men, however,
have been broken down more by the world than by time, and so Matt's encounter with them is a bit melancholy, as they stir memories not just of youth
but of a remembered social and political past that seems golden by comparison with the present.

Matt is rarely visual because he usually lacks the detachment necessary for
it. He responds to the world not just with his eyes, but with all of his senses at
once, and his way of rendering its impact upon him is by a manner that
reflects his feeling of being surrounded, beset, overcome. If Jery's characteristic style as a correspondent is cool, measured, and contained, Matt's is hot, full
of urgency, explosive. Damian Grant has accurately described his use of language as "a species of linguistic prodigality," [24] and indeed he is like an older,
more articulate Roderick Random, firing off words as though they were defensive weapons. His attacks on the excesses of Bath and London are so well

known, and have been so often quoted and discussed, that it almost seems a
redundancy for me to take them up here. I shall do so as briefly as I can. The
former city he finds so changed that he hardly recognizes it after a thirty-year
absence, and the changes are not for the better in his view. "This place," he
complains, "which Nature and Providence seem to have intended as a re-
source from distemper and disquiet, is become the very center of racket and
dissipation" (p. 34). Its boasted new architecture is disappointing when it is
not downright pretentious and ugly to the point of decadence,[25] and many of
its recently completed buildings are in his estimation shabbily constructed.
The waters of the city are so vile that they make him sick—he can neither
bathe in them nor drink them: the King's Bath, he fears, may be infected by
floating matter of "scrophulous ulcers" or by "the king's-evil, the scurvy, the
cancer, and the pox"; if he drinks the waters drawn from the cistern below the
Pump Room, he may "swallow the scourings of the bathers" in a "delicate
beveridge" "medicated with the sweat, and dirt, and dandriff; and the abominable discharges of various kinds, from twenty different diseased bodies, par-
boiling in the kettle below"; and if he has recourse to water from the spring
that supplies other baths, he will be drinking the "strainings of rotten bones
and carcasses," as it runs through an old Roman burial ground (pp. 44–45).[26]
If he cannot drink the water, the wine is almost as bad—it is "an adulterous
mixture, brewed up of nauseous ingredients, by dunces, who are bunglers in
the art of poison-making" (p. 45). The smells of the place are perhaps worst
of all. "Imagine to yourself," Matt enjoins Dr. Lewis, "a high exalted essence
of mingled odours, arising from putrid gums, imposthumated lungs, sour
flatulencies, rank arm-pits, sweating feet, running sores and issues, plasters,
ointments, and embrocations, hungary-water, spirit of lavender, assafœtida
drops, musk, hartshorn, and sal volatile. . . . Such, O Dick! is the fragrant
æther we breathe in the polite assemblies of Bath" (p. 63).

Everything at Bath makes Matt nearly crazy with indignation, provoking
outbursts so violently written that they more than replicate feeling; his words,
throbbing with their relentless rhythms and hard consonants and jarring jux-
tapositions, almost become what they describe. The effects they achieve could
never be pictured, as the visual would be far too limiting. Worst of all for Matt
is the abstraction he calls the "mob," created by "the general tide of luxury"
(p. 36) into what he calls "a monster I never could abide, either in its head, tail,

midriff, or members: I detest the whole of it, as a mass of ignorance, presumption, malice, and brutality; and, in this term of reprobation, I include, without respect of rank, station, or quality, all those of both sexes, who affect its manners, and court its society" (p. 37). Here Matt comes very close to a personification of the mob as a sinister grotesque. The image is not new to *Humphry Clinker;* Smollett uses it repeatedly in the *Adventures of an Atom,* where he represents the mob as a many-headed hydra with an actual shape and a real voice. For Matt, it is almost as though the public—clamorous, socially ambitious, greedy, grasping, crushing everything in its way as it rushes headlong to fulfillment of its desire for wealth, station, power—takes on animate life and becomes a hideous, active presence in the world, frightening and enraging him. His references to the "mob" in the London letters are comparably graphic and disturbing. The city itself, he writes, "is become an overgrown monster; which, like a dropsical head, will in time leave the body and extremities without nourishment and support" (p. 86). London, in his mind, is inseparable from the people who inhabit it, and he characterizes it whole as a diseased body expanding into a grotesque bloatedness. The reasons for the unrestrained growth which fills him with such horror are not difficult to assign, for they "may be all resolved into the grand source of luxury and corruption," while the boundaries among classes have broken down, and "there is no distinction or subordination left" (p. 87), just "this incongruous monster, called *the public*" (p. 88).

It is excess that so troubles Matt, which is of course ironic because he is himself a man of excesses, at least in his language and his sensibilities. He will have to learn how to govern and moderate them if he is ever to be happy. Matt reflects Smollett's own attitudes toward contemporary English life, which troubled him deeply as the tide of luxury eroded class differences to create an increasingly homogeneous society. Luxury was for Smollett a moral issue of profound importance, as John Sekora has shown so convincingly,[27] while the aggressive new mercantilism of a developing market-based economy greatly disturbed his conservative soul, as John Zomchick has demonstrated more effectively than anyone else who has discussed the matter.[28] Lest we identify Smollett too closely with Matt, however, we ought to remember that he is the author who also created Jery; he understood the need, finally, to allow the comic—as a kind of defense—to prevail over the satiric, which leaves the self vulnerable to the objects of its judgment. Still, he must have had a fine and satisfying time imagining Matt's outbursts. There are many others besides those mentioned. The London letters especially go on and on with them in a litany of attacks on everything worthy of being scorned or despised—corrupt politics, city air, foul water, tasteless and polluted food, putrid wine, and nauseous beer. In London, he concludes, "every corner teems with fresh objects of detestation and disgust" (p. 117); at the end of the last letter he writes there he declares his "aversion to this, and every other crowded city" (p. 122). With this final outburst from Matt, Smollett brings to a dramatic conclusion his lifelong obsession with the city as emblem of the dangers and confusions of modern life. As he follows his travelers northward toward Scotland he leaves this image of the city behind him for the last time.

Before taking up the Scottish episodes I want to return briefly to Lydia. If the register of Matt's voice is satiric, and Jery's comic, Lydia's voice is heard in a register of its own. It is a strong voice, as I have argued earlier, and it proves capable of lyrical notes early on, long before the excursion to Scotland moves her uncle and brother to discover the lyricism in their own voices. Lydia writes a quite elegant description of the Downs at Clifton, where she is bedazzled by the springtime sight of "the furze in full blossom; the ground enamelled with daisies, and primroses, and cowslips; all the trees bursting into leaves, and the hedges already clothed with their vernal livery; the mountains covered with flocks of sheep" (p. 28). Matt finds the place ugly and irritating, as he later does Bath, while Jery is preoccupied with observing its human oddities. From the outset the dynamic of their multiple voices is apparent, and it does not change significantly until the passage through Scotland has modulated the tones of all three. Against Matt's ragings at Bath we hear Lydia saying that to her the city is "a new world——All is gayety, good-humour, and diversion. The eye is continually entertained with the splendour of dress and equipage; and the ear with the sound of coaches, chaises, chairs, and other carriages. *The merry bells ring round,* from morn till night" (p. 38). We know that she is naive and impressionable, yet there is a certain truth in the honest wonder of her girlish effusion. London also takes her fancy, and she is struck by its size and extent, by the bustle of its people, by the grandeur of its bridges, and by the enchantments of its splendid oases of pleasure and entertainment at Ranelagh and Vauxhall. She acknowledges that her view of the city clashes with the views of others in her family, especially her uncle: "People of experience and infirmity," she remarks to her friend Letty Willis, "see with very different eyes from those that such as you and I make us of" (p. 92). If later she expresses a weariness with the traveler's life and its constant movement through the busy world, it is partly because she has grown wiser, touched by the lovely serenity of Scotland and chastened by anxiety over her as yet unfulfilled love for Dennison.

The entire Bramble party, including Tabitha and Win, is a tableau on display before the reader's eye, a community divided initially by separate needs and sensibilities but in motion toward a condition of harmony and equilibrium. In Scotland they approach nearer to this condition. Its cities of Edinburgh and Glasgow, though by no means represented as sites of social perfection or ideal urban design, are both beautiful and hospitable, full of alluring sights and interesting, inviting people. The countryside is in some places grand and sublime, in others quiet and idyllic. For Matt, even for Jery, and certainly for their author, Scotland represents the best of an old and better way of being in the world. For the first and only time in his career as a novelist, Smollett permits himself the indulgence of a tribute to the beauty and tranquility of his native region of Dumbartonshire. Matt grows lyrical, describing the sweet sights of the fields, pastures, and woodlands along Loch Lomond: "Every thing here is romantic beyond imagination," he writes from Cameron House, a Smollett family seat. "This country is justly stiled the Arcadia of Scotland" (p. 241). In the same letter he encloses a poem "by Dr. Smollett," the lovely "Ode to Leven-Water" (pp. 241–42).

In Scotland Matt finds his bodily complaints fading away, to Jery's delight and his own. "I never saw my uncle in such health and spirits as he now enjoys," Jery observes with real gladness in his heart (p. 253). Matt, in his turn, proclaims that he now has begun "to feel the good effects of exercise——I eat like a farmer, sleep from mid-night till eight in the morning without interruption, and enjoy a constant tide of spirits, equally distant from inanition and excess" (p. 211). Later, in his very last letters, he gladly reports that his gout, rheumatism, and constipation are as much things of his past as his irascible temperament, and he celebrates the journey that has cured all of his ills. "We should sometimes increase the motion of the machine, to *unclog the wheels of life*" (p. 324), he writes to Dr. Lewis, echoing the hilarious connection be-

tween physical health and spiritual well-being drawn in the opening para-
graphs of his very first letter. In the last sentence of his final letter he declares,
once and for all, "I intend to renounce all sedentary amusements" (p. 336).

From the Scottish episodes onward, *Humphry Clinker* progresses steadily
toward its resolution. Except for the extended Baynard interlude, it also progresses very quickly. It is hardly necessary to argue further that the members
of the Bramble party grow closer together during and especially after their
time together in Scotland, until finally all that has divided them—differences
in experience, character, and voice—is simply dissolved away. As a microcosmic community they come to signify the hope of a broader harmony in the
greater world beyond them. It is a hope only imagined, but its expression is
unlike what we find in any of Smollett's other novels. Increasingly in the letters written after the family's return to England, the focus is upon Matt. As
the internal divisions that have pained him for years go away, he sees more
clearly than he ever could have done before the possibility of reconciliation in
the external world as well—reconciliation within his family; reconciliation
between old ideas and new, between the individual and society, between the
ancient and admired traditions associated with Scotland and the progressive
ways of England. All of these reconciliations actually occur before the novel
reaches its last page. Matt assists his old friend Baynard in the rescue of his
dashed fortunes by persuading him to organize the affairs of his estate on the
well-regulated model of another friend, Dennison, who is a practitioner of
modern English agricultural economy but whose estate equals the best of
Scotland in the important respects of beauty, productivity, hospitality to
guests, and communal harmony among its residents. He even finds himself
promoting the idea of the 1707 Act of Union, though he must do so over the
strenuous objections of Lismahago, who laments the loss of Scottish national
identity and the political sacrifice it had entailed, proclaims the dangers of increased freedoms and the inevitable excesses of growing commercial prosperity, and insists on praising the good dietary effects of the oats that Matt
would have a prosperous Scotland feed to its livestock instead of its people
(pp. 265–70).

The debate between Matt and Lismahago takes place as the novel approaches its festive conclusion in the several weddings that will actually join
Welsh and English estates, unite people of different nationalities, and alter the

structure of relations among classes. Lydia will marry young Dennison, the son of her uncle's English friend; Tabby will marry the Scottish Lismahago; Win Jenkins will marry Matt's natural son, the hybrid English/Welsh Clinker, now Matthew Loyd. Not all members of the traveling party will go home to Wales; as Win announces in her last letter, "our satiety is to suppurate" (p. 337). But those who do not go home—Jery, Lydia, and her new husband—will, as Matt gladly announces, "visit us in their return from the Bath" (p. 336), where they propose to enjoy themselves for an unspecified period of time—with Matt's blessing. The overall effect is unifying despite the impending separations, not least because the families created by the marriages replicate the configuration of the recently formed United Kingdom, but in an idealized version that Byron Gassman has described as mythic.[29] There is a distinctly personal note in all this too, and it is Smollett's own. The angry young Scot who arrived in England full of hope and ambition, suffered through dislocation, alienation, and disappointment, and then spilled out his indignation in *Roderick Random,* has in his maturity achieved exactly the same balance as Matt Bramble.

This is a commonplace; every reader of *Humphry Clinker* who knows anything at all of Smollett's biography is aware of it. I repeat it here only because I wish to give it a slightly revised statement and a new emphasis. What Smollett seems to have recognized as he wrote his last novel is the futility of continual outrage against an imperfect world. As a political man he had already accepted that Scotland was now a part of England, but at last he was able to feel the meaning of that reality and to pass beyond all sense of alienation; on a deep personal level he arrived at the understanding that a Scot could be English without giving up his native identity altogether—through Matt, he was able to remember Dumbartonshire, the Highlands, and the cities of Glasgow and Edinburgh, but still return imaginatively to England. He knew now that the integration of identity and consciousness was possible, and that irascibility, one form of sensibility, could be melted into benevolence, another form, without sacrificing energy, wisdom, or sharp awareness of the world. The divided self portrayed in the dedication to *Ferdinand Count Fathom* could thus be made whole.

I must not end this chapter, and with it this book, before adding a final word on *Humphry Clinker* as a *novel.* The work does not continue to hold our

interest because it explains its author's life, or because it comments so memo-
rably on his times; neither its biographical nor its historical value is enough to
make us want to continue reading it, though one might think so from the
quantity of ink (some of it my own) spilled over such matters by critics and
scholars. We keep on reading—and admiring—*Humphry Clinker* because it is
a great story, well told, and because it manages a remarkable disparateness—
of narrative forms, of characters and episodes, of voices and sensibilities, of
portraits and tableaux—without flying apart into chaotic scatterings. It keeps
our imagination always on the stretch. The reconciliations it achieves at the
end provide enormous emotional satisfaction, and they are equally satisfying
aesthetically and intellectually. John M. Warner has rightly claimed that, in
Humphry Clinker, Smollett achieved nearly total synchronicity of multiple narrative elements, creating a coherent vision and a wholeness of overall effect.[30]
I am not entirely sure just how much Smollett would care about all this praise
for having—finally—written a novel that everyone can agree is unified. Of
course it is unified, we can imagine him saying; for he surely meant it to be just
that, as he clearly meant his other novels to defy principles of formal unity in
the interest of promoting an entirely different vision of life and the world.

   Humphry Clinker creates its particular principles of unity as it draws its five
correspondents toward the meaningful closure of their individual and collec-
tive stories. They are not the principles governing the novels of Sterne, or
Fielding, or Richardson, but Smollett's own. No other novel of his century, or
for a long time afterward, even attempts them. Indeed, there simply is no
other novel quite like *Humphry Clinker.* Without denying that the world is and
always will be a disordered place, and while acknowledging that all human experience is nothing but a crazed accumulation of sensations, emotions, and
memories, it proclaims—utterly without sentimentality—a faith in the capacity of people to join in the creative act of living together harmoniously. Somehow the novel manages to be both a tribute to the human spirit of endurance
and a luxurious celebration of its sources in a troubling world. What vexes us
most, Smollett obviously believed, also stirs us to vital life, fixes our attention,
and inspires us to exercise our humanity in the fullest possible way. *Humphry
Clinker* is also, and finally, an exuberant celebration of the spatial form that
arose naturally from Smollett's manner of apprehending experience—the
form to which he was always committed as a novelist whose imagination, like

that of the painter whom he repeatedly called "incomparable" and "inimitable," was so intensely visual that he could not help responding to life in terms of the pictures relentlessly generated by its defining moments. In the last analysis it is clearly the Hogarthian pictures he drew with his words that he cared most about as an artist, for he gave them his greatest energy and the best efforts of his genius. They are the very heart and life—the thematic, moral, and aesthetic centers—of every novel he wrote. It is the pictures, I believe, that Smollett would most want us to remember. And we do.

NOTES

Introduction

1. *The Regicide: A Tragedy* was never performed, but Smollett published it by subscription in 1749. *The Reprisal: Or, The Tars of Old England* was produced at Drury Lane Theater in January 1757 and, after a modest initial run, was several times revived during the remaining years of the eighteenth century. There is no evidence that it has been performed since.

2. Smollett also translated, among other works, Voltaire's *Micromegas* and *Zadig* (both in 1752), and possibly his *Candide*—the last for his massive edition of Voltaire, published in collaboration with Thomas Francklin, 1761–69. His translation of Archbishop Fénélon's *Adventures of Telemachus* appeared posthumously in 1776.

3. Both the *Complete History* and the *Continuation* went through numerous editions during Smollett's lifetime and after; they were usually published together in a continuous series. The *Complete History,* originally projected as competition for the early installments of Hume's *History of Great Britain* (1754–62), actually outsold the rival work, at least initially; later, Smollett's two histories were frequently conflated with Hume's, resulting in considerable confusion as to the actual contribution of each writer. Smollett also produced (as editor, writer, or both) other historical works, including *The Modern Part of the Universal History* (1759–65) and *The Present State of All Nations: Containing a Geographical, Natural, Commercial, and Political History of All the Countries in the Known World* (1768–69); to the latter he contributed long essays on England and Scotland, and probably several other shorter pieces as well.

4. *Roderick Random* was published in January 1748, the translation of *Gil Blas* in the following October (dated 1749).

5. The phrase is Alan Dugald McKillop's, from the title of his extremely important book, *The Early Masters of English Fiction* (Lawrence: University of Kansas Press, 1956), which was published at a time when scholarly interest in the eighteenth-century novel was undergoing a vigorous revival—to which McKillop contributed significantly. The book includes seminal essays on Daniel Defoe, Samuel Richardson, Henry Fielding, Smollett, and Laurence Sterne.

6. In the interest of accuracy I should note that Smollett's fiction has been the subject of many articles and book chapters over the years; the number and frequency of these has lately increased. Several of the books about his work focus importantly on his nonfictional writings or other topics, with the following worthy of special notice: Louis L. Martz, *The Later Career of Tobias Smollett* (New Haven: Yale University Press, 1942); George M. Kahrl, *Tobias Smollett: Traveler-Novelist* (Chicago: University of Chicago Press, 1947); Fred W. Boege, *Smollett's Reputation as a Novelist* (Princeton: Princeton University Press, 1947); and James G. Basker, *Tobias Smollett: Critic and Journalist* (Newark: University of Delaware Press, 1988). Lewis M. Knapp's *Tobias Smollett: Doctor of Men and Manners* is still the standard biography. The full record of scholarly and critical work on Smollett through the 1970s may be traced in two comprehensive bibliographies: Robert D. Spector, *Tobias Smollett: A Reference Guide* (Boston: G. K. Hall, 1980); and Mary Wagoner, *Tobias Smollett: A Checklist of Editions of His Works and an Annotated Secondary Bibliography* (New York: Garland, 1984).

7. Spector, *Smollett's Women: A Study in an Eighteenth-Century Masculine Sensibility* (Westport, CT: Greenwood Press, 1994); Douglas, *Uneasy Sensations: Smollett and the Body* (Chicago: University of Chicago Press, 1995); Skinner, *Constructions of Smollett: A Study of Genre and Gender* (Newark: University of Delaware Press, 1996); Grant, *Tobias Smollett: A Study in Style* (Manchester: Manchester University Press, 1977); Boucé, *The Novels of Tobias Smollett* (London: Longman, 1976). Two other books, both very slight, have appeared from the publishing house of Peter Lang in Frankfurt am Main during the last decade: Susan Bourgeois, *Nervous Juyces and the Feeling Heart: The Growth of Sensibility in the Novels of Tobias Smollett* (1986); William Robert Adamson, *Cadences of Unreason: A Study of Pride and Madness in the Novels of Tobias Smollett* (1990).

8. The inaugural volume, *The Adventures of Ferdinand Count Fathom,* appeared in 1988. The edition includes Smollett's five novels, the major translations and historical works, and all of the other important writings.

9. Douglas, *Uneasy Sensations,* xix.

10. See M. Dorothy George, *London Life in the Eighteenth Century* (New York: Harper Torchbooks, 1965), especially chaps. 1, 2, and 5. See also J. H. Plumb, *England in the Eighteenth Century* (London: Penguin, 1950), and Derek Jarrett, *England in the Age of Hogarth* (London: Hart-Davis, MacGibbon, 1974).

11. *Present State,* 2:104. These sentiments are echoed in *Humphry Clinker,* Jery Melford to Sir Watkin Phillips, September 3 (p. 231). I have written elsewhere of Smollett's lifelong sense of displacement; see "Tobias Smollett: The Scot in England," *Studies in Scottish Literature* 29 (1997): 14–28. The present discussion draws heavily upon this essay. Opposition between the town and the country was a common motif in

eighteenth-century literature generally, and particularly in the fiction; see Jeffrey L. Duncan, "The Rural Ideal in Eighteenth-Century Fiction," *Studies in English Literature* 8 (1968): 517–35, and A. S. Knowles, Jr., "Defoe, Swift, and Fielding: Notes on the Retirement Theme," in *Quick Springs of Sense: Studies in the Eighteenth Century,* ed. Larry S. Champion (Athens: University of Georgia Press, 1974), 121–36. Smollett's use of the town-country motif is unusual in that his representation of the city is so graphic and his tone so often intensely personal.

12. After his departure in 1739, Smollett traveled home to Scotland only three times, in the summer and fall of 1753, in the summer of 1760, and again in the summer of 1766.

13. In an apparent fit of homesickness, Smollett raised the issue of his divided loyalties rather bitterly in a letter of 1 March 1754, addressed to his friend Alexander Carlyle. "I do not think I could enjoy Life with greater Relish in any part of the world than in Scotland among you and your Friends," he wrote; "I am heartily tired of this Land of Indifference and Phlegm" (*Letters,* 33). On the broad subject of the cultural dislocation felt by Smollett and other transplanted North Britons, see Kenneth Simpson, *The Protean Scot: The Crisis of Identity in Eighteenth-Century Scottish Literature* (Aberdeen: Aberdeen University Press, 1988), especially the introduction and chap. 1.

14. The best evidence that this was a crucial issue for Smollett is his decision to eliminate Scotticisms that had crept into *Roderick Random* before allowing the novel to go into a second edition. On the broader matter of language as a source of anxiety for Scots writing in England, see James G. Basker, "Scotticisms and the Problem of Cultural Identity in Eighteenth-Century Britain," *Eighteenth-Century Life* 15 (1991): 81–95.

15. Constantly beset by perceived threats of disorder and by his worry that Chance actually ruled in human affairs, Smollett wrote as follows to David Garrick on 5 April 1761: "I am old enough to have seen and observed that we are all playthings of fortune, and that it depends upon something as insignificant and precarious as the tossing up of a halfpenny whether a man rises to affluence and honours, or continues to his dying day struggling with the difficulties and disgraces of life" (*Letters,* 98).

16. In the *Complete History* and *Continuation,* and most notably in the essays on England and Scotland written for the *Present State,* Smollett maintained a carefully balanced view of the opposed values he always associated with his native and adopted lands. In these works he was clearly writing as an Englishman, and in a very public capacity, and so he was able to suppress the private feelings that captivated his imagination as a writer of fiction. See Beasley, "Tobias Smollett: The Scot in England," 18–22.

17. Smollett's personal religious beliefs remain something of a mystery, as he was

very private about them, but in all of his fiction he subscribed to an essentially Christian notion of human history and of the trajectory of the individual life directed by faith. See Thomas R. Preston, *Not in Timon's Manner: Feeling, Misanthropy, and Satire in Eighteenth-Century England* (University: University of Alabama Press, 1975), 2.

18. The fullest account of the relations between Smollett's life and his writings is found in Knapp. For a briefer but still extensive account see Robert Donald Spector, *Tobias George Smollett,* Updated Edition (Boston: Twayne, 1989). See also Jerry C. Beasley, "Tobias Smollett," in *Dictionary of Literary Biography: British Novelists, 1660–1800,* ed. Martin C. Battestin (Detroit: Gale, 1985), 39:440–70.

19. That is, *Roderick Random* and *Peregrine Pickle.* The latter novel attacks many other enemies besides; by the time of its second edition in 1758 many of Smollett's old antagonisms had subsided, and he deleted most of the passages in which he had originally exercised himself over them.

20. The expedition was undertaken as part of the so-called War of Jenkins' Ear launched against Spain as a first stage in what eventually developed into the long, widespread, and disastrous War of the Austrian Succession. The expedition was very badly managed, and it ended in a major defeat for the British fleet.

21. He set up first in Downing Street, and thereafter moved to Chapel Street in May Fair, to Beaufort Street (near Somerset House), and finally to fashionable Chelsea, where he thought he might have better success in attracting patients than he had enjoyed in the other locations. None of the moves brought him the business he needed to flourish as a physician.

22. From the date of its publication, *Roderick Random* has often been taken as much more than incidentally autobiographical; Smollett himself protested vigorously against this interpretation in a letter to Alexander Carlyle of 7 June 1748 (*Letters,* 7–9). On the autobiographical elements of the shipboard chapters see Lewis M. Knapp, "The Naval Scenes in *Roderick Random,*" *PMLA* 49 (1934): 593–98, and Louis L. Martz, "Smollett and the Expedition to Carthagena," *PMLA* 56 (1941): 428–46; on the Melopoyn story as a record of Smollett's prolonged frustrations with *The Regicide,* see Knapp, *Tobias Smollett: Doctor of Men and Manners,* 53–57. The best recent discussion of Smollett's uses of autobiography in *Roderick Random* may be found in John Skinner's *Constructions of Smollett,* chap. 2; Skinner moves effectively from questions of fact to matters of form, arguing the much greater significance of the latter.

23. Smollett felt an intense rivalry with Fielding, which culminated in his publication of a scurrilous pamphlet, *A Faithful Narrative of the Base and Inhuman Arts That Were Lately Practiced upon the Brain of Habbakkuk Hilding* (1752). In the same year of this pamphlet's appearance he was charged with criminal assault upon Peter Gordon and

Edward Groom (he had lent money to Gordon, who refused to pay him back) and eventually forced to pay damages in excess of twenty pounds; a few years later, in 1760, he was thrown into the King's Bench Prison for a libelous attack on Admiral Charles Knowles (published in the May 1758 number of the *Critical Review*), whom he accused of misconduct in a naval expedition of 1757. His earlier *Essay on the External Use of Water* (1752) angered the medical establishment by its broadside against the common practice of prescribing the mineral waters at Bath and other spas as a cure for disease. In the early 1760s Smollett agreed to edit the weekly *Briton* (May 1762–February 1763), launched in support of the administration of Lord Bute, a fellow Scot, and found himself painfully embroiled with the hostile *North Briton,* edited by his former friend John Wilkes. He abandoned the *Briton* in exasperation, but got off a ferocious last political sally in his prose satire, *The History and Adventures of an Atom* (1769).

24. The relocation did not help Smollett's health, for he died at Leghorn in September 1771, just three months after the publication of *Humphry Clinker.* He had earlier (in June 1763) journeyed to Italy and the south of France, and he actually lived at Nice from November 1763 to April 1765, with only slight improvement in his consumptive condition.

25. Between September 1749 and the summer of 1750 he did travel twice to the Continent, touring France and the Low Countries.

26. This was a compilation. For details of its preparation, publication, and reception, see Martz, *The Later Career,* 16–18, 23–52.

27. The *Travels* was based on the journals Smollett kept during his extended trip to the Continent from 1763 to 1765. See above, n. 24.

28. Adams, *Travel Literature and the Evolution of the Novel* (Lexington: University Press of Kentucky, 1983); see especially chaps. 1 and 2. Defoe, Fielding, and Sterne all wrote important travel books. Defoe's three-volume *Tour thro' the Whole Island of Great Britain* (1724–27) went through many editions during the eighteenth century and after; Fielding's *Journal of a Voyage to Lisbon* (1755) and Sterne's novelistic *Sentimental Journey through France and Italy* (1768) are, like Smollett's *Travels,* justly regarded as among the most original and compelling contemporary works of their kind.

29. For extended discussion of the important relations between historical contexts and episodic narrative structure see my essay, "Life's Episodes: Story and Its Form in the Eighteenth Century," in *The Idea of the Novel in the Eighteenth Century,* ed. Robert W. Uphaus (East Lansing, MI: Colleagues Press, 1988), 21–45.

30. In addition to Adams see Charles Batten, *Pleasurable Instruction* (Berkeley: University of California Press, 1978), and Barbara Maria Stafford, *Voyage into Substance:*

Art, Science, Nature, and the Illustrated Travel Account, 1760–1840 (Cambridge, MA: MIT Press, 1984).

31. Admiral George Anson, Captain James Cook, and others made celebrated voyages around the world, and accounts of the adventures of such travelers were widely available and eagerly read.

32. Walpole became prime minister in 1721. Controversial and unscrupulous, he was a brilliant politician who, for many years, held greater power than the two monarchs (George I and George II) under whom he served. A Whig, he was reviled by many in his own party, who joined with the Tory Opposition in a coalition to unseat him; after long frustration, the Opposition effort finally succeeded in February 1742. Walpole was pilloried by John Gay in *The Beggar's Opera* (1728) and by Fielding in *The Life of Mr. Jonathan Wild the Great* (1743). The "Great Man," as he was called derisively, was a favorite subject of fiction writers, who produced no fewer than three dozen narratives about him, all of them satirical and some of them scurrilous; for discussion of these see my essay, "Portraits of a Monster: Robert Walpole and Early English Prose Fiction," *Eighteenth-Century Studies* 14 (1981): 406–31.

33. The Godwin circle included, besides Wollstonecraft, the novelists Thomas Holcroft, Robert Bage, Elizabeth Inchbald, and Mary Hays. For the best discussion of this group of radical thinkers as literary figures see Gary Kelly, *The English Jacobin Novel, 1780–1805* (Oxford: Clarendon Press, 1976).

34. These works, a species of confessional writing, were encouraged by the clergy as a devotional practice; among the most famous of them is Bunyan's own spiritual autobiography, *Grace Abounding to the Chief of Sinners* (1666). The practice of writing such narratives continued well into the eighteenth century, and in fact John Wesley all but required it of ministers in his Methodist movement. See Leopold Damrosch, *God's Plot and Man's Stories: Studies in the Fictional Imagination from Milton to Fielding* (Chicago: University of Chicago Press, 1985), chap. 2, for discussion of seventeenth-century examples of the type; for a consideration of mid-eighteenth-century spiritual "lives," see my *Novels of the 1740s* (Athens: University of Georgia Press, 1982), chap. 5.

35. See Ian Watt, *The Rise of the Novel: Studies in Defoe, Richardson, and Fielding* (London: Chatto and Windus, 1957), chaps. 3 (on *Robinson Crusoe*) and 4 (on *Moll Flanders*). The connections between Defoe's fiction and the tradition of spiritual biography and autobiography are very strong, as has been convincingly demonstrated by G. A. Starr in *Defoe and Spiritual Autobiography* (Princeton: Princeton University Press, 1965), and by J. Paul Hunter in *The Reluctant Pilgrim: Defoe's Emblematic Method and Quest for Form in Robinson Crusoe* (Baltimore: Johns Hopkins University Press, 1966).

36. *Clarissa. Or, The History of a Young Lady,* ed. Florian Stuber et al. *The Clarissa Project* (New York: AMS Press, 1990), 7:175. She means heaven, of course. In *Novels of the 1740s* I have discussed *Clarissa* at length as a record of spiritual life bearing important features of devotional literature; see chap. 5, especially pp. 144–56.

37. The principal offending latitudinarians were Isaac Barrow and John Tillotson, while the deism of Matthew Tindal and the third earl of Shaftesbury was seen as even more hostile to orthodoxy; the natural theology of Samuel Clarke was an extension of both of the other major currents of Anglican rationalism. Barrow and Tillotson rose to prominence in the final years of the seventeenth century, the latter serving as archbishop of Canterbury; Tindal and Shaftesbury were important voices during the first three decades of the eighteenth century, as was Clarke, who went beyond their deism to argue that divine truth was accessible to human understanding without the benefit of Scripture. For a helpful general consideration of all these theological backgrounds see Martin C. Battestin, *The Moral Basis of Fielding's Art: A Study of Joseph Andrews* (Middletown, CT: Wesleyan University Press, 1959), chap. 2; see also G. R. Cragg, *From Puritanism to the Age of Reason: A Study of Changes in Religious Thought within the Church of England, 1660–1700* (Cambridge: The University Press, 1950).

38. One might make a similar claim for eighteenth-century French fiction in its own culture, which endured similar anxieties for similar reasons. The parallels in cultural experience surely help to explain why so many French novels—by Madame de La Fayette, Pierre Marivaux, the Abbé Prévost, Voltaire, and others—were so well received in England and so influential in helping to shape the new English novel. But all of this is another subject, beyond my scope here.

39. This is especially true of *Clarissa,* as every informed student of the novel knows. Following the first edition of 1747–48, Richardson—worried that the character of Lovelace was being wrongly understood by his audience—revised extensively and added numerous footnotes for the purpose of restricting the range of interpretive possibilities.

40. *Selected Letters of Samuel Richardson,* ed. John Carroll (Oxford: Clarendon Press, 1964), 41. For extended discussion of the claims of originality made by mid-eighteenth-century novelists, see William Park, "What Was New about the 'New Species of Writing'?" *Studies in the Novel* 2 (1970): 112–30.

41. John M. Warner has convincingly made the case for Smollett's relevance to modern fiction in his recent book, *Joyce's Grandfathers: Myth and History in Defoe, Smollett, Sterne, and Joyce* (Athens: University of Georgia Press, 1993).

42. Between 1831 and 1833 Cruikshank prepared illustrations for all of Smollett's

novels except *Ferdinand Count Fathom;* he also illustrated the translation of *Don Quixote.* Browne was the illustrator for a popular edition of the novels published in 1857 and reprinted many times thereafter.

43. Rowlandson, like Cruikshank after him, illustrated all of the novels except *Ferdinand Count Fathom,* a work apparently regarded by both as uncongenial to their art, as it includes relatively fewer of the eccentrics and grotesques they liked to draw.

44. I depart here from what seems to me a mistaken judgment in Ronald Paulson's otherwise authoritative essay, "Smollett and Hogarth: The Identity of Pallet," *Studies in English Literature* 4 (1964): 351–59. Paulson concludes that Smollett did indeed mean to mock Hogarth. But in fact he explicitly praises the artist in *Peregrine Pickle* itself, thirty chapters prior to the appearance of Pallet; and he does likewise in all of his other novels except *Ferdinand Count Fathom; The History and Adventures of an Atom* also contains an admiring allusion. See Robert Etheridge Moore, *Hogarth's Literary Relationships* (Minneapolis: University of Minnesota Press, 1948), 164–67, for discussion of all these references; see the entire fifth chapter of Moore's book (pp. 162–95) for extended consideration of the general affinities with Hogarth displayed in Smollett's novels.

45. See Robert Halsband, "Hogarth's Graphic Friendships: Illustrating Books by Friends," in *Johnson and His Age,* ed. James Engell (Cambridge, MA: Harvard University Press, 1984), 333–66. See also Jack Lindsay, *Hogarth: His Art and His World* (New York: Taplinger, 1979), passim. The standard works on Hogarth's life and career are by Ronald Paulson: *Hogarth's Graphic Works,* rev. ed. (New Haven: Yale University Press, 1970), and *Hogarth: His Life, Art, and Times* (New Haven: Yale University Press, 1971). Lindsay, Moore (see above, n. 44), and Paulson all provide detailed accounts of Hogarth's interest in important works of literature, and of his extensive personal and professional connections with contemporary writers. It is not known whether he had any personal relationship with Smollett; Hogarth studies are silent on this point, as is Smollett's biographer Knapp, and there is no mention of Hogarth in Smollett's surviving letters. The two men did have a mutual friend, William Huggins, the distinguished translator of *Orlando Furioso* (see Halsband, pp. 337–44), and so it is likely that they were at least acquainted.

46. The serial publication of Smollett's fourth novel in his new periodical venture, the *British Magazine* (January 1760–December 1761), contained two illustrations by Anthony Walker, the first magazine illustrations for a work of fiction in England. *Sir Launcelot Greaves* was itself the first full-length English novel to be written expressly for publication in a magazine. See Robert D. Mayo, *The English Novel in the Magazines 1740–1815* (Evanston: Northwestern University Press, 1962), 276–88. Both *Roderick*

Random and *Peregrine Pickle* were illustrated during Smollett's lifetime, but not for their first editions. Francis Hayman furnished frontispieces for each volume of the former in its second edition (1748), and an unnamed illustrator (probably it was Henry Fuseli) provided several drawings for the fourth edition of the latter (1769). See Brian Allen, *Francis Hayman* (New Haven: Yale University Press, 1987), 189, and John Knowles, *The Life and Writings of Henry Fuseli* (London, 1831), 32–33; see also M. G. Sutherland, "Illustrated Editions of Tobias Smollett's Novels" (Ph.D. diss., University of Edinburgh, 1974). Smollett's translations of *Gil Blas* and *The Devil upon Crutches* were both published with engravings in their first editions, as was his translation of *Don Quixote* (for this work Hayman prepared twenty-eight drawings, including a frontispiece). Various others of his works were also illustrated: the *Compendium* of voyage narratives, the *Complete History* (by Hayman), and the *Present State*.

47. On *caricatura* as a form, and on Smollett's adaptations from it in his fiction, see Milton Orowitz, "Smollett and the Art of Caricature," *Spectrum* 2 (1958): 155–67, and George Kahrl, "Smollett as a Caricaturist," in *Tobias Smollett: Bicentennial Essays Presented to Lewis M. Knapp,* ed. G. S. Rousseau and P.-G. Boucé (New York: Oxford University Press, 1971), 169–200. Kahrl has pointed out (pp. 174–76) that Hogarth, for all his contributions to popularizing the art of caricature, publicly dissociated his work from it and did not like to be called a caricaturist.

48. Moore, *Hogarth's Literary Relationships,* 167–72.

49. Pamela Cantrell has argued convincingly that Hogarth's example had an even greater effect upon Smollett than upon Fielding. See her recent essay, "Writing the Picture: Fielding, Smollett, and Hogarthian Pictorialism," *Studies in Eighteenth-Century Culture* 24 (1995): 69–89. "Fielding owes much to Hogarth's influence," Cantrell observes (p. 72), but "he rarely achieves the visual acuity of a Hogarth print. Tobias Smollett on the other hand, often does."

50. Richardson, in his way as visually oriented as Smollett, regularly constructed scenes using the elements of specific paintings, though his preference was for representational and mythic styles. He also arranged for illustration of many of his works, including (besides the novels) his edition of *Aesop's Fables* (1739). See Janet E. Aikins, "Richardson's 'speaking pictures,'" in *Samuel Richardson: Tercentenary Essays,* ed. Margaret Anne Doody and Peter Sabor (Cambridge: The University Press, 1989), 146–66; see also two essays by Murray L. Brown, "Learning to Read Richardson: *Pamela,* 'speaking pictures,' and the Visual Hermeneutic," *Studies in the Novel* 25 (1993): 129–51, and "*Emblematica Rhetorica:* Glossing Emblematic Discourse in Richardson's *Clarissa,*" *Studies in the Novel* 27 (1995): 455–76.

51. Moore, *Hogarth's Literary Relationships,* 166.

52. *Travels,* 289–91 (Letter XXXIII). The comparison is not so favorable to Guido as Moore seems to believe.

53. Walpole was a great collector of contemporary and earlier art, and he wrote extensively and authoritatively about the works he admired. See especially his *Aedes Walpolianae; or, A Description of the Collection of Pictures at Houghton Hall in Norfolk* (1748) and his four-volume *Anecdotes of Painting in England* (1762–80).

54. Smollett started the series very ambitiously, with five features in the first five numbers of the magazine, but allowed it to slack off afterward to an average of two per year, published at irregular intervals. Still, the cumulative total of the features for about a decade was substantial, unrivaled by the efforts of any other contemporary periodical. See Basker, *Tobias Smollett: Critic and Journalist,* 143–46, for more detailed discussion of the *Critical*'s contemporary arts series and Smollett's part in it. Interestingly, when Smollett ceased writing for the magazine in the mid-1760s, the series quickly disappeared.

55. Knapp, 167–69.

56. Knapp, 168.

57. *Critical Review* 1 (January–July 1756): 387. I am relying on the attributions of items published in the *Critical* established by Basker in *Tobias Smollett: Critic and Journalist;* in the back matter of Basker's book may be found a list of the attributions and a record of the evidence supporting them.

58. *Critical Review* 1 (January–July 1756): 479. The altar painting was completed probably in July 1756, as Hogarth was paid for it in August of that year; see Lindsay, *Hogarth,* 194. Lindsay does not share Smollett's enthusiasm for the work. Smollett's praise for the triptych as potential inspiration for a *"British* school of painters" was very likely intended as an enthusiastic tribute to Hogarth's long history of strong—and very public—support for native art.

59. *Critical Review* 7 (January–June 1759): 375–77.

60. *Critical Review* 9 (January–June 1760): 400. The first notice of Frye's work is only one page long. The second and third notices, also brief, appear in volume 11 (January–June 1761): 331–32 and volume 12 (July–December 1761): 312–13, respectively.

61. *Critical Review* 9 (January–June 1760): 197–205.

62. For more detailed discussion of Smollett's heroines and their rhetorical function in the novels, see my essay, "Amiable Apparitions: Smollett's Fictional Heroines," in *Augustan Subjects: Essays in Honor of Martin C. Battestin* (Newark: University of Delaware Press, 1997), 229–48.

63. The opening chapter of my *Novels of the 1740s* reviews the background in popular fiction against which Richardson, Fielding, and Smollett made their claims of originality. See also William Park, "What Was New about the 'New Species of Writing'?" Here it is necessary to notice Margaret Anne Doody's recent book, *The True Story of the Novel* (New Brunswick, NJ: Rutgers University Press, 1996), which argues vehemently that the novel was not "new" in the eighteenth century, that the English certainly did not invent it as a literary form, that its classical and other antecedents were much more formative than has been heretofore recognized. Doody's version of the novel's story is indeed true in its broad outlines, but incomplete, misleading, and even inaccurate in certain particulars, as it ignores the essential fact that the innovative novelists of Smollett's generation were writing within a specific context of prose fiction familiar to them as a result of its recent or current popularity. Their "newness" was real, in other words; it was largely conceived against an immediate background of contemporary narrative without any sense of a perceived tradition; and it certainly did help to bring the modern novel into being.

Chapter 1: *Roderick Random*

1. Beattie, *Dissertations Moral and Critical* (Dublin, 1783), 2:316.

2. Paul-Gabriel Boucé, in *The Novels of Tobias Smollett* (London: Longman, 1976), provides (pp. 101–4) a useful brief review of early commentary on *Roderick Random* (much of it negative), from James Beattie in Smollett's own century to David Herbert and G. K. Chesterton in the next. For more comprehensive coverage see Lionel Kelly, *Tobias Smollett: The Critical Heritage* (London: Routledge & Kegan Paul, 1987). See also the bibliographies by Robert D. Spector, *Tobias Smollett: A Reference Guide* (Boston: G. K. Hall, 1980); and Mary Wagoner, *Tobias Smollett: A Checklist of Editions of His Works and an Annotated Secondary Bibliography* (New York: Garland, 1984).

3. Rymer's *The Tragedies of the Last Age Considered* (1678) and *A Short View of Tragedy* (1692) were both very influential, leading to revisions of Shakespeare (to make his tragedies conform to the unities of time, action, and place) by Dryden, Nahum Tate, and others.

4. Frank, "Spatial Form in Modern Literature," *Sewanee Review* 53 (1945): 221–40, 433–56, 643–53.

5. The most important evidence of its continued influence is a collection of essays published some years ago, all inspired by Frank and many of them still consulted as authoritative extensions of his argument: *Spatial Form in Narrative,* ed. Jeffrey R. Smit-

ten and Ann Daghistany (Ithaca: Cornell University Press, 1981). The collection includes a lengthy bibliography of related writings, suggesting the degree to which the
idea of spatial form has become central to critical thinking about narrative.

6. Mickelsen, "Types of Spatial Structure in Narrative," in *Spatial Form,* ed. Smitten
and Daghistany, 69.

7. Bakhtin, *The Dialogic Imagination,* ed. Michael Holquist, trans. Caryl Emerson and
Michael Holquist (Austin: University of Texas Press, 1981), 84.

8. Smollett admitted this himself, in a letter of 17 June 1748 addressed to his Scottish friend Alexander Carlyle: "the whole," he wrote of *Roderick Random,* "was begun
and finished in the Compass of Eight months, during which time several Intervals
happened of one, two, three and four Weeks, wherein I did not set pen to paper . . ."
(*Letters,* 8).

9. Bunn, "Signs of Randomness in *Roderick Random,*" *Eighteenth-Century Studies* 14
(1981): 452.

10. Boucé, *The Novels of Tobias Smollett.*

11. See, for example, Ronald Paulson, *Satire and the Novel in Eighteenth-Century England* (New Haven: Yale University Press, 1967), 178.

12. I should note here that the plates in the published versions of Hogarth's serial
works, because they were produced from engravings, were mirror images of the original paintings. The painting for scene three is reproduced here, and the overall composition is intended to be "read" from left to right, as though it were in a book. Apprehended in this order, the details of the narrative indicate very clearly how the final
phase of Tom's night of debauchery is to begin (the whore, the candle, and the platter). The reversal in the engraving does not undermine the overall narrative effect of
the painting, but it does alter it.

13. Kayser, *The Grotesque in Art and Literature,* trans. Ulrich Weisstein (New York:
McGraw-Hill, 1966); Kahrl, "Smollett as a Caricaturist," in *Tobias Smollett: Bicentennial
Essays Presented to Lewis M. Knapp,* ed. G. S. Rousseau and P.-G. Boucé (New York: Ox-
ford University Press, 1971), 169–200; McAllister, "Smollett's Semiology of Emo-
tions: The Symptomatology of the Passions and Affections in *Roderick Random* and
Peregrine Pickle," *English Studies in Canada* 14 (1988): 286–95, and "Smollett's Use of
Medical Theory: *Roderick Random* and *Peregrine Pickle,*" *Mosaic* 22 (1989): 121–30.

14. Kayser, *The Grotesque,* 31. Here Kayser is actually citing the German poet and
novelist Christoph Martin Wieland, whose *Unterredungen mit dem Pfarrer von * * * (1775)
was an important early commentary on caricature and the grotesque.

15. Kahrl, "Smollett as a Caricaturist," 180, 183.

16. Smollett, like many others of his century, was much interested in the study of

physiognomy, and though he repudiated its formal practice as a pseudo-science, he nevertheless adapted some of its principles in representing faces that could be "read." See Graeme Tytler, *Physiognomy in the European Novel: Faces and Fortunes* (Princeton: Princeton University Press, 1982).

17. McAllister, "Smollett's Semiology of Emotions," 287–88. McAllister notes that the conservative mainstream of eighteenth-century medical thought (to which Smollett belonged) was broadly mechanistic, equating signs or symptoms with diseases themselves and treating them accordingly. The rudimentary psychology that grew from such mechanistic theory was morally based, and it "read" outward appearances as symptomatic of both character and personality. For much more extensive technical discussion of early symptomatology than McAllister is able to provide in his fine essay, see L. J. Rather, *Mind and Body in Eighteenth-Century Medicine* (London: The Wellcome Historical Medical Society, 1965).

18. See especially Albrecht B. Strauss, "On Smollett's Language: A Paragraph in *Ferdinand Count Fathom*," in *Style in Prose Fiction: English Institute Essays,* ed. Harold C. Martin (New York: Columbia University Press, 1959), 25–54.

19. Crab is the first of a whole crowd of medical charlatans to figure in Smollett's novels; his portraits of them are, like this one, most often fiercely critical.

20. Such juxtaposition of names was of course a common practice with Smollett, who used it for the title characters of all of his novels and for many other personages besides. The usual effect of the juxtaposition is to create a tension between the grand and the absurd, leading either to a joke, dark or light (Launcelot Crab, Humphry Clinker), or to a quite straightforward judgment (Ferdinand Fathom).

21. I have discussed these associations at some length in *Novels of the 1740s* (Athens: University of Georgia Press, 1982), 119–21.

22. See, for example, Roderick's description of the apothecary Lavement in chap. 18 (p. 97); Lavement is another scoundrel whose appearance in the novel reinforces the judgment against corrupt medical practitioners started with the portrait of Crab.

23. The Rowlandson illustration reproduced on p. 50 is the best early drawing of Weazel (it dates from 1790), though it gets the narrative details wrong; Roderick does not see the Captain at all when first hearing his refusal to allow any additional passengers to board the wagon (p. 48).

24. Mrs. Sagely (or Smollett) errs in her Italian; the form should be *virtuosa* (the feminine of *virtuoso*). The description is not altogether kind, for the word was commonly used in the eighteenth century to mean trifler, dilettante, dabbler (*OED*).

25. But in his portrait of her Smollett merely expresses a conventional attitude of his day; see, for example, Mrs. Western in Fielding's *Tom Jones.*

26. I have quoted from Talbot's letter as excerpted in Kelly, *Tobias Smollett: The Critical Heritage,* 38–39. The letter is dated 15 February 1748, and so it was written within a month after the publication date of *Roderick Random.*

27. Moore, in *Hogarth's Literary Relationships* (Minneapolis: University of Minnesota Press, 1948), suggests (p. 165) that the image of Strap in this scene was modeled upon that of the imbecile servant in the final scene (VI) of *Marriage à la Mode,* but there is actually very little resemblance between the two figures at all except that both stand dazed, with staring eyes.

28. Kahrl, "Smollett as a Caricaturist," 184.

29. Grant, *"Roderick Random:* Language as Projectile," in *Smollett: Author of the First Distinction,* ed. Alan Bold (London: Vision Press, 1982), 143.

30. For example, the scene in chap. 30 when Roderick is again accused of spying and is subjected to an inquisitorial examination after his diary is found; the diary is written in Greek characters, and none of his examiners will admit that they cannot read it.

31. *Novels of the 1740s,* 121–22.

32. Mickelsen, "Types of Spatial Structure in Narrative," 76.

33. Bunn, "Signs of Randomness in *Roderick Random.*"

34. Boucé, *The Novels of Tobias Smollett,* 103.

35. Bunn, "Signs of Randomness in *Roderick Random,*" 469.

Chapter 2: *Peregrine Pickle*

1. The first edition was published 25 February 1751, the second in March 1758. Until fairly recently, reprints of the novel have typically used the text from the second edition, which, besides its omission of much of the satirical commentary on Smollett's contemporaries, also deletes other personal material and, in some places, cleans up the style; the whole is some eighty pages shorter than the original version of the novel. Scholars now agree that the first edition best represents the authentic Smollett, and my discussion of the work is based on that version of it. See Howard Swazey Buck, *A Study in Smollett: Chiefly Peregrine Pickle* (New Haven: Yale University Press, 1925), and O M Brack, Jr., "Toward a Critical Edition of Smollett's *Peregrine Pickle,*" *Studies in the Novel* 7 (1975): 361–74.

2. In the advertisement prefixed to the second edition Smollett alluded directly to his suspicions about the fate of the first, complaining of the "art and industry" used against it by "certain booksellers and others, who were at uncommon pains to misrepresent the work and calumniate the author." There seems to have been at least some

justification for his complaint. Smollett held the copyright of the novel to himself (an unusual practice at the time), no doubt angering booksellers; he certainly made enemies by his rough treatment of prominent people in its pages, generating a considerable paper war that embroiled him with, among others, his rival Fielding. There was only one substantial early review, a generally enthusiastic one by John Cleland, in the *Monthly Review* 4 (1751): 355–64. For a detailed account of the novel's initial reception see Knapp, 118–21; see also Kelly, *Tobias Smollett: The Critical Heritage* (London: Routledge & Kegan Paul, 1987), 47–89, for an extensive selection of contemporary commentary in pamphlets and private letters.

3. See my essay, "Smollett's Art: The Novel as 'Picture,'" in *The First English Novelists: Essays in Understanding*, ed. J. M. Armistead (Knoxville: University of Tennessee Press, 1985), 159, 160.

4. See line 122. *Reproof* is included in *Poems, Plays, and The Briton*, ed. Byron Gassman (Athens: University of Georgia Press, 1993), 37–46.

5. Putney, "The Plan of *Peregrine Pickle*," *PMLA* 60 (1945): 1051–65; Boucé, *The Novels of Tobias Smollett* (London: Longman, 1976), chap. 4, especially pp. 124–44.

6. The five articulations are (as Boucé outlines them, pp. 124–25): the opening fifty pages detailing the "social and economic milieu in which young Peregrine will develop"; the succeeding chapters (through 36) accounting for Perry's childhood and adolescence; the European travels, which take the story to chapter 70; the attempted seduction of Emilia, extending over the next dozen chapters; and finally, the "long social and moral decline of the hero and his rehabilitation."

7. Grant, *Tobias Smollett: A Study in Style* (Manchester: Manchester University Press, 1977), 48. John Skinner, in *Constructions of Smollett: A Study of Genre and Gender* (Newark: University of Delaware Press, 1996), chap. 2, discusses the jokes and pranks of *Peregrine Pickle* from the perspective of Bakhtinian carnivalesque and modern game theory. Skinner's argument is valiant and ingenious, and it works admirably as a theoretical explanation of the novel's particular satiric practice, but it does not overturn Grant's accurate assessment of the total effect.

8. Smollett is never explicit about Perry's illegitimacy, but he certainly gives almost unmistakable hints of it at the beginning of chap. 3 (p. 13) and at the very end of chap. 4 (p. 18). See Aileen Douglas, *Uneasy Sensations: Smollett and the Body* (Chicago: University of Chicago Press, 1995), 90; see also R. G. Collins, "The Hidden Bastard: A Question of Illegitimacy in Smollett's *Peregrine Pickle*," *PMLA* 94 (1979): 91–105.

9. See my essay, "*Roderick Random*: The Picaresque Transformed," *College Literature* 6 (1979): 211–20.

10. Earlier, in chap. 97, Smollett launches a more dramatically appropriate—and

thus more seemly—attack on Sir Robert Walpole (the "Great Man" of the chapter heading) by aligning him with the unseen figure of Sir Steady Steerwell, the prime minister who will eventually disappoint Perry with false promises. Walpole fell from power in 1742 and then died in 1745, six years before the publication of *Peregrine Pickle,* but in the public consciousness he was still the archetype of the political villain; the characterization of him as Sir Steady, though anachronistic, was clearly intended as a slam against all powerful, corrupt ministers.

11. *Letters,* 103.

12. Hill's *Lady Frail* appeared in print 8 February 1751. For an account of the competition between Hill and Smollett over the story of Lady Vane, and of the broad reception of Smollett's version, see Knapp, 117–24.

13. In addition to Putney and Boucé (above, n. 5), see John M. Warner, "The Interpolated Narratives in the Fiction of Fielding and Smollett: An Epistemological View," *Studies in the Novel* 5 (1973): 271–83. Felicity Nussbaum, in *The Autobiographical Subject: Gender and Ideology in Eighteenth-Century England* (Baltimore: Johns Hopkins University Press, 1989), chap. 8, interestingly discusses Lady Vane's story in a larger context of "scandalous memoirs" by contemporary female writers (Teresa Constantia Phillips, Laetitia Pilkington, Charlotte Charke, and numerous others), though she has little to say about its place in the structure of *Peregrine Pickle.*

14. Probably their length, even more than their topical obscurity, most daunts the modern reader. Knapp has calculated (p. 117, n. 47) that of the approximately 380,000 words in the four volumes of the first edition of *Peregrine Pickle,* some 50,000 are devoted to Lady Vane's memoirs; in the Oxford World's Classics edition of the novel the memoirs extend over more than 100 pages (432–539) of the total of 781. Any reader may be forgiven for finding them an annoyance and an obstacle. The history of MacKercher is much shorter, but at 45 pages it is still a considerable intrusion, coming as it does when Smollett has Perry, now bankrupt, demoralized, and in prison, poised to begin the resolution of his story.

15. See Knapp, 121–25, for fuller details of Smollett's knowledge of the Annesley case and of both MacKercher and Lady Vane.

16. In chap. 46, for example, the narrator remarks that Peregrine has now "resided about fifteen months in France" (p. 223).

17. See above, chap. 1, pp. 42–43, and the illustration on p. 43.

18. His name, drawn from naval terminology, suggests exactly this about him. A hawser is a cable or rope used to moor a ship; a trunnion is a pin or gudgeon, two of which were attached to a cannon to form an axis on which it might pivot in its carriage while firing (*OED*).

19. See above, chap. 1, p. 57 and n. 28.

20. Ronald Paulson, in "Smollett and Hogarth: The Identity of Pallet," *Studies in English Literature* 4 (1964): 351–59, takes the description of Pallet's speech and dress as the primary evidence that he is a portrait of Hogarth, who was known both for his talkativeness and his jaunty attire. It was long ago established that the physician is modeled on Mark Akenside, a doctor and poet of greater gifts and higher achievement than Smollett's fictional character, certainly, but sometimes criticized for arrogance and pretentiousness; see Howard Swazey Buck, "Smollett and Dr. Akenside," *Journal of English and Germanic Philology* 31 (1932): 10–26. The Rowlandson illustration reproduced on p. 98 accurately catches Smollett's picture of Pallet, who stands at the far right—looking very much like Hogarth.

21. As Paulson notes in "Smollett and Hogarth," 357–58, Hogarth launched a lottery scheme for his *March to Finchley* in April 1750, and its details exactly coincide with Pallet's plan, including the price of half a guinea per chance. Hogarth's lottery, unlike Pallet's, was a great success, bringing him £1,200.

22. See Paulson, "Smollett and Hogarth," 355–58, for a brief summary of the criticism typically leveled at the painter on all these counts.

23. See, for example, the letter to Garrick quoted above, in the introduction, n. 15.

24. McAllister, "Smollett's Use of Medical Theory: *Roderick Random* and *Peregrine Pickle*," *Mosaic* 22 (1989): 126–27.

25. Kahrl, "Smollett as a Caricaturist," in *Tobias Smollett: Bicentennial Essays Presented to Lewis M. Knapp,* ed. G. S. Rousseau and P.-G. Boucé (New York: Oxford University Press, 1917), 191.

26. Moore, *Hogarth's Literary Relationships* (Minneapolis: University of Minnesota Press, 1948), 169–70.

27. The work was completed in oil on canvas in 1730–31, and as an engraving in 1732. The latter, a superior composition, is more dense, with the figures in the scene brought up much closer to the viewer's eye, making the whole effect much more ominous and more emphatically admonitory. Smollett would certainly have been most familiar with the engraving, which is reproduced on the title page of this book.

28. *Critical Review* 1 (January–July 1756): 479. See above, the introduction, p. 26.

29. Moore, in *Hogarth's Literary Relationships,* 184–85, has made the same connection between Smollett's "Entertainment" episode and Hogarth's later work, though without developing it.

30. Kahrl, "Smollett as a Caricaturist," 193.

31. Grant, *Tobias Smollett: A Study in Style,* 141.

32. Boucé, *The Novels of Tobias Smollett,* chap. 4.

33. McAllister, "Smollett's Use of Medical Theory," 129.

Chapter 3: *Ferdinand Count Fathom*

1. *Monthly Review* 8 (1753): 206–7.

2. *Ferdinand Count Fathom* was published in London by W. Johnston in February 1753. Except for a Dublin printing (probably authorized) in the same year, it did not appear again until 1771, when Johnston put out a second edition. From that time forward the popularity of the novel increased somewhat, and by the end of the eighteenth century a half-dozen separate new editions had issued from the shops of various booksellers. The work was included in the seventh volume of Harrison's *Novelist's Magazine* in 1782. There were also during this same period translations into French, Italian, German, and Dutch.

3. The letters were written on 24 March, 7 April, and 21 April 1753; they are excerpted in Lionel Kelly, *Tobias Smollett: The Critical Heritage* (London: Routledge & Kegan Paul, 1987), 95.

4. See Saintsbury, introduction to *The Adventures of Ferdinand Count Fathom,* in *The Works of Tobias Smollett* (London, 1895), 8: xviii; and Boucé, *The Novels of Tobias Smollett* (London: Longman, 1976), 158.

5. Aileen Douglas, in *Uneasy Sensations: Smollett and the Body* (Chicago: University of Chicago Press, 1995), chap. 5, effectively but restrictively treats *Ferdinand Count Fathom* as an anomaly in Smollett's work because of its lack of interest in the physical body of its protagonist; John Skinner, in *Constructions of Smollett: A Study of Genre and Gender* (Newark: University of Delaware, 1996), chap. 3, focuses narrowly but productively upon the novel as satire, emphasizing its generic adaptations from the picaresque. Several studies of the issue of structural unity are worthy of mention: T. O. Treadwell, "The Two Worlds of *Ferdinand Count Fathom,*" in *Tobias Smollett: Bicentennial Essays Presented to Lewis M. Knapp,* ed. G. S. Rousseau and P.-G. Boucé (New York: Oxford University Press, 1971), 131–53; David K. Jeffrey, "'Ductility and Dissimulation': The Unity of *Ferdinand Count Fathom,*" *Tennessee Studies in Literature* 23 (1978): 47–60; and K. G. Simpson, "Tobias Smollett: The Scot as English Novelist," in *Smollett: Author of the First Distinction,* ed. Alan Bold (London: Vision Press, 1982), 64–105. I should mention here three essays of my own in which I have dealt with questions of Smollett's compositional strategies: "Smollett's Novels: *Ferdinand Count Fathom* for the Defense," *Papers on Language and Literature* 20 (1984): 165–84; "Smollett's Art: The Novel as 'Pic-

ture,'" in *The First English Novelists: Essays in Understanding*, ed. J. M. Armistead (Knoxville: University of Tennessee Press, 1985), 143–83; and the introduction to the Georgia Edition of *Ferdinand Count Fathom*. Parts of the present chapter rely extensively upon these three essays.

6. Grant, *Tobias Smollett: A Study in Style* (Manchester: Manchester University Press, 1977), 65–67.

7. George Kahrl, "Smollett as a Caricaturist," in *Tobias Smollett: Bicentennial Essays Presented to Lewis M. Knapp*, ed. G. S. Rousseau and P.-G. Boucé (New York: Oxford University Press, 1971), 182.

8. McKillop, *The Early Masters of English Fiction* (Lawrence: University of Kansas Press, 1956), 164–65.

9. See especially Pamela Cantrell, "Writing the Picture: Fielding, Smollett, and Hogarthian Pictorialism," *Studies in Eighteenth-Century Culture* 24 (1995): 69–89. Aileen Douglas, in *Uneasy Sensations*, chap. 5, gives considerable emphasis to the purposefully pictorial qualities of *Ferdinand Count Fathom*.

10. M. A. Goldberg, in *Smollett and the Scottish School: Studies in Eighteenth-Century Thought* (Albuquerque: University of New Mexico Press, 1958), chap. 4, argues at great length that *Ferdinand Count Fathom* sets out deliberately to be a dualistic work insistently portraying the collision between artifice and natural sensibility, and that whereas architectonics suffer from Smollett's awkward management of an actual four-part structure, the book finally succeeds in meeting its ethical and didactic aims. I find Goldberg's argument persuasive, despite its stridently unsympathetic comments on the compositional form of the novel. See K. G. Simpson, "Tobias Smollett: The Scot as English Novelist," for a similar but more congenial discussion suggesting that Smollett's dualism—his purposeful exploration of the sentimental and the magical in a study of almost inhuman evil, all finally balanced by rational reduction—reflected an early Scottish tradition, and that it is a source of unity and coherence achieved through apparent divisiveness.

11. Paulson, *Satire and the Novel in Eighteenth-Century England* (New Haven: Yale University Press, 1967), 228.

12. Celebratory military biographies of these two men began to appear early in the second decade of the eighteenth century, often within the covers of a single work. The most ambitious and lavish of these biographies came later, in fact many years after the greatest triumphs of their subjects: *The Military History of the Late Prince Eugene of Savoy, And of the Late John Duke of Marlborough* (London, 1736), printed in 2 vols. and gorgeously illustrated by Claude Du Bosc; and *Memoirs of the Lives and Conduct of those Illustrious Heroes Prince Eugene of Savoy, and John Duke of Marlborough* (London, 1742).

13. The best account of the life and sorrows of this melancholy figure may be found in the biography by André Le Glay, *Theodore de Neuhoff Roi de Corse* (Monaco: Imprimerie de Monaco, 1907). Smollett apparently felt Theodore's plight very keenly, and actually went to visit him in prison; see Knapp, 157–58.

14. Walpole published an appeal on Theodore's behalf in *The World,* No. 8 (22 February 1753). "This island," he wrote, "ought to be as much the harbour of afflicted majesty, as it has been the scourge of offending majesty."

15. Earl Wasserman was the first to make a convincing case for the identity of Sir Mungo as a caricature of Hutchinson; see "Smollett's Satire on the Hutchinsonians," *Modern Language Notes* 70 (1955): 336–37.

16. The Banks portrait and the MacArdell print are described in F. G. Stephens, *Catalogue of Political and Personal Satires Preserved in the Department of Prints and Drawings in the British Museum* (1978), 3. pt. 1, nos. 2852, 3092.

17. Besides the works of Shakespeare and Milton, together with *Don Quixote,* Minikin's library includes Thomas Mozeen's farcical play drawn from *Le Roman Comique,* called *Young Scarron* (London, 1752), and the following novels: John Hill, *The Adventures of Mr. Loveill* (London, 1750), and by the same author *The History of a Woman of Quality: Or, The Adventures of Lady Frail* (London, 1751) and *The Adventures of Mr. George Edwards, a Creole* (London, 1751); Edward Kimber, *The Life and Adventures of Joe Thompson* (London, 1750); *An Apology for the Life of Bampfylde-Moore Carew* (London, 1749); and Eliza Haywood, *The History of Miss Betsy Thoughtless* (London, 1751). The reference to *Lady Frail* is a private joke, for Hill's subject is of course the Lady Vane whose "memoirs" were included in Smollett's own *Peregrine Pickle.*

18. Knapp has suggested (p. 154), not very convincingly, that Joshua was inspired by a similar character in Christian Gellert's *Das Leben des swedischen Graffin G. xxx,* which was published in English translation in March 1752; see also H. R. S. Van Der Veen, *Jewish Characters in Eighteenth Century English Fiction and Drama* (Batavia: J. B. Wolters, 1935), 41–46.

19. *Letters,* 69. The letter to Huggins is dated 2 July 1758, and it was occasioned by publication of Smollett's *Complete History of England.*

20. For extended discussion of Smollett's echoes of *The Mourning Bride* see Catherine L. Almirall, "Smollett's 'Gothic': An Illustration," *Modern Language Notes* 68 (1953): 408–10. For more general discussion of the theatricality of Smollett's novels, especially *Ferdinand Count Fathom,* see Thomas R. Preston, "The 'Stage Passions' and Smollett's Characterization," *Studies in Philology* 71 (1974): 105–25; and see also Lee Monroe Ellison, "Elizabethan Drama and the Works of Smollett," *PMLA* 44 (1929): 842–62.

21. See Robert Donald Spector, *Tobias George Smollett,* Updated Edition (Boston: Twayne, 1989), 72–74, for a convincing (if brief) argument that Smollett actually conceived Fathom as a "spiritual heir" to Iago. On the larger matter of Smollett's general indebtedness to Shakespeare see George M. Kahrl, "The Influence of Shakespeare on Smollett," in *Essays in Dramatic Literature: The Parrott Presentation Volume,* ed. Hardin Craig (Princeton: Princeton University Press, 1935), 399–420.

22. The four Stothard illustrations were included in Harrison's *Novelist's Magazine,* 1782 (vol. 7, no. 4), the four by Clennell in a collection entitled *British Novelists,* 1810 (vol. 2, no. 2). All eight of these illustrations are reproduced in the Georgia Edition of *Ferdinand Count Fathom.*

23. Moore, *Hogarth's Literary Relationships* (Minneapolis: University of Minnesota Press, 1948), 168.

24. See above, chap. 2, pp. 109–10.

25. See Preston, "Disenchanting the Man of Feeling: Smollett's *Ferdinand Count Fathom,*" in *Quick Springs of Sense: Studies in the Eighteenth Century,* ed. Larry S. Champion (Athens: University of Georgia Press, 1974), 223–39.

26. Douglas, *Uneasy Sensations,* 97.

Chapter 4: *Sir Launcelot Greaves*

1. For a summary of the details of what is known about the composition of *Humphry Clinker* see Thomas R. Preston's introduction to the Georgia Edition of the novel, xxi–xxiii.

2. The *Briton* began its weekly run on 29 May 1762 and abruptly ceased publication with the number for 12 February 1763. For full discussion of the circumstances of Smollett's editorship of this magazine see Byron Gassman's introduction to the work in the Georgia Edition of Smollett's *Poems, Plays, and The Briton* (Athens: University of Georgia Press, 1993), 221–40.

3. Sterne, *A Sentimental Journey,* ed. Graham Petrie, intro. A. Alvarez (Harmondsworth: Penguin Books, 1967), 51.

4. Douglas, *Uneasy Sensations: Smollett and the Body* (Chicago: University of Chicago Press, 1995), 116.

5. See Leavis, *The Great Tradition* (London: Chatto and Windus, 1948), chap. 5. *Hard Times* was the only novel by Dickens allowed into Leavis's "great tradition," which he defined very narrowly, emphasizing organic form and moral seriousness above all else.

6. Boucé, in *The Novels of Tobias Smollett* (London: Longman, 1976), chap. 5, discusses *Sir Launcelot Greaves* and *Ferdinand Count Fathom* together, seeing them as "moral

antipodes"; Douglas, in *Uneasy Sensations*, chap. 5, also discusses the two novels together, and is particularly effective in her consideration of the issues of the law, madness, and moral violence in Smollett's supposedly mellow fourth novel; Skinner, in *Constructions of Smollett: A Study of Genre and Gender* (Newark: University of Delaware Press, 1996), chap. 3, reads *Sir Launcelot Greaves* as a satiric work whose strongest generic affiliation is with romance.

7. At about 85,000 words, the work is less than half the length of *Ferdinand Count Fathom* (155,000 words) and *Humphry Clinker* (180,000 words), and only a little more than one-third as long as *Roderick Random* (220,000 words); it is just under a quarter of the length of *Peregrine Pickle* (380,000 words).

8. See Mayo, *The English Novel in the Magazines 1740–1815* (Evanston: Northwestern University Press, 1962), 280–82, for full discussion of the chapter divisions in *Sir Launcelot Greaves* and for comparisons between Smollett's practice and that of other contemporary writers of magazine fiction.

9. Scott, "Prefatory Memoir," *The Novels of Tobias Smollett, M.D.* (London and Edinburgh, 1821), 2:xxiii.

10. Price, "Smollett and the Reader in *Sir Launcelot Greaves*," in *Smollett: Author of the First Distinction*, ed. Alan Bold (London: Vision Press, 1982), 195.

11. Skinner, *Constructions of Smollett*, 147–58.

12. For discussion of these forms of romance and of the reactions of Smollett and his immediate contemporaries to them, see chap. 2 of my *Novels of the 1740s* (Athens: University of Georgia Press, 1982). See also Thomas Philip Haviland, "The 'Roman de Longue Haleine' on English Soil" (Ph.D. diss., University of Pennsylvania, 1931).

13. See Jack Lindsay, *Hogarth: His Art and His World* (New York: Taplinger, 1979), 186–89, for discussion of the reception given the *Analysis*.

14. See above, the introduction, n. 46.

15. See above, the introduction, pp. 25–28.

16. See James R. Foster, "Smollett's Pamphleteering Foe Shebbeare," *PMLA* 57 (1942): 1053–1100, for a thorough discussion of the hostile relations between the two men.

17. See above, chap. 2, pp. 111–12, for discussion of the parallel between the "Entertainment" episode in *Peregrine Pickle* and Hogarth's picture. The picture is reproduced on p. 112.

18. The best and most detailed discussion of the law as an issue in *Sir Launcelot Greaves*, particularly as it bears on the hero's quixotism, may be found in Douglas, *Uneasy Sensations*, 119–27.

19. *Continuation* (London, 1766), 1:317.

20. Gaunt, *The World of William Hogarth* (London: Jonathan Cape, 1978), 78.

21. See Pamela Cantrell, "Writing the Picture: Fielding, Smollett, and Hogarthian Pictorialism," *Studies in Eighteenth-Century Culture* 24 (1995): 80–84, for a slightly different reading of the relations between Smollett's election scenes and Hogarth's prints.

22. Grant, *Tobias Smollett: A Study in Style* (Manchester: Manchester University Press, 1977), 125.

23. The new buildings of the King's Bench, located in Saint George's Fields south of Westminster Bridge, were opened in November 1758; the prison was formerly situated in Southwark.

24. In the May 1758 number of the *Critical Review* Smollett published a severe attack on a pamphlet in which Admiral Charles Knowles defended his conduct during the failed expedition to Rochefort in the preceding year. Knowles sued for libel. The case came to a conclusion after two years of delays, and on 24 November 1760 Smollett was convicted, fined £100, and sentenced to three months in prison. See Knapp, 213–14, 230–36.

Chapter 5: *Humphry Clinker*

1. See especially Louis L. Martz, *The Later Career of Tobias Smollett* (New Haven: Yale University Press, 1942), 68–73, 132–35. It is worth noting here that, like Matt Bramble after him, the persona of the *Travels* leaves home bad-tempered but returns softened, in a gentler frame of mind, healed and happy.

2. I cannot prove what I claim here, as only a few scattered copies of the weekly numbers have survived. But the rhythm I have detected will, I think, be apparent to anyone else who reads the relevant portions of the *Present State* from a knowledge of its original mode of publication.

3. Martz, *The Later Career,* 127–29, 136–67. The English and Scottish sections of the *Present State,* according to Martz, were probably first drafted early in the 1760s. Busy as he was, Smollett no doubt revised and put them into final form prior to their appearance in the serial format, and so their contents must have been much in his mind as he worked on *Humphry Clinker.*

4. See Paulson, *Satire and the Novel in Eighteenth-Century England* (New Haven: Yale University Press, 1967), 165–218, and Skinner, *Constructions of Smollett: A Study of Genre and Gender* (Newark: University of Delaware Press, 1996), chaps. 1–3.

5. Preston, *Not in Timon's Manner: Feeling, Misanthropy, and Satire in Eighteenth-Century England* (University: University of Alabama Press, 1975), 69. Preston first uses this phrase to describe Smollett himself.

6. Jery writes twenty-eight letters, Matt twenty-seven. On Matt's renunciation of satire at the end of the novel see Preston, *Not in Timon's Manner,* 119.

7. Baker, "*Humphry Clinker* as Comic Romance," *Papers of the Michigan Academy of Sciences, Arts, and Letters* 46 (1961): 645–54. The crucial phrase ("comic romance") is from Fielding, who used it in the preface to *Joseph Andrews* as a way of distinguishing his work from a parallel kind, the "serious" romance. In a second essay, "The Idea of Romance in the Eighteenth-Century Novel," *Papers of the Michigan Academy of Sciences, Arts, and Letters* 49 (1963): 49–61, Baker focuses upon *Humphry Clinker* as his primary illustration of the influence of romance upon Smollett and other contemporary novelists.

8. Lydia Languish is the apparently empty-headed heroine of Sheridan's comedy *The Rivals,* 1775.

9. It is possible, even likely, that Smollett took at least one of his cues for the form of *Humphry Clinker* from Christopher Anstey's popular *New Bath Guide: or, Memoirs of the B——r——d Family. In a Series of Poetical Epistles* (1766). Anstey's book also includes multiple correspondents, though their characters are little developed and they are not really travelers. See Martz, *The Later Career,* 133–34.

10. See Reid, "Smollett's Healing Journey," *Virginia Quarterly Review* 41 (1965): 549–70.

11. See Beasley, "Smollett's Art: The Novel as 'Picture,'" in *The First English Novelists: Essays in Understanding,* ed. J. M. Armistead (Knoxville: University of Tennessee Press, 1985), 168–69.

12. See Folkenflik, "Self and Society: Comic Union in *Humphry Clinker,*" *Philological Quarterly* 53 (1974): 204.

13. See the Georgia Edition, xxi–xxiii, and Knapp, 295–96. Of the eleven reviews that appeared within a year of the novel's original publication date, only one—for the *Monthly Review* 45 (1771): 152—was negative.

14. The *Universal History,* begun in about 1730, was a comprehensive chronicle of all human history from ancient to modern times; Smollett contributed substantial portions of the *Modern Part* (1759–65), and during the last years of his life was busy revising the entire work for a new edition. See Martz, *The Later Career,* 7–8.

15. Thomas R. Preston has identified these in his introduction to the Georgia Edition, xxv–xxvi. Only one letter is undated—Jery Melford's, for October 6. The absence of a date for this letter may simply have been a slip on Smollett's part, but see G. S. Rousseau, "Beef and Bouillon: A Voice for Tobias Smollett, with Comments on His Life, Works, and Modern Critics," *British Studies Monitor* 7 (1977): 42 and n. 91.

16. There is no need to detail *Humphry Clinker*'s historical allusions here; there are

too many of them to treat meaningfully, and in any case they are amply accounted for by Preston in his introduction to the Georgia Edition, and in his notes to the text. What I wish to emphasize is their sheer abundance. For interpretive commentary beyond what Preston is able to offer, see Byron Gassman, "*Humphry Clinker* and the Two Kingdoms of George III," *Criticism* 16 (1974): 95–108; see also Robert Mayer, "History, *Humphry Clinker,* and the Novel," *Eighteenth-Century Fiction* 4 (1992): 239–55.

17. Martz, in *The Later Career,* 136–46, provides a detailed analysis of the close parallels between the two accounts of Scotland.

18. For the best available discussion of the biographical dimensions of Matt's character see Lewis M. Knapp, "Smollett's Self-Portrait in *The Expedition of Humphry Clinker,*" in *The Age of Johnson: Essays Presented to Chauncey Brewster Tinker,* ed. Frederick W. Hilles (New Haven: Yale University Press, 1949), 149–58.

19. Paul-Gabriel Boucé, in *The Novels of Tobias Smollett* (London: Longman, 1976), 199, has also observed this difference between Smollett's last novel and all of his others. "*Humphry Clinker,*" says Boucé, "marks the splitting-up of the principal character and its quintuple fragmentation." The "relativity" of the views expressed by the novel's correspondents, "sometimes superimposed, sometimes overlapping, now confirming, now contradicting each other, is better fitted to convey the organic multiplicity of life, physical or mental, which Smollett strove to capture with the avidity of his passionate nature."

20. See Cantrell, "Writing the Picture: Fielding, Smollett, and Hogarthian Pictorialism," *Studies in Eighteenth-Century Culture* 24 (1995), 79–80.

21. I should note, however, that Win's language has generated a great deal of scholarly and critical interest, most importantly from W. Arthur Boggs, who, in a series of ten articles, has studied everything from her eccentric usages, to her echoes of Shakespeare, to her archaisms and proverbial expressions, to her appearances in the *OED*. The most comprehensive and generally useful of these articles is "A Win Jenkins Lexicon," *Bulletin of the New York Public Library* 68 (1964): 323–30, which defines 133 "Winisms." The entire series of articles is listed in Mary Wagoner, *Tobias Smollett: A Checklist of Editions of His Works and an Annotated Secondary Bibliography* (New York: Garland, 1984), Nos. 2637–46.

22. I have developed the comparisons between Lydia and Smollett's other heroines at some length in "Amiable Apparitions: Smollett's Fictional Heroines," in *Augustan Subjects: Essays in Honor of Martin C. Battestin* (Newark: University of Delaware Press, 1997), 229–48.

23. See pp. 254–56, where the scene is described in the kind of detail Jery elsewhere lavishes on comic moments. Pamela Cantrell, in "Writing the Picture," 74–76, has

carefully and expertly analyzed this description as a pictorial representation exactly in the manner of Hogarth. Obviously, Jery's visual acuity is not limited in range only to what amuses him.

24. Grant, *Tobias Smollett: A Study in Style* (Manchester: Manchester University Press, 1977), 165.

25. John F. Sena, in "Ancient Designs and Modern Folly: Architecture in *The Expedition of Humphry Clinker*," *Harvard Library Bulletin* 27 (1979): 86–113, has elaborated upon the importance of architectural styles in Matt's Bath letters, and in many of his others as well, including those from Scotland that express such pleasure in the older, more traditional buildings of Glasgow and (especially) Edinburgh. Sena concludes, very persuasively, that Matt judges buildings against classical ideals of proportion and utility and finds many modern structures symptomatic of social and moral decay.

26. Matt's railings against the Bath waters accurately echo a contemporary debate about them, to which Smollett himself had contributed earlier in his *Essay on the External Use of Water* (1752). For a comprehensive discussion of the entire debate see George S. Rousseau, "Matt Bramble and the Sulphur Controversy in the XVIIIth Century: Medical Background of *Humphry Clinker*," *Journal of the History of Ideas* 28 (1967): 577–89.

27. See Sekora, *Luxury: The Concept in Western Thought, Eden to Smollett* (Baltimore: Johns Hopkins University Press, 1977), especially chaps. 7 and 8.

28. See Zomchick, "Social Class, Character, and Narrative Strategy in *Humphry Clinker*," *Eighteenth-Century Life* 10 (1986): 172–85.

29. See Gassman, "*Humphry Clinker* and the Two Kingdoms of George III." One of the "two kingdoms" of Gassman's title is the perfected model implied by the social and political harmonies of the novel's ending. See also Mayer, "History, *Humphry Clinker,* and the Novel," especially pp. 248–50; and my own essay, "Tobias Smollett: The Scot in England," *Studies in Scottish Literature* 29 (1997): 14–28.

30. See Warner, *Joyce's Grandfathers: Myth and History in Defoe, Smollett, Sterne, and Joyce* (Athens: University of Georgia Press, 1993), 86–88. For other views on the aesthetic unity of *Humphry Clinker* see Eric Rothstein, *Systems of Order and Inquiry in Later Eighteenth-Century Fiction* (Berkeley: University of California Press, 1975), 109–53, and Frederick M. Keener, "Transitions in *Humphry Clinker*," *Studies in Eighteenth-Century Culture* 16 (1986): 149–63.

INDEX

—